THE POWER OF CORPORATE COMMUNICATION

Crafting the Voice and
Image of Your Business

Paul Argenti

Janis Forman

Boston, Massachusetts   Burr Ridge, Illinois
Dubuque, Iowa   Madison, Wisconsin   New York, New York
San Francisco, California   St. Louis, Missouri

Library of Congress Cataloging-in-Publication Data

Argenti, Paul A.
  The power of corporate communication / Paul Argenti & Janis Forman.
    p. cm.
  Includes bibliographical references.
  ISBN 0-07-137949-5
  1. Communication in management.   2. Corporations—Public relations.
  3. Communication in organizations.   I. Forman, Janis.   II. Title.
  HD30.3 .A73 2002
  658.4'5—dc21
                                                            2002003744

McGraw-Hill

A Division of The McGraw·Hill Companies

2 3 4 5 6 7 8 9   BKM BKM   0 9 8 7 6 5 4

ISBN 0-07-137949-5

This book was set in Palatino by Patricia Wallenburg.

With much love to our children—Benjamin, Julia, and Lauren.

May you continue to thrive and reach for the stars.

ACKNOWLEDGMENTS

W E WROTE THIS BOOK between the fall of 1999 and the fall of 2001. Much has happened to Americans and to the world—for that matter—in that period. We have seen the highs and lows of the dot.com phenomenon, the proliferation of new communication technologies, the shift from a Democratic to a Republican Administration, and, most important, the movement from peace to a new kind of war—one initiated by terrorist attacks at the heart of American institutions, the World Trade Center and the Pentagon.

Like all Americans, we have been anguished and grief stricken by the attacks. As we completed this book, we asked ourselves, "What can words do in the face of a violence that struck down people just trying to go about doing their daily business?" Taking a retrospective glance, we could see the foreshadowing of the violence in the increasing verbal attacks on corporate America, especially the anticorporate jamming that floods the Internet, and the envy of our freedom and prosperity as seen in the worldwide media.

Words accompany war. We have known this since the very early poetic expression of Western civilization in Homer's *Iliad*—the epic song of battle between the Trojans and the Greeks. We hope that words will also supersede war and replace it with civil discourse.

We are both teachers of civil discourse—public organizational discourse that aims to support and extend respectful, honest exchanges between companies and their constituencies—and we have both worked for years with MBA students who struggle to discover and develop their individual voices alongside and within the organizations they represent. We hope that this book moves them a bit further along in that direction, and we thank our students for the many conversations about language, organizations, ethics, and strategy.

As with any satisfying coauthorship, we have each contributed to the design and scope of this book and to the creation of a single voice. Each of us has had a hand in every chapter. Paul was primarily responsible for Chapters 4, 6, 7, 9, and 10 and Janis for Chapters 1, 2, 3, 5, and 8.

We are grateful to many individuals and companies for their contributions to this book. We would like to thank the following executives for sharing their expertise with us: Elizabeth Heller Allen of Dell, Ron Culp and Penny Cate of Sears, David Drobis and Peter Fleischer of Ketchum, Daryl Fraser of TRW, Steve Harris of General Motors, Bill Margaritis of FedEx, Rob Frazier of Colgate-Palmolive, David McCourt of RCN, Jim Murphy of Accenture, Bill Nielsen of Johnson & Johnson, John Onoda of Schwab, Steven Parrish of Philip Morris, and Dennis Signorovitch of Honeywell. Our special thanks go to Jack Bergen of the Council of Public Relations Firms and the immediate past and current presidents of the Arthur Page Society, Jim Murphy of Accenture and David Drobis of Ketchum, for their continued support of our work. Several companies also permitted us to include samples of their corporate advertising in the book: Absolut, Accenture, AT&T, Credit Suisse First Boston, Disney, Dun & Bradstreet, Hitachi, Pfizer, and Philip Morris.

We also want to thank our research assistants at the Tuck School: Kimberley Tait, who was integral to the development of Paul's chapters, and Abbey Nova, whose assistance is impossible to measure—and Peter Marino of the Anderson School at UCLA.

Finally, we want to express our love and appreciation to our families—to Paul's wife, Mary Munter, and to Janis' husband, Don Brabston. Busy and highly productive professionals in their own right, each of them also gave us the space and support to complete this project.

We have dedicated this book to our children—Benjamin Kenneth Forman Brabston, Julia Louise Argenti, and Lauren Jeane Argenti as a small expression of our love and hopes for their progress and prosperity as they move toward adulthood.

CONTENTS

WHY BOTHER WITH CORPORATE COMMUNICATION?

B EFORE WE ANSWER THE QUESTION posed by the title of this chapter, we would like to make one thing perfectly clear: The purpose of our book is to address the imbalance between the importance of corporate communication and its relative neglect, to make the field of corporate communication visible, and to demonstrate its influence on the bottom line. In other words, we want to put the spotlight on what has been placed inappropriately in the background of corporate life. First, however, we think it appropriate to introduce this subject broadly to you.

With so many competing demands on your time, why should you bother with corporate communication? A glance at the headlines of today's major newspapers should quickly provide you with an answer: You need to pay attention to corporate communication because missed opportunities and potentially serious threats to your business are the rather costly alternatives.

A variety of constituencies, including investors; employees; customers; competitors; current and potential partners; special-interest groups; government; local, national, international communities; and, of course (who could forget), the media, are hounding today's businesses. To illustrate this point we chose a random two-week period in late August and early September of 1999—the period in which we began to draft this book—and found many top stories about business and its constituencies in a single publication, *The Wall Street Journal*.

During NATO air strikes, McDonald's had to "Serbify" their corporate image in Yugoslavia to avoid ostracism by a major client. They changed their logo, lapel pins, and posters to reflect their sympathies; the Golden Arches sported a Serbian cap.[1] Another article in *The Wall Street Journal* exposed discrimination issues at Merrill Lynch. Not only was the organization refusing to abide by the court's stipulations, rulings, and so forth that came out of a gender discrimination suit, but they were also lashing back at women filing for restitution who claimed to have been affected by the organization's gender bias.[2] Discrimination is a touchy subject, and as another *Wall Street Journal* article stated, "Networks need to find a better balance with minority roles." The NAACP unleashed criticisms toward the top TV networks, arguing that representation of minorities in their shows was too limited.[3]

In yet another *Journal* article, we read that stock prices for companies associated with Linux, a computer operating system, seem to rise sharply in tandem with Internet chat room discussions of Linux and to fall as sharply when discussion stops.[4] In another article, large corporations like Ford, Dunkin' Donuts, and Raytheon are challenged by employees and consumers—critics who are using the Internet to expose proprietary company information that has been hidden from the public and the competition.[5] By contrast, companies such as LucasFilms have been able to capitalize on Web-site discussions, using talk about their products to stimulate further interest.

An overriding theme we can see from these stories is that the American public's attention to businesses is widespread and persistent. This attention, however, is by no means limited to the printed word. Television also serves as a medium for corporate scrutiny.

Within the same random time period, the *Today Show* featured a provocative exchange between a spokesperson from Kaiser Permanente, a large Health Maintenance Organization (HMO), and a representative for a paramedics and firefighters group. The latter accused the HMO of choosing profits over patient care, forcing its members to seek clearance from Kaiser before ordering an ambulance in potentially life-threatening situations.

Another medium provided us with yet another example. Late-summer entertainment on airline flights included a movie based on the best-selling, award-winning novel *A Civil Action*. The story revolves around a lawyer's quest to prove that the deaths of several children are due to the dumping of mysterious, cancer-causing contaminants into the water supply of a small Massachusetts town by two large, blank-faced corporations. This movie justifiably condemns the guilty parties, but it also contributes to the impression that corporate America as a whole is to blame, especially companies in the chemical industry.

Finally, to commemorate a major holiday—Labor Day—*The Wall Street Journal* invited its readers to view a series of films on the topic of the evil boss, beginning with Charlie Chaplin's 1936 *Hard Times* and including the 1987 Oliver Stone film *Wall Street*, which features the infamous "Greed is Good" speech delivered by Michael Douglas, who plays the role of a ruthless investment banker.

This quick media review of business from a random two-week period represents only a snapshot of the highly dynamic situation we face in a new millennium. Try a similar test of the media for another two-week period, and we think you will also find a considerable amount of attention (mostly negative) paid to companies by their constituencies. For both internal and external constituencies, corporate America is a huge blip on the radar screen.

In fact, when we fast-forward two years later to the summer and fall of 2001 (as we began to wrap up this book), communication challenges, some old and some new, demand our attention as well. To name just a few:

- The Justice Department and individual states continue to scrutinize Microsoft for unfair monopolistic practices, and the future of the company is still in the balance.
- Televised images of defective tires exploding damages the reputations of both Ford and Firestone.
- Consumer groups demand that California legislators abandon rescue plans for Southern California Edison and allow it to fall into bankruptcy.
- Drug maker Eli Lilly faces lawsuits for failing to warn patients that the company's cancer drugs may have been diluted by an unscrupulous pharmacist.
- After its spectacular run in 2000, the academy-award–winning *Erin Brockovich*, a film about a single, out-of-work mother who successfully took on a major public utilities company and its cover-up of contaminated water, has become readily available in video stores (and is already used in our MBA classes on Corporate Communication).

As our research, consulting work, and teaching in executive programs at Dartmouth and UCLA confirm, to shed the role of victim during this attention frenzy, companies need to take active measures to construct and send out their corporate communications. To clarify our subject matter further, a definition follows.

CORPORATE COMMUNICATION: AN EXTENDED DEFINITION

By *corporate communication* we mean the corporation's voice and the images it projects of itself on a world stage populated by its various audiences, or what we refer to as its constituencies. Included in this field are areas such as corporate reputation, corporate advertising and advocacy, employee communications, investor relations, government relations, media management, and crisis communications.

We look at corporate communication from several vantage points. It is most visibly a *function* that may be centralized or dispersed across a company's units. The majority of U.S. companies have departments of corporate communication that appear on their organizational charts along with traditional functions like marketing or accounting.

In addition, corporate communication is also the *processes* a company uses to communicate all its messages to key constituencies—a combination of meetings, interviews, speeches, reports, image advertising, and online communications. Ideally, corporate communication is *an attitude toward communication* or a *set of mental habits* that employees internalize. The result is good communication practices that permeate an organization and are present in all its communications with constituencies.

Corporate communications are defined as the products of communication, be they memos, letters, reports, Web sites, e-mails, speeches, or news releases. The aggregate of these messages is what a company sends to its constituencies, whether internal or external.

Finally, we also think it's important to distinguish corporate communication from "spin." This quackery, most recently associated with politicians, actually has a legacy of dishonesty dating back more than two millennia to the Greek philosopher Plato. He went so far as to ban poets and dramatists from the city-state for fear that their gift with words and detachment from ethical concerns would undermine the values of the community. While masquerading as ethical corporate communication, "spin" really peddles lies. As public relations expert Robert L. Dilenschneider has argued, "spin doctors" attempt "to alter the facts through a deliberate and reckless disregard for the truth."[6] Like Dilenschneider, we strongly endorse the need for companies to align their voice and image with who they are, to have integrity, to listen as well as speak, and, when they speak, to do so honestly. In other words, we see ethics as a necessary component of corporate communication. Now that we have defined the what, we return to the why.

CORPORATE COMMUNICATION: YOUR ATTENTION PLEASE!

At a Macro Level

The news items identified at the beginning of this chapter suggest only a few of the reasons you should take time to consider your company's corporate communication strategy. In addition, corporate communication can be one of the major ways to counteract the persistent scrutiny and negative attention that businesses face. Second, a good strategy can offset the technological advances that enhance the scope of the publicity barrage discussed above. Third, numerous lessons from corporate America demonstrate the harsh consequences of avoiding corporate communication. And, finally, corporate communication can serve as a differential advantage for your organization. So few companies practice this art that they leave those that do, and do it well, standing out from the crowd.

At a Micro Level

Corporate communication has a direct impact on your work, no matter where you're located on the organizational chart. Every manager needs to understand corporate communication, not just those officially in charge of public relations or communications. Think for a moment about the ways that corporate communication may affect your work life. Most obviously, as an employee, your company's internal communications influence your attitude toward the workplace: Do you work in an atmosphere of trust or anxiety? Are you confident that the messages you hear about your organization are timely and honest? Are there forums for voicing your concerns and offering your perspective?

If you work with constituencies external to your company—and this applies to most of us—corporate communication influences these relationships. For instance, your company's reputation can affect your ability to buy equipment, negotiate a contract, or make a sale. Your communications with a community can affect whether attempts to extend the business *into* that community are greeted with enthusiasm or hostility. Solid relations with investors can cushion or accentuate the reaction of financial markets to union unrest, reports of defective products, and announcements of anticipated failures to meet projected financial goals. Even those of you in start-up companies have to take into account corporate communication because the very survival of entrepreneurial organizations depends on their ability to manage communications with investors, potential and current partners, employees, suppliers, and customers.

Consider for a moment how the communications of your company affect your ability to be successful in your job. Who are your organization's key constituencies? What might improve company communications with them? How does your organization's corporate communications assist you in your work? All these questions take on even greater importance in light of the scrutiny with which business is regarded.

THE CRITICS AND THEIR NEGATIVE ATTITUDE TOWARD BUSINESS

Despite the overall health of our economy, criticism of business remains loud and persistent. One major source of negative perception is the ever-widening pay gap between CEOs and almost every other working individual. Public frustration grows as the press broadcasts the steep rise in executive pay at significantly higher rates than the salaries of other employees. These increases are primarily due to CEO stock options and seem to occur regardless of company stock market performance.[7] A survey of executive pay from 1990 to 2000 emphasizes its astronomical rise of 571 percent, a growth rate that looms even larger when compared to the modest rise in workers' paychecks of 37 percent during the same period.[8] Public advocacy groups and company shareholders alike decry what they view to be excessive compensation for those at the top and rally around the idea of "decompensation"—or the process by which executives are made to return portions of their huge compensation packages.[9] Technology has made this issue more visible as well. A Web site called "Executive Pay Watch"[10] has been developed for the purpose of monitoring top managers' compensation.

Beyond the outcry surrounding CEO compensation, surveys of attitudes toward business confirm a more general antibusiness sentiment on the part of the public. When responding to a series of questions about business in a 2000 Yankelovich[11] survey, the people polled were highly negative. When asked about:

Quality of products of big business: "The quality of products made by the very big companies has been slipping"—66% strongly agree or agree

Reliability: "The giant companies have gotten too big to give
   reliable service to their customers"—67% strongly agree
   or agree
Attitudes toward integrity of business: "Even well-known, long-
   established companies cannot be trusted to make safe,
   durable products without the government setting industry
   standards"—67% strongly agree or agree

The Yankelovitch survey found that the American public feels
business puts profits ahead of integrity. Employees also hold a strong
belief in the untrustworthiness of corporations. According to a survey
of 2000 employees by Walker Information, the majority of employees
believe that while senior management claims to act ethically, their
actions show something quite different.[12] Obviously, if employees, the
potential "ambassadors of goodwill" for a company, hold such views,
the image of business among external constituencies is bound to
decline.

Of course, public distrust of business is also fueled by an accumulation of media reports about irresponsible corporate behavior: charges of
sexual harassment brought by female employees against Mitsubishi;
accusations about Prudential selling unnecessary policies to clients; government and competitor charges against Microsoft for monopolistic
practices. The fallout from these incidents, however, seems to go beyond
individual organizations to hit big business as a whole. This is similar to
another phenomenon. If an organization in your industry engages in
neglectful behavior, then your entire industry is somehow tainted. Even
if your company abhors the bad practices of the offending corporation, if
you remain silent, your name will inevitably be affected by the negative
publicity.

Industry is also portrayed negatively in books and films. Michael
Moore followed up his 1989 film *Roger & Me*—a scathing exposé of
General Motors for its layoff of 30,000 workers in Moore's hometown—
with his 1996 book *Downsize This! Random Threats from an Unarmed
American.* The book, which was on the *New York Times Business Bestseller
List* for five months, continues Moore's critique of corporate aggression
against the American worker. From the start, he points out the chasm
between the larger-than-ever corporate profits and the increased worker
fear of downsizing.

The cinema provides a third medium for negative scrutiny. In the
1997 blockbuster film *Titanic,* the rich are depicted as villains and the

poor as suffering heroes. The male lead is a poor artist traveling in steer-age, and the main villain, J. Bruce Ismay, is the chairman of the shipping line, later infamous for his cowardice. To save himself, Ismay steals a lifeboat seat, leaving women and children to their watery fate. The movie perpetuates the belief that rich business guys are bad guys.

Commenting on both *Titanic* and a larger Hollywood trend, *Boston Globe* reporter Robert Krumer asserts that "In countless movies, the vil-lain is a corporate lawyer, a corrupt politician, an evil merger artist or the CIA. The subtext is almost Naderish: Little guy good, powerful guy bad. This theme dates to the infancy of talking pictures in the Great Depression."[13] Another example of this bias is the acclaimed 1999 film *The Insider*, a story about a top research scientist and executive at Brown & Williamson, one of the largest tobacco firms, who blows the whistle on the industry for lying about the dangers of smoking. To drive home its point, the movie continuously returns to the contrasting images of the seven CEOs from the top tobacco companies claiming ignorance of tobacco's harmful effects before Congress and then the whistle-blower condemning them for perjury.

And then there's the inimitable 2000 release, *Erin Brockovitch*, starring Julia Roberts as a twice-divorced, impoverished mother of three young children who, despite her lack of formal legal training, successfully defeats the corporate behemoth Pacific Gas & Electric Co., exposing their cover-up involving contaminated water. As a result of the film's success, the real Erin Brockovitch has been moved to further social action.

On a lighter note—but just as negative and damaging in its own way—is the popular "Dilbert" cartoon strip and its depiction of imper-sonal management at an anonymous corporation. Dilbert's inept boss victimizes his employees, leaving them powerless and frustrated through his inability to listen, his general incompetence, and his mind-numbing doublespeak by which he "rightsizes," "downsizes," "re-engineers," and "quality controls" the organization. The universal appeal of the comic strip's message is evident from its frequent appear-ance in corporate presentations and on office doors, and from the claims of "Dilbert" readers at many different companies that the anonymous corporation depicted in the cartoon is their own work-place. From the portraits of CEO greed to Dilbert's work life of quiet desperation, corporate America continuously appears in a very unflat-tering light. With so much negative attention focused on them, it is a wonder that organizations do not do everything in their power to refute this damaging commentary. Here we take a closer look at the rationale behind the silence.

THE COSTS OF DENIAL: PAY NOW OR PAY LATER

So, why do organizations refuse to look at the consequences of reported bad behavior or of bad publicity, even in the absence of wrongdoing? The answer may, in fact, be deeply psychological. From Freud to the present, psychologists have argued that when people confront a painful situation, they tend to deny its existence rather than to face it. They make believe it isn't happening because the pain is too great to bear. This phenomenon can even be seen operating with a "group mentality." As one expert describes it, the psychological life of groups offers "splendid opportunities for evasion and denial."[14] An excellent example of denial on the part of individuals is smoking.

Do you know people who still smoke? Researchers examining the best ways to get smokers to stop have yet to come up with an adequate solution. What impetus is most motivational? Arousing smokers' fear? Identifying the consequences of not changing this self-destructive behavior?

Antismoking advertising and huge taxes on cigarette sales notwithstanding, people continue to smoke. Despite the warnings from the surgeon general and the family doctor, the social ostracism from many circles, and the ban on trendy cartoon characters like Joe Camel, 25 percent of smokers make no attempts to stop and of the 16 million Americans who do try to stop each year, 14 million fail.[15]

Just like the smoker, companies in crisis do not really have the luxury of unresponsiveness. If they don't act thoughtfully now to mitigate potential damage (e.g., quit smoking), they will have to pay more later to correct the consequences of their neglect (e.g., mouth cancer, lung cancer, heart disease). Numerous historical examples and even current practices demonstrate this lesson. Let's look, for instance, at a classic case of corporate denial: Hooker Chemical Company and the Love Canal—the first major U.S. environmental crisis created by a corporation.

Hooker Chemical: America's First
Environmental *Cause Celèbre*

In the late 1970s, allegations arose that the Hooker Chemical Company had been using a site near Niagara Falls as a waste disposal dump. The Love Canal, as the area was called, began to leak carcinogens. Once the crisis became public knowledge, miscarriages, birth defects, and cancer deaths, among other things, were attributed to the company's actions. The controversy expanded as the Love Canal story became national news. It was picked up by *New York Times* reporter Don McNeil on the same day that the New York State government ordered an evacuation of the area. National and local newspapers conveyed vivid images of chemical sludge and sick mothers and children, and reported the impassioned pleas of the frightened citizenry as well as the demands of legislators for explanation and retribution.

Meanwhile, Hooker made no comment on the controversy—a deafening silence, in sharp contrast to the clamorous 13 months of attention given to the story by the local press, the *Niagara Gazette*. New York Governor Carey even focused on the incident in his campaign for reelection. Following these events, Hooker offered to pay $280,000 (or one-third the estimated cleanup costs) and put together an internal task force to communicate information to the public. These actions were, however, too little, too late.

Jim Green, manager of public relations for Hooker at the time, later reflected on the controversy:

> Love Canal is, and was, a disaster. It contains all the elements that could go into one of the longest running soap operas in history. For openers, it has that wonderfully sexy name: Love Canal. Then there is the magic appeal of a Niagara Falls dateline. Mix in mothers and fathers frightened into emotional peaks of hysteria by the hype of media reporting, both print and electronic.
>
> Add a laundry list of real, imagined, or suspected diseases and illnesses, miscarriages, and birth defects. Throw in a daily barrage of questions to which no responsible medical or regulatory authorities had the answers. And blame it all on indifferent-appearing local authorities and the alleged misdeeds of a corporate giant.[16]

Two decades after the dispute began, Hooker's parent company, Occidental Chemical, was still in the news. In 1995, the company agreed to pay $129 million to the federal government for cleanup, $102 million to the EPA's Superfund account, and $27 million to the Federal Emergency Management Agency, a family relocation service. Many people still believe that these payments were inadequate. They think Niagara Falls also deserves its share of the money for reputation damage; it may now be thought of as the "dump capital of the US" rather than the "honeymoon capital."[17]

Nike's Troubles in Asia

Twenty years after the Love Canal crisis, a similar story of denial unfolded at Nike when the company failed to respond to allegations that its suppliers were using child labor in Southeast Asia and paying less than subsistence wages. When the charges were first made, Nike Chairman Philip Knight denied them. Later he offered a weak rationalization—other companies abused overseas workers as well—that only served to inflame public opinion against the company. The media's perception of Nike became increasingly negative, and U.S. television networks encouraged public criticism by showing images of malnourished Asian children working in sweatshops. Even Gary Trudeau's comic strip "Doonesbury" portrayed Nike in a bad light. Only after several years—in May of 1998—did Knight institute a plan to remedy the problems, promising to raise wages and improve working conditions. The silence cost his company an enormous amount of goodwill.

Nike's limited response to criticism was especially surprising for two reasons. First, according to research conducted at the Tuck School of Business at Dartmouth, Nike workers in Vietnam were paid above-average wages and treated very well relative to the local economic conditions in Southeast Asia.[18] Second, although unresponsive to the negative press, Nike was astute in using external communications to its advantage. It had done a great job of building its popular image among consumers with its "Just Do It" advertising campaign and the use of famous spokespeople such as Michael Jordan and Tiger Woods. In all likelihood, the company found it much easier to promote its brand than to respond to bad publicity.

The costs to Hooker and Nike of doing too little too late were substantial. The lesson here—for us as individuals as well as for companies—is that if you don't pay now, you pay later and you pay a whole lot more. Yet, in many instances, companies are unwilling to take preventive measures by launching and sustaining credible defenses for their actions. If initiated properly, these actions can actually result in shaping positive impressions in the minds of a company's key constituencies.

The costs of denial have also risen in recent years because new communication technologies make a corporation's activities increasingly open to public scrutiny. Internet chat rooms and advocacy groups, along with the proliferation of cable TV channels, allow for the immediate dissemination of potentially damaging information about companies and for the repeated airing of these accusations. Investor groups, environmental activists, and economic isolationists can gain support for their antibusiness causes in a broadcast forum. Companies now have to deal with both legitimate and false claims against them in this rapid-fire, technologically assisted environment.

12

THE POWER OF CORPORATE COMMUNICATION

THAT PRESSURED, OUT-OF-CONTROL FEELING: THE NOISE ABOUT CORPORATIONS

Let's say that companies recognize the scrutiny with which they are regarded, the antibusiness bias, and the costs of denial. Even then they have another communication challenge to address: the amount of company information that's quickly and easily available to nearly anyone with Internet access and a subscription to cable or satellite television. With the growth of the Internet and the proliferation of TV channels, information can be disseminated more widely and more quickly than ever before. Just consider the leisurely pace at which the Watergate scandal unfolded on television and in the press during the mid-1970s, compared to the frenzied clip at which details of the Monicagate scandal hit cyberspace in the late 1990s. Indeed, *Reputation Management* has called today's business environment an "Age of Transparency," that is, "a time in which business will be forced to operate on the premise that all of its actions (and many of its thoughts) will ultimately be made public, and in which corporate reputation will be based less on the information that a company's professional communicators can shape and control and more on third-party perceptions...."[19]

Internet chat rooms and Web sites intensify the out-of-control feeling that companies experience in the face of transparency. These information portals have already exhibited some spectacular successes in influencing the fortunes of corporations: driving stock prices of companies up and down; providing timely data on executive pay that support negative perceptions of top management; serving as an electronic forum for employees and consumers to complain about management practices; and, as a result, acting as a tool to force change. Television also avidly seeks content about business controversies as this communication channel spawns an increasing number of stations and programming that include breaking business news, investigative reports, interviews with CEOs, and panel discussions with business leaders and reporters.

In *Faster: The Acceleration of Just about Everything*, cultural critic James Gleick warns that the multiplicity of communication channels and the information that flows across them create a perception of speed in our culture that denies us sufficient time and mental space to think. Our culture is moving toward increasing pressure and mindlessness. He argues, "The Web facilitates information consumption much as the remote control facilitates television watching. Reading on-line becomes another form of channel-flipping."[20] Certainly all of us have experienced the mind-numbing procession of e-mails that crosses our computer screens, and we have felt the pressure of being unable to respond thoughtfully to communications in the face of this overload. But, when we ourselves, or our organizations, are the topic of attention in e-mails and on the Web, the consequences may be much worse than discomfort or annoyance. Investor, consumer, and many other advocacy groups can affect the bottom line, dictating what a company must do on the basis of the group's interests, strength, and persistence.

There is so much noise in the mental environment that the *Los Angeles Times* drew attention to the mass of verbiage in a spoof announcing the launch of a new magazine called *Oh Shut Up!*. According to the "editors" of this apocryphal publication, its single, but sufficient, virtue is that "We are a major force of taciturnity."[21] What causes even greater "noise" about a corporation is the frequency with which communications about corporations amount to a set of deceptive, orchestrated theatrics—staged events with no underlying substance to them. Of course, the use of the staged event has been a staple of public relations for years, but what if your company is involved in a "play" that's not of its own making—or liking? For instance, in the case of one of our clients, a small high-tech firm, we learned about a staged event, a big public reception funded by a larger company hoping to enter into an agreement with our client. At the reception, the larger company announced to the press and to the greater high-tech community that an alliance had been formed between the two firms. Our client company had signed nothing; the announcement was staged with great fanfare simply to force the agreement. When deceptive theatrics are at work, how does a corporation use communications to counteract? How does it replace lies with the truth?

In such a noisy and chaotic business environment, corporations must have a coherent, consistent voice and image. The whole of the organization needs to speak with one voice. In light of new communication channels and the messages that flow across them (and in response to deceptive theatrics), companies need to monitor their constituencies' views. They need to become adept at articulating their own voice and getting that voice heard. Understanding how to craft an effective corporate voice and image is the main focus of the rest of this book.

MAKING THE "INVISIBLE" VISIBLE

Despite the scrutiny corporate behavior receives, antibig-business attitudes, and the proliferation of communication channels for voicing criticism, the importance of corporate communication to the life of big business has been given short shrift. As we have shown in this chapter, the attention of key constituencies to corporations has become ubiqui-tous, but businesses rarely take a look at the voice and image they proj-ect. We know that if left unaddressed, issues of corporate communication can come back to haunt a company; when addressed, they can extend its success.

From one perspective, the reason for neglect may be the absence of corporate communication as a subject in undergraduate and graduate business education programs. In other words, what is not studied sys-tematically is invisible. Anyone who studies business in college has taken courses in marketing, organizational behavior, finance, and even business communication skills, such as how to give an effective presen-tation or write a good report. (In fact, businesspeople are getting good at producing and responding to individual communications, and a large body of knowledge has developed about communication at this micro level.) Yet, issues of corporate communication are still conspicuously invisible, perhaps because the field has been unfairly and incorrectly downgraded as a "soft skill" unconnected to the bottom line. We hope this book will help to dispel that myth.

You may want to turn first to the chapters that address your organi-zation's current communication challenges—be they issues of reputa-tion, corporate advertising, crisis management, etc. Remember, though, that whatever corporate communication issue is your most current con-cern, any single issue is likely to be connected to others. For instance, an immediate crisis brings into play your company's management of its reputation and image advertising as well as how its corporate commu-nication function is designed and how its communications with all its constituencies are managed.

CONCLUSION

American business progressed more rapidly in the twentieth century than at any other time in history; yet, surprisingly, business has been scorned and vilified in what is, by any measure, the most successful cap-italist nation in history.

While we do not pretend to offer all the answers about how the rep-utation of a business can be transformed from the negative to the posi-tive, we do believe that a company's corporate communication, what we are describing as the voice and image of an organization, offers a unique opportunity for companies and individuals to present themselves as con-tributing partners in society. Our book offers you and your company an opportunity to gain the kind of respect that other institutions seem to have implicitly.

Our hope is that you will use this book as a field guide in building your company's reputation. Try to keep an open mind in reading the chapters to follow, and we think you will have a leg up on the competition.

2

THE ROOTS OF CORPORATE COMMUNICATION

Although corporate communication is a relatively new arrival in the workplace and in business education, it has a fascinating but somewhat tainted history. In fact, corporate communication can claim historical links to the field of public relations, which has been concerned with the voice and image of big business for nearly a century. In this chapter, we look selectively at the history of public relations, not for its own sake and not in any encyclopedic sense, but, rather, to identify those elements of the past that come into play today whenever decisions are made about a corporation's presentation of itself and its key messages. Because our interest is in corporate communication today, the chapter is, by no means, a full account of the history of public relations.

We begin with a brief assessment of the public's attitudes toward big business at the turn of the twentieth century, the context in which the field of public relations emerged. Then we turn to highlights in the careers of Ivy Ledbetter Lee and Edward L. Bernays, who competed for the title of "Father of Public Relations," to identify the issues these pioneers began to address that still concern us today in corporate communication:

- Keeping track of the larger social, political, economic, and cultural climate in which corporations create images and project their voices

- Taking advantage of the "opportune moment," or creating the circumstances for corporate communications
- Understanding and capitalizing on the psychology of constituencies
- Choosing the best mix of communication channels (e.g., video-conferences, e-mail, reports)
- Taking responsibility for the ethics of corporate communications.

We then consider these five issues in greater detail, especially as they inform us about how the voice and image of today's corporations are shaped.

Paradoxically, although we credit public relations for raising some of the issues central to corporate communication today, our goal is to *pull* corporate communication *out* of that tradition, usually taught in schools of journalism and communication, and to place it squarely within management education and within business practice where we think corporate communication belongs. We would like to see corporations develop *internal* managerial expertise in corporate communication and to learn how to use the outside expertise of public relations agencies wisely. From the outset, even as we explore the history of public relations, we want to affirm the importance of corporate communication as part of every manager's essential toolkit, as a set of mental habits shared by the leadership and understood at every level of management.

BIG BUSINESS UNDER ATTACK

Let's suppose we could take a satellite photo of the American landscape in the first years of the twentieth century. What would we find? At the center of our photo, we might see head shots of the captains of industry, such as William H. Vanderbilt, J. P. Morgan, John D. Rockefeller, Jr., that feature their serious-minded, detached, and even arrogant expressions. In the background, we might find increased urban density, the buildup of factories and railroads, and the closing of the American frontier.

Although such a photo would have been impossible at that time, we would have been able to pick up one of the new, cheap, popular American magazines to read about these tycoons' excessive wealth and untempered ambition for corporate power as well as the havoc they were wreaking on their more humble constituencies—farmers, laborers, railroad customers and employees, apartment dwellers, and home owners. The new magazines, including *McClure's* and *Munsey's*, and the investigative journalists, known as "muckrakers," who wrote antibig-business articles, were contributing to a change in the American landscape.

In contrast to the tolerance and even the support for business expansion in the 1890s, at the turn of the new century many Americans were beginning to see a dark side to the unrestrained economic growth and ruthless acquisition of power in the hands of a few wealthy men. Worries grew because, despite the Sherman Anti-Trust Act of 1890 which was intended to curb the growth of trusts (companies controlled by a central board of trustees to manipulate prices and destroy competition), their numbers continued to rise at the turn of the twentieth century. By 1904, about 5300 plant mergers had resulted in 318 industrial trusts valued at over $7 billion.[1] As historian C. C. Regier explains:

> ...people, partly because of the facts which the muckrakers revealed, partly because of the visions of better things which the reformers [political advocates in favor of improving economic conditions for the many] held before them, partly because of chastening personal experiences, began to regard the corporations as enemies rather than as friends. In particular, the comfortable middle classes, who had viewed the earlier stages of the growth of monopoly with considerable complacency, now began to fear the power of the trusts.[2]

Who, then, were the muckrakers singling out for public scrutiny? At center stage, the muckrakers placed the generic "Business Man." Muckraker Lincoln Steffens had this to say about the subject in his 1904 book, *Shame of the Cities*:

> The typical business man is a bad citizen; he is busy. If he is "big business man" and very busy, he does not neglect, he is busy with politics, oh, very busy and very businesslike. I found him buying boodlers [thieves or swindlers] in St. Louis, defending grafters in Minneapolis, originating corruption in Pittsburgh, sharing with bosses in Philadelphia, deploring reform in Chicago, and beating good government with corruption funds in New York. He is a self-righteous fraud, this big business man. He is the chief source of corruption, and it were a boon if he would neglect politics.[3]

Muckrakers also provided a voice for grievances against the abuses of specific industries: John D. Rockefeller's illegal attempts to control the oil industry, exposed in Ida Tarbell's *The History of the Standard Oil Company*, which became a contributing factor in the breakup of the Standard Oil Trust; the terrible sanitation problems in the meat-packing industry, graphically shown in Upton Sinclair's *The Jungle*; and the dishonest practices of the railroad trusts featured in Frank Norris's *The Octopus*. In addition, the new communication channels for the muckrakers' work—city newspapers and inexpensive magazines—enjoyed a large circulation.[4]

Along with alerting the public to the excesses of big business, the journalists supported regulatory laws championed by then President Teddy Roosevelt, among others, and demanded by a public seeking protection from large corporations. From 1900 to 1915, regulatory laws were passed to support reform in areas such as child labor, food safety, land conservation, worker's compensation, and prison reform.[5]

Under attack by the muckrakers and reforming politicians, big business began to question its attitude toward the public, an attitude captured by an exclamation attributed to multimillionaire businessman Cornelius Vanderbilt—"The public, the public be damned"—when he was asked whether the public should be taken into account when making corporate decisions.[6] Beginning in the 1890s, big business reevaluated this arrogant laissez-faire attitude as it became clear that such a corporate image was an economic threat to industry. Walter Lippman, a noted social commentator of the first decades of the twentieth century, tracked this shift in attitude in one of the first industries subjected to public scrutiny—the railroads: "They [big business men] are talking more and more about 'responsibilities,' their 'stewardship.' It is the swan-song of the old commercial profiteering and a dim recognition that the motives in business are undergoing revolution...."[7]

Whether interested in social responsibility or in merely appearing to seem so, big business needed strategies and techniques to articulate and convey this new voice and image. It is from this set of conditions that the fledgling discipline of public relations emerged and the careers of Ivy Ledbetter Lee and Edward L. Bernays began.

"THE FATHER OF PR"

Ivy Ledbetter Lee (1877–1934) grasped the importance of public opinion to the big businesses he served and used it to their advantage. Over the course of his career, Lee worked for some of the major industrial leaders of his time, including George Westinghouse (electronics), J. P. Morgan (banking), the Guggenheims (mining), and the Rockefellers (oil).

After working as a journalist in New York City, Lee created a public relations firm with George Parker in 1904. Lee had his first major opportunity to demonstrate the skills that made him famous when anthracite coal mine operators hired the firm in 1906.[8] The mine operators were already suffering from bad publicity they had brought upon themselves by their arrogant silence in the face of questions from the press during an employee strike in 1902. To remedy their bungled management of that crisis, they turned to Lee to handle the public relations of the company as another strike loomed in 1906.

To improve the mine owners' image and that of his own line of work, Lee put together a *Declaration of Principles* that he distributed to the press, a statement that spelled out the ethical conduct he expected of his own agency and his clients. Included in it was Lee's promise to the public and the press of open, timely, and complete information about the client. He suggested that a public informed by the facts would act rationally and respond favorably to a business that conducted itself ethically. Although the ethics of Lee and his clients would be scrutinized and condemned in other endeavors, in this instance his client, with Lee's guidance, made an abrupt change in behavior that yielded good results. The mine operators began to distribute to the press information about conditions in the mines, statements that were signed by specific operators to whom the information could then be attributed. Using Lee as their representative, the operators even invited further requests for information from the press and anticipated the needs of the press for copy. (Among other things, Lee provided reporters with materials they could readily use in their newspapers.) The result of this proactive, open approach was that the mine operators—and not just the potential strikers who had earlier developed good relations with the press—were able to get a hearing in the court of public opinion and to create the conditions for resolving the conflict that took into account the views of both parties.

Lee's next big client was the Pennsylvania Railroad Company.[9] Like the mine operators, top management at the nation's railroads habitually suppressed information from their constituencies. At the same time, the railroads were under attack by muckrakers, unions, government, the press, and the public for a variety of perceived ills, including high rates, secret rebates and other special privileges for favored consumers, increases in accidents, and poor management. The swell of complaints against the railroads led to passage of restrictive legislation, the Hepburn Act of 1906, and a string of other laws intended to curtail abuses by the railroad.

In this climate, the Pennsylvania Railroad Company attempted to resist government regulation in 1906 but made little headway because it lacked public support. Once hired by the company, Lee immersed himself in learning about the industry and then launched a public relations campaign in efforts to get out the company's point of view to counter the opposition's view that, among other things, the railroad was engaging in kickbacks, preferential treatment to favored clients, and unfairly high local rates.

At the heart of the campaign was Lee's insistence on open communications with the press. The railroad industry was known for poor press relations, especially when the breaking news involved an accident on one of their lines. Lee, having been a reporter himself, realized how important it was to cooperate with the press. He began the practice of inviting reporters to the scene of an accident, even paying for them to come, and setting up special facilities at the site for photographers and newspaper reporters.[10] Even in the wake of a disastrous accident, this new practice earned the Pennsylvania Railroad Company positive press coverage. As part of his campaign, Lee also published extensive analyses of the industry and its contribution to society.

Later, as representative of several railroads in the fight against government regulation, Lee extended his public relations efforts to include in-depth analyses of the railroads, a speakers' bureau composed of railroad executives who brought the railroad's cause to the public, and exhaustive distribution of material targeted to specific constituencies.[11]

While still employed by the Pennsylvania Railroad Company, Lee's services were sought by John D. Rockefeller, Jr. to help manage corporate response to the negative press and the resulting reputation for brutality that the Rockefellers had garnered following a bloody strike by their workers at the Colorado Fuel and Iron Company. (Ida Tarbell had earlier damaged the Rockefeller name in her critical exposé on the practices of Rockefeller's Standard Oil.) The event, which came to be known as the "Ludlow Massacre," took place on August 20, 1914, when the men hired by the Rockefellers to control the strike used physical force to suppress it. The fighting resulted in the deaths of several people and injuries to miners, their wives, and children. Before the public knew about his appointment, Lee worked clandestinely to support Rockefeller's cause, sending out press releases and articles on behalf of the Rockefeller organization under a third party's name. These activities broke one of his own pronouncements about public relations: the need for open communications. Moreover, he was also responsible for spreading misinformation about the Rockefellers' opposition; whether the result of hasty work or intentional lying, his actions in this regard flew in the face of another of his pronouncements: the need to convey accurate information to the public.[12]

Following the Ludlow incident, the U.S. Congress's Commission on Industrial Relations conducted hearings to explore the event more carefully. Because of Lee's high-profile role advising Rockefeller, Lee was asked to appear. His testimony revealed his total disregard for the accuracy of the material he had put before the public and his primary concern for presenting his client's case in a positive light.[13]

Lee further defined his ideas about public relations in his firm's newsletter of April 3, 1925: "What an individual or corporation tells of its doings, voluntarily and in advance, acts much more favorably upon every mind concerned than in the way of explanation after the fact. It is indeed the best use of publicity to prevent misapprehensions before they appear."[14] Unfortunately, his advice—disclose information proactively— which Lee gave so religiously to his clients was not always the guiding light in his own affairs.

The scandal that would cloud his reputation involved his decision to work as a public relations counsel for the powerful German company I. G. Farben, known in the United States as the German Dye Trust in 1934.[15] Farben hired Lee to help counter the anti-German feeling that permeated America in reaction to Hitler's persecution of the Jews. In essence, Lee was working for the Nazi government through his work with Farben, having been introduced to both Hitler and the infamous Nazi propaganda chief Joseph Goebbels. The fact that Lee asked the advice of the U.S. State Department before taking the account is a testament to Lee's naiveté; he was never accused of trying to hide his involvement with I. G. Farben. A year after beginning work with the German company, Lee was brought before a U.S. House Special Committee on the infusion of Nazi propaganda in America. Although his name was cleared of any wrongdoing by this investigation, the story was sensationalized in headlines such as this one in the *New York Mirror*: "ROCKEFELLER AIDE NAZI MASTER MIND."

Throughout Lee's career he was affiliated with some of the largest, most well-known American industries and organizations. He handled accounts for Macy's, American Tobacco, Lever Brothers, Chrysler Corporation, and General Mills, among others.[16] Despite the prestige of the companies he served, his own reputation was at best mixed, especially because of his involvement with I. G. Farben at the end of his life.

Was Lee primarily shrewd and dishonest, or was he a man of wisdom, broad learning, and an ability to apply his theoretical statements to the practice of public relations? The final judgment is ambiguous. Investigated by the federal and state governments and frequently maligned by the press, he nonetheless had his supporters.[17] One of them, *New York Mirror* reporter Henry Pringle, argued that much of the criticism heaped on Lee derived from his willingness to take on the legitimate public relations role of serving as spokesperson for the businesses he represented. Ironically, Lee was better at defending his clients' reputations than his own, refusing to answer his critics directly and promptly. In one of Lee's last statements about his profession, he stressed its role in helping companies create policy as well as communicating it—a significant addition to the scope of the profession and one that forward-thinking corporate communication experts engage in today. In Lee's words, this expanded role required the public relations counsel to "bring an intelligent, detached, outside point of view, based on a multitude of experience and contacts, and a keen, up-to-date study of trends, of new forces, of new currents of opinion.... Our business is becoming potentially a miniature brain trust for the business we are working with."[18]

Another widely known figure and a rival for the title "Father of Public Relations," Lee's contemporary, Edward L. Bernays, dominated the field during and after Lee's career.

A RIVAL CLAIMANT TO THE TITLE "FATHER OF PR"

The life of Edward L. Bernays spanned nearly the entire twentieth century. Born in the early 1890s, he lived over 100 years and worked in public relations for about 80 of those years. Not only was he continuously employed for his public relations services by a broad range of corporations, but he was also extremely prolific, tracking the concerns of his field from its early days, promoting his own reputation through his publications, and identifying some key ideas that experts in corporate communication are still grappling with today.

Bernays's first job in public relations—a field that had no real identity at the time—was to publicize a play called *Damaged Goods*, which dealt with society's refusal to acknowledge sexually transmitted diseases.[19] Two of the big challenges in producing this play in the early 1900s were to persuade New York City authorities to permit a public performance on a taboo subject and to gain the public's financial support for the play's production. To gain acceptance and support for the play, Bernays set up a committee of well-respected members of society to voice the importance of the play's message in testimonials to the press and to provide financial support for the play's production. This alignment of the play with respected members of the community—including a performance for President Woodrow Wilson and his cabinet—gave the play's controversial subject legitimacy through association and led to its success. Throughout Bernays's career, he would use this strategy of building credibility for his clients through association with respected members of society.

With this experience behind him, Bernays went on to serve as the publicity agent for another play, *Daddy Long-Legs*.[20] As with the earlier play, Bernays promoted *Daddy Long-Legs* by establishing alliances with respected members of the community who were concerned about a social issue—the institutionalization of orphans—and he went further by encouraging promotional tie-ins like Daddy-Long-Legs dolls. He then moved on to work as publicity agent for a number of artists, trying to build an audience for them in the United States. Among them were Diaghelev's Russian Ballet and its top performer, Waslaw Nijinski, and the great opera star Enrico Caruso.[21] In building the avalanche of attention for Caruso in the press of the cities on his tour, Bernays was struck by the aura surrounding the opera singer and the celebrity status that resulted from very little factual material. Bernays explained in his autobiography:

> I was impressed with the power an image has in affecting people; for the overwhelming majority of the people who reacted so spontaneously to Caruso had never heard him before. Some few may have listened to his recordings, but the attitudes of the mass had been formed by what they had read and heard about him. The public's ability to create its own heroes from wisps of impressions and its own imagination and to build them almost into flesh-and-blood gods fascinated me.
>
> The influence of Caruso on America cannot be measured accurately. Historically, it was like that of all great men who stimulate change. They make their appearance, the time is ripe and the public responds; then the engines of communication spread the news of change. The public gains new standards and criteria, and the culture pattern is changed. He became the symbol of serious music to millions of Americans....[22]

When the United States entered World War I, Bernays worked for the U.S. Committee on Public Information (CPI) to support its ambitous efforts to sell the war to the American public.[23] Following this stint, he teamed up briefly with a fellow employee at CPI, Carl Byoir, another giant in the field of public relations, to win the support of the American public for Senate passage of a resolution in favor of Lithuanian independence from Russia, an effort that succeeded in the early 1920s. This PR campaign was conducted primarily in the print media through newspaper articles, trade publications, editorials, and telegrams soliciting the vote of politicians. Bernays used two important new elements in his campaign—writing feature stories for a variety of target audiences, for instance, features about the Lithuanian theater for American theater lovers, and providing copy for newspapers that helped the editors fill empty space and PR specialists advance their clients' agendas.[24]

Bernays's career in public relations moved into high gear following his work for the theater and the government. Several high-profile engagements for prestigious corporations in the 1920s established his mark in the field of public relations and point to his contributions to corporate communication today: the Ivory Soap campaign for Procter and Gamble, the Torches of Freedom March for the American Tobacco Company, and Light's Golden Jubilee for General Electric.

Procter and Gamble and the Campaign for Ivory Soap

Procter and Gamble hired Bernays in 1923 to help promote some of their products, including Ivory Soap and Crisco. Upon hearing that Brenda Putnam, a sculptor, had asked the company for large amounts of soap to use for her work, Bernays came up with an unusual, creative scheme: Why not popularize soap sculpting as a new pastime for American children who typically couldn't care less about staying clean? Bernays wrote about the campaign: "Children, the enemies of soap, would be conditioned to enjoy using Ivory. And nothing would be wasted—soap shavings could be used for washing. The coincidence of public and private interest in the mingling of soap and art was so incongruous that it was bound to be newsworthy."[25] The campaign, then, created common ground between the company and its customers: the company's interest in selling soap and the public's interest in having clean kids engaged in wholesome artistic activity.

The Torches of Freedom March and the American Tobacco Company

Bernays's work for the American Tobacco Company, maker of Lucky Strikes, is filled with stories of wacky public relations campaigns, some more successful than others.[26] The most notable of his efforts was his attempt to make modern women aware of the social prejudice against women smoking in public, with the objective of increasing sales of cigarettes to women. (Men had already taken up the habit in large numbers during World War I when cigarettes were included in the soldiers' rations.[27]) The CEO of American Tobacco, George Washington Hill, worked closely with Bernays to mastermind this effort. Masking their direct involvement, they sponsored a "Torches of Freedom" March in 1929 in which a group of New York City debutantes, liberated "flappers" of the 1920s, walked down Fifth Avenue during the Easter Sunday

Parade, their lit cigarettes symbolizing women's assertion of their freedom to smoke openly in the streets. According to a psychoanalyst Bernays consulted for the campaign, "'Cigarettes, which are equated with men, become torches of freedom.'"[28] To enlist the participation of the debutantes, Bernays sent 30 of them the following telegram under the signature of his secretary who was not identified as a member of Bernays's staff:

IN THE INTERESTS OF EQUALITY OF THE SEXES AND TO FIGHT ANOTHER SEX TABOO I AND OTHER YOUNG WOMEN LIGHT ANOTHER TORCH OF FREEDOM BY SMOKING CIGARETTES WHILE STROLLING ON FIFTH AVENUE EASTER SUNDAY. WE ARE DOING THIS TO COMBAT THE SILLY PREJUDICE THAT THE CIGARETTE IS SUITABLE FOR THE HOME, THE RESTAURANT, THE TAXICAB, THE THEATER LOBBY BUT NEVER NO NEVER FOR THE SIDEWALK. WOMEN SMOKERS AND THEIR ESCORTS WILL STROLL FROM FORTY-EIGHTH STREET TO FIFTY-FOURTH STREET ON FIFTH AVENUE BETWEEN ELEVEN-THIRTY AND ONE O'CLOCK.[29]

Bernays scripted the event, suggesting where marchers should join the route of the parade and advising that some of the women should be escorted by men.[30] The event attracted national media attention and contributed to a change in women's smoking habits.

General Electric and Light's Golden Jubilee
In 1929 General Electric sought to mitigate the bad press it was suffering for its monopolistic practices in the lamp manufacturing industry. To improve its public image, the company hired Bernays to help orchestrate an event honoring Thomas Edison on the occasion of the fiftieth anniversary of the light bulb.[31] Henry Ford, a big admirer of Edison's, became thoroughly involved in the event as well, conceiving of and funding a facility to honor Edison, even transferring and reconstructing the original buildings in New Jersey where Edison had conducted his experiments. The culminating moment for honoring Edison's invention was Light's Golden Jubilee Celebration at the newly constructed Edison Institute of Technology, which included a technical school and a museum of Edison memorabilia.

Primarily from behind the scenes, Bernays staged a national public relations campaign that built excitement and anticipation for the event. Sensing that the country was ripe for celebrating an American hero, Bernays created a sponsoring committee, headed by President Hoover, that drew from respected leaders in government, the sciences, education, labor, and business. The establishment of the committee allowed Bernays to work

from behind the scenes. As a result, he created the impression that the esca-
lating waves of enthusiasm for Edison were spontaneously generated.

Bernays also orchestrated the pace and spread of publicity for the
event, releasing materials on all aspects of Edison's work to the press in
the six months prior to the celebration, hosting luncheons, providing a
speakers' bureau to give talks to local civic groups, and accelerating publicity in other cities as the fall date approached for the Dearborn celebration. All the while he tried to make the publicity he was crafting appear
spontaneous and unrehearsed, as if it were the genuine outpouring of
the nation's feelings for Edison's achievements. In the publicity drive
leading up to the event, the Post Office issued a two-cent stamp in honor
of Edison's achievements, a decision initiated by a letter from Bernays.
Through his orchestration of the publicity, Bernays also realized that he
had so built up public interest that the press had taken upon itself the
task of picking up on local and national events that had anything to do
with the anticipated celebration. He reflected upon the campaign later:

> From the grass roots to Broadway the spirit of ballyhoo took
> over. Mayors and Governors issued proclamations to celebrate
> Light's Golden Jubilee. Universities offered lectures on Edison
> and the implications of his discovery. Educational groups con-
> ducted essay contests. Librarians displayed books about Edison.
> Museum heads arranged exhibits that would illustrate the his-
> tory of light. Women's clubs throughout the country held
> exhibits honoring the Jubilee. Dining-car menus on leading
> trains mentioned the event. And to be sure that laggards acted,
> we sent copies of every dining-car menu that carried the
> announcement to superintendents of dining-car service who had
> not yet acted. Edison was the hero of the day.[32]

Consulting with Henry Ford, who had taken over the Dearborn celebration, Bernays advised about a whole range of details—the guest list,
the selection of members of the press corps who should receive special
accommodations to make their work easy, and even the use of horses
rather than cars to carry guests to the celebration as a way to underscore
the progress in science and engineering of the 50-year period and the
roles of Edison and Ford in creating these improvements. Among the distinguished guests at the ceremony were President Hoover, Will Rogers,
Madame Curie, and John D. Rockefeller, Jr. In summarizing Bernays's
role in the event, public relations historian Stuart Ewen wrote, "Bernay's
efforts were, at once, brilliant and invisible; as events unfolded, it was as
if history was simply running its course."[33]

In tandem with his public-relations practice, Bernays carved out time to write several books on his work and profession. He was often criticized for exaggerating his role in public-relations campaigns and for bragging about his contributions to the field. In his book *Public Relations*, he tended to confuse the history of modern public relations with his own career achievements, and in his *Biography of an Idea*, he quoted frequently from critics' favorable reviews of his work. Despite his personal grandstanding, Bernays did contribute some important ideas to the field of public relations that we can look to today as we consider corporate communication: concepts about group psychology, the staging of PR events, the need for a broad-based understanding of the public's attitudes, the relative merits of different communication channels, and the need for ethical behavior. Let's look now at two of his major books on public relations.

Crystallizing Public Opinion (1923) and *Propaganda* (1928)

In *Crystallizing Public Opinion*, Bernays defined the newly established profession of what he calls the "public relations counsel" (although many say that Ivy Lee had already used the term). Crediting the rise of pubic relations to the public's increased demand for information about companies and to growing competition for the public's dollars, he asserted that "the public relations counsel is the pleader to the public of a point of view. He acts in this capacity as a consultant both in interpreting the public to his client and in helping to interpret his client to the public. He helps to mould the action of his client as well as to mould public opinion."[34]

In this work Bernays discussed the counsel's special ability to understand the psychology of people and the techniques for influencing them. Bernays saw the public as divided into many groups, each of which reacts to circumstances emotionally and without reflection. Believing in a kind of "crowd-mentality," he argued that people are driven by primitive emotions, such as anger, fear, and the desire to flee, and are subject to the prejudices of the groups to which they belong. Bernays thought that the public-relations counsel—unlike everyone else—could set himself apart from the groups to which he belonged and objectively analyze the constituencies whom his client tries to influence:

> Perhaps the chief contribution of the public relations counsel to the public and to his client is his ability to understand and analyze obscure tendencies of the public mind.... It is his capacity for crystallizing the obscure tendencies of the public mind before they have reached definite expression, which makes him so valuable.

His ability to create those symbols to which the public is ready to respond; his ability to know and to analyze those reactions which the public is ready to give; his ability to find those stereotypes, individual and community, which will bring favorable responses; his ability to speak in the language of his audience and to receive from it a favorable reception are his contributions.[35]

Although Bernays did not refer specifically to his family relationship to Freud—he was Freud's double nephew (related through his father and mother)—the importance he gave to the psychology of primitive emotions in this early book suggests his respect for his uncle's work.

Bernays believed that the analysis of group life was important to a public-relations counsel because it provided the foundation for the strategies he devised for his clients. Such strategies, Bernays contended, had to bring into play the best mix of communication channels (which in Bernays's day included newspapers, magazines, lectures, conversation, the stage, and movies) and should include the creation of news: "The public relations counsel must lift startling facts from his whole subject and present them as news. He must isolate ideas and develop them into events so that they can be more readily understood and so that they may claim attention as news."[36]

Along with the privileges of his special kind of understanding, Bernays thought that the public-relations counsel needed to adopt a high standard of ethics, that "he must never accept a retainer or assume a position which puts his duty to the groups he represents above his duty to his own standards of integrity—to the larger society within which he lives and works."[37]

Propaganda (1928) extended some of the themes identified in the earlier work: the elite status and potential leadership roles of the public-relations counsel, the counsel's understanding of mass psychology used to help shape campaigns for clients, the counsel's talent for designing "created circumstances" or the invention of events to serve his client's goals, and the importance of ethics to the profession. In *Propaganda*, Bernays also attempted to define a "new propaganda" and the special powers of the public-relations counsel for managing it:

It is the purpose of this book to explain the structure of the mechanism which controls the public mind, and to tell how it is manipulated by the special pleader who seeks to create public acceptance for a particular idea or commodity. It will attempt at the same time to find the due place in the modern democratic scheme for this new propaganda and to suggest its gradually evolving code of ethics and practice.[38]

And, as he further explained, "Any society, whether it be social, religious, or political, which is possessed of certain beliefs, and sets out to make them known, either by the spoken or written words, is practicing propaganda."[39] Of course, from our perspective, this attempt to strip the term *propaganda* of its negative connotations was a dismal failure. Indeed, Bernays's use of the term in the 1920s to explain the effort of the public relations counsel to "create or shape events to influence the relations of the public to an enterprise, idea or group"[40] was quickly superseded by its use as a term of condemnation to refer to the diabolical manipulation practiced by totalitarian systems beginning with Hitler's in the 1930s and continuing to this day. In the corporate world, the association of PR with propaganda is long-standing and quite damaging to those in the profession who conduct themselves ethically.

ISSUES IN CORPORATE COMMUNICATION

The careers and thinking of Lee and Bernays, pioneers in the field of public relations, suggest several issues that those interested in corporate communication should consider today:

- The larger social, political, economic, and cultural climate in which corporations create their images and project their voices
- The "opportune moment" or the creation of circumstances for corporate communications
- The need to understand and capitalize on the psychology of constituencies
- The best mix of communication channels (e.g., videoconferences, e-mail, reports)
- The ethical dimension of corporate communication

The Big Picture: The Social, Political, Economic, and Cultural Climate

As we saw earlier in this chapter, the concern of corporations about their image with constituencies began more than 100 years ago as muckraker journalists shone a spotlight on the monopolistic wealth and unrestrained expansion of big business. Aware of the public's negative attitude toward big business, Lee looked out on this world and saw that the unrestrained actions taken by tycoons like John D. Rockefeller, Jr. would have to be tempered by both responsiveness to his constituencies and by an image of corporate responsibility. In fact, throughout Lee's career, his business associates remarked on his ability to attend to a wide range of social, political, economic, and cultural currents and their implications for the public image and voice of his clients.

Like Lee, Bernays was a keen observer of the big picture in which corporate America operates. As his orchestration of the Torches of Freedom March demonstrates, Bernays could capitalize on this under- standing to support the agendas of his clients, in this case, harnessing feminist interest in expanding the freedom of women to get them to par- ticipate—albeit unwittingly—in the marketing of American Tobacco's cigarettes. In his reflections on public relations, Bernays himself linked his work to the larger context in which big business operates. Remarking on the early years of his field in terms of the climate in which business operated, he said:

> ...many large corporations were employing public relations counsel under one title or another, for they had come to recog- nize that they depended upon public good will for their contin- ued prosperity. It was no longer true that it was "none of the public's business" how the affairs of a corporation were man- aged. They were obliged to convince the public that they were conforming to its demands as to honesty and fairness.[41]

Moreover, although he observed that the climate for business was friendly in the 1920s (the time of his writing *Propaganda*), Bernays warned—prophetically, given the hostility toward business in the Depression of the 1930s—that "it would be rash and unreasonable to take it for granted that because public opinion has come over to the side of big business, it will always remain there."[42]

One lesson to be drawn from the work of Lee and Bernays, then, is that as managers, we need to become astute "readers" of our culture. We need to cast a very wide net to locate those aspects of American society, politics, economics, and culture that can influence how our organizations are perceived and how best to get our image seen and our voice heard. As individual communicators, many managers have learned to take into account their image and voice for a particular speech or written commu- nication by "reading" the particular audience: Will they be bored or engaged? Informed or ignorant? Biased or neutral? These are the basics of individual communication.

For corporate communication today, "reading" the culture means paying attention to issues that impinge on your particular firm and industry. For example, if you're working for an Internet firm, user pri- vacy and security are concerns for your key constituencies, especially customers. If you're in the defense industry, U.S. relations with foreign countries are critical: Following the terrorist attacks of September 11, 2001, on the World Trade Center and the Pentagon, how will public opinion and federal policy influence the competitive structure and product lines of the industry? If you work for an established multinational firm, how will Gen Xers' interest in entrepreneurship, with their accompanying desire for quick acquisition of wealth and a balance between workplace and family life, affect your ability to hire and retain managers? We invite you to think about your organization and industry and to track the broader issues that may affect your corporate communications.

The "Opportune Moment" and the Staged Event

Along with an awareness of the larger climate in which organizations operate, Lee and Bernays developed the strategist's talent for sensing the right moment for their clients to communicate their messages and the dramatist's gift for, in Bernays's words, "created circumstances," that is, establishing scenes, actions, actors, props, and drama that craft an impression of the organization in the minds of its constituencies. When orchestrated well, these "created circumstances" become media events, attention-getting activities of newsworthy quality. Moreover, though staged and contrived, these events can be made to appear to be spontaneous and natural. We need only think of two classic examples of this talent: Bernays's work for the Torches of Freedom March and Light's Golden Jubilee. Corporate communication today is replete with such events as well: for instance, the huge annual investor or employee meetings that large corporations hold, such as Sun Microsystems and Microsoft; and the Avon Breast Cancer Walkathons in support of research and treatment. Think about your organization in this regard. What are the "opportune moments" you can take advantage of to enhance your company's image?

The "Psychology" of Constituencies

Although not formally trained in psychology, Lee and Bernays held certain beliefs about the psychology of their clients' constituencies, and these beliefs influenced how these PR pioneers put together a public relations campaign. For Lee, his clients' constituencies seemed to be capable of rational decision making and so should be provided the facts on which to base decisions.[43] Bernays, who formally addressed the issue of mass psychology, believed that the public was driven by primitive emotions. As a result, the public could be persuaded by symbols, such as the lit cigarette (a sign of independence in the Torches of Freedom March) or national figures turned into symbols, that is, into celebrity heroes like Caruso or Edison. Symbols, by their nature, appeal to the emotions, not to the judgment or intellect. On the basis of his views, Bernays also thought that the public was susceptible to the entertainment value of news events, even when they were contrived.

Today, it makes sense for managers interested in corporate communication to ask themselves: What's my view of human nature as I apply it to my company's constituencies? Are they rational and astute in their judgments or driven, instead, by their emotions?Are my constituencies similar to one another, or are some likely to be persuaded by logic and others by emotional appeals?

Communication Channels and the Role of Technological Innovation

Looking back over the last century, we can see how technological innovation spawned new communication channels that served as conduits for corporate communications. For instance, the emergence of inexpensive magazines with large readerships created an audience for the muckrakers' antibusiness messages. In the early decades of the twentieth century, corporate communication relied heavily on print media. In the 1920s and 1930s, radio and motion pictures were the innovative communication channels. Edison's voice was heard over the radio around the nation during the Light's Golden Jubilee, publicizing the event far beyond its physical location and thereby contributing to his celebrity status. In the political arena, President Franklin Roosevelt's "fireside chats" rallied a nation in the depths of the Depression. Winston Churchill's words inspired a country to hold firm against the Nazis. And as television took hold in the 1960s, John F. Kennedy was elected president, at least in part, as a result of his performance in the debates against Richard Nixon. Today, Internet Web sites, chat rooms, computer bulletin boards, e-mail, FAX-800 numbers, and an expanded number of radio and television stations have joined the mix of communication channels that managers can choose for their corporate communications. For managers, there are a host of questions to address: What are the relative merits of different channels for conveying communications? When is old-fashioned face-to-face communication preferable? Where would a video clip on an Internet Web site be most powerful? When would it be best to use several channels in concert? Over the course of this book, we look at numerous scenarios in which managers choose among communication channels to convey their company's image and voice.

The Ethics of Corporate Communication: Snake Oil or Honest Representation?

The fathers of public relations were so concerned about the ethics and reputation of their profession that each published explicit statements about professional ethics, for example, Lee's treatise, *Declaration of Principles*, and Bernays's many books which dealt with this subject. The most cynical critics might say that these published statements were just "smoke and mirrors" to mask the real nature of their acts. Even the most sympathetic critic would have to say that some of their practices were shady at best. Think of Lee's work for I. G. Farben and Bernays's theatrics in support of the American tobacco industry. Indeed, the long saga of the ongoing tobacco wars is, from one vantage point, a study of the distortion and manipulation practiced by Lee, Bernays, and many public-relations agencies that followed them as counsels to the big tobacco companies, which are still vigorously engaged in masking or minimizing the health hazards of their product to continue making profits.[44] Moreover, as watchdog and governmental oversight groups have revealed, the activities of several public-relations agencies are mired in lies and distortion, and even in the malpractice of infiltrating groups whose task it is to expose and curtail unethical company practices, such as the creation of environmental hazards and unsafe food and drugs.

In the hands of people with questionable ethics, the strategies and techniques of corporate communication can serve evil ends. At worst, corporate communication is the practice of publicity stunts and spin, managed by modern-day "snake-oil salesmen" interested in covering up the real activities and intentions of the companies they serve. By contrast, a corporate reputation that is built by honest, open corporate communications can be better than cash in the bank, as we will see in, among other examples, the discussion of Johnson and Johnson's management of the Tylenol poisoning in Chapter 10 on crisis communication.

The final question this chapter poses, then, is one that goes beyond the bounds of this book: Will you as a manager use what you learn about corporate communication for ethical or illegitimate ends? Will your company "walk the talk" or just talk in a way that masks the truth? This is an ethical choice. The strategies and techniques of corporate communication are morally neutral.

CONCLUSION

A look at the roots of corporate communication brings into focus a number of issues that managers face today when they consider how to craft the voice and image of their organization: an understanding of the larger social, political, economic, and cultural climate; a talent for finding or creating the circumstances for organizations to be seen and heard as they wish; an ability to capitalize on the psychology of constituencies; the need to discover the best communication channels; and the inextricable links between corporate communication and ethical choice. The chapters that follow echo and extend these issues in light of the contemporary scene for big business. Rather than merely dead and gone, history offers lessons about and an important prelude to today's corporate communication challenges.

3

How Corporate
Communication Works

MOST MANAGERS TODAY RECOGNIZE the need to develop their speaking and writing skills and their ability to communicate effectively in groups. But for those who aspire to the top ranks of leadership, understanding how to craft their organization's voice and image to get buy-in from key constituencies matters at least as much. The experts in corporate communication whom we interviewed confirm emphatically the importance of communication with a big "C"—Corporate Communication—to the success of senior management. A sampling of opinions makes this quite clear.

From Phyllis J. Piano, vice president of corporate communication at Raytheon, we heard: "If you want to be a top leader, you need to understand your obligations to the various audiences in terms of communication. You need to tell your story effectively. The difference between those who are at a high level and those who can't get there is the ability to articulate vision and strategy to a broad audience."[1] Steven J. Harris, vice president of communications at General Motors, explained: "If leaders are successful, they will spend an increasing amount of time on communication issues. Just pick up *Fortune*, for example, and you'll see executives explaining what their company is doing."[2] Elizabeth Heller Allen, vice president of corporate communication at Dell Computer Corporation, advised: "You will never be a corporate leader without understanding corporate communication. There is no corporate leader who is bad at it. Analytical skills alone won't get you to the top. Public opinion and employee opinion count."[3] Lewis Platt, former CEO of Hewlett-Packard, reflecting on his tenure there, expressed regret for not having communicated proactively, and praised some of today's CEOs for putting themselves in the public eye and recognizing the need to do so:

> In retrospect, I wish I was more rebellious. We live in a world where visibility and what you say have become more important. Leaders in the industry—Michael Dell, Scott McNealy [of Sun Microsystems]—generate a lot of interest. There's a positive aura that surrounds their companies because they're upfront. I was brought up in a world that said, "Do great things and the world will notice."[4]

As Platt went on to explain, actions alone are insufficient. They must be accompanied by carefully honed and focused communications.

So if you want to succeed in your organization or to start your own business, knowing how corporate communication can work successfully takes on even greater importance because the higher you rise in an organization, the more you'll be responsible for the voice and image your organization projects. Entry-level managers need to give credible performances in pitching their ideas to those they report to, but a CEO speaks for the company as a whole about strategic issues that shape the organization's future.

In this chapter, we look at how corporate communication can work, exploring the multiple meanings of corporate communication—as the voice of the corporation and the images it projects to key constituencies, as a set of mental habits to be internalized by all employees, as a function that may be centralized or decentralized across a company's units, and as the products of communication. We offer two vantage points from which to view how corporate communication can function. We begin at the top from the eagle's perch, with the example of GE's former CEO Jack Welch, who retired in 2001. Welch, a master of corporate communication, ably served his organization as a spokesperson for its key strategies and values as well as inculcated the importance of communication in his employees. Then we navigate from the top down to consider corporate communication as a function, looking at the role of corporate communication experts in assisting the CEO, as well as the scope of activities that the corporate communication function can perform and where it may be best placed.

Before you read further, however, try to get an understanding of how corporate communication works in your own organization:

• How would you assess the CEO's skills as a corporate communicator?

- What communication expertise does the organization provide to assist the CEO? For instance, is there a department of corporate communication with a staff of experts? If so, what does the department do, and how well does it work?

- Is communications expertise an integral part of your organization, or is it brought in only when there is a crisis?

As you will now see, not only must managers acquire skills in communication with a big "C" to advance to the highest ranks of their organizations, but, to be successful, organizations must have at their helm CEOs who are masters of corporate communication.

A LESSON FROM THE TOP

Across the many interviews we conducted with communication experts in the workplace, we repeatedly heard a single idea: that the CEO must be the force behind corporate communication and must lead by example. This idea marches with the force of a drum beat through the interviews and led us to put the spotlight on those CEOs who can be characterized as great communicators. At the top of our list is Jack Welch, who was CEO of General Electric (GE) for over 20 years from the early 1980s to the fall of 2001. As he prepared to leave his position, the company's year-2000 earnings of $12.7 billion were more than eight times larger than its 1980 profits of $1.5 billion. Revenue more than quintupled to $129.9 billion. GE shares had grown more than 5 percent, inclusive of dividends, since Welch's first day on the job. The S&P 500 increased 1433 percent over the same period, or around 14.3 percent a year.[5]

GE's Jack Welch: The Great Corporate Communicator

There have been volumes written about Jack Welch, whose management practices have made him one of the most celebrated and respected leaders and educators in corporate America. Indeed, many top managers of Fortune 500 companies, including CEOs at over a dozen U.S. companies,[6] got their training by working at senior management positions under Welch.

Our purpose here is to focus on his genius for corporate communication and what we might take away from his example for our own use. From this perspective, four interrelated themes emerge from his activities as CEO of GE: the strong partnership between communication and strategic planning, the place of communication as a core organizational value in transforming the company and sustaining its vitality, the role of communication for GE as a "learning organization," and the importance of streamlining communications by reducing unnecessary bureaucracy.

Communication as Part of Strategic Planning.   For Welch, communication took center stage in all his efforts to create strategic change at GE. Were we to follow him through a typical year's planning cycle, we'd see that he scheduled numerous opportunities for informal, intense dialogues with his 35 direct reports, who were held accountable for explaining and defending their strategic recommendations for their businesses.

As described to shareholders in the GE Annual Report for 2000, Welch's meetings with senior management, known as the "GE Operating System," represent a "series of intense learning sessions in which business CEOs, role models and initiative champions from GE as well as outside companies, meet and share the intellectual capital of the world: its best ideas."[7] In Corporate Executive Council (CEC) meetings, which typically begin at 8 A.M. and run until 10 P.M., talk ranges from reviews of performance targets to discussions of best practices, customer impact, and succession planning, including selection of candidates for leadership training.

The Welch calendar of meetings may be planned ahead with goals and agendas, but the meetings themselves are anything but formal in tone. As a firsthand observer reported,

> These sessions earn descriptions from executives like "food fights" and "free-for-alls." They are where Welch collected unfiltered information, challenged and tested his top players, and made sure that the organization's triumphs and failures were openly shared. "I may be kidding myself,'" says Welch, "but going to a CEC meeting for me is like going to a fraternity party and hanging around friends. When I tell my wife I can hardly wait to go, she says, 'Well, why wouldn't you? You hired them all!' If you like business, sitting in that room with all these different businesses, all coming up with new ideas, is just a knockout.[8]

Moreover, important strategic issues—like acquiring new businesses or selling old ones—were typically addressed at one session and scrutinized again and again at later meetings of the full CEC or in smaller groups. When CEC was not in session, Welch could be found traveling to each of the separate GE businesses for a closer review of their operations. Welch met many of his employees, and

...every one of Welch's direct reports—from three vice-chairmen to each of the operating heads of GE's 12 businesses...receives a handwritten, two-page evaluation of his performance at the end of the year. "I do the evaluations on Sunday nights in my library at home," says Welch. "It gives me a chance to reflect on each business." Attached to the detailed notes are his jottings from a year earlier, with new comments written in red pencil in the margins. "Nice job." "Still needs work."[9]

As his work with senior management indicates, Welch takes a hands-on approach, motivating through compelling words and actions.

Communication as a Core Value: Repeat! Repeat! Repeat!   The company's chief strategist and communicator, Welch was the teacher, role model, and coach for all his employees. As biographer Robert Slater described him:

> He is the communicator par excellence. Of all his management secrets, his uncanny ability to communicate, to engender an enthusiasm in employees, may be his greatest. He knows that it is not enough to simply raise an idea with employees. He's not naïve enough to believe that all 270,000 of his workers will absorb his ideas the first time around. He knows that he will have to keep repeating an idea until it finally sinks in with everyone at the company.[10]

Repeating ideas ensured that they were heard broadly, but, as important, Welch was selective in what he broadcast, choosing to communicate ideas at the heart of his vision for GE, core values he wanted to inculcate in his employees. He expressed these ideas simply and with passion, and disseminated them across the company's key constituencies—in the shareholder's letter in the company's annual report, in talks with employees and financial analysts, in interviews with the press.[11] Rather than "hot-house" ideas that die as soon as they are uttered, through the force of selective repetition, Welch's messages had high impact, functioning as guidelines for action.

Welch, however, could not do it all. Rather, he taught by example: going out into the field, leading the communications effort, and establishing expectations that management would follow his lead. His job was to motivate senior management, and they, in turn, motivated the ones below them—and on and on in this way through the ranks. The communication process might be described as a kind of cascading movement:

As if in lockstep, each business chieftain... emulates the behavior of the boss, and their reports, in turn, do the same. After Welch's Boca meeting [a CEC meeting] in January, for instance, Lloyd G. Trotter, CEO of GE's electrical-distribution and -control business, had his own 2-1/2 day leadership conference in Orlando with his top 250 people. And in February, after Welch gave him his bonus and reiterated the targets for the remainder of this year, Trotter then followed through in similar fashion with the 97 people in his organization who received cash bonuses. Other GE businesses follow the same format.[12]

Not surprisingly, some of Welch's most memorable ideas are themselves about communication as a core value. Several of these GE values appear on a wallet-size card that all employees are supposed to carry: "GE Leaders...Always with Unyielding Integrity Create a Clear, Simple, Reality-Based Vision...and Communicate It to All Constituencies."[13] Here Welch stressed how important it is for leaders to express themselves succinctly and clearly. Using this style of communication maximizes the possibility that key strategic ideas will make sense to a broad base of constituents and have a positive impact on all of them. "GE Leaders...Always with Unyielding Integrity Have the Self-Confidence to Involve Everyone and Behave in a Boundaryless Fashion." Here Welch emphasized the entrepreneurial aspects of communication, that is, the need for leaders to pay serious attention to new ideas that come from any source, including not only those of senior executives but also those of workers at the lowest ranks. As an advocate of the "democratization" of communication, Welch established a climate in which people from the lowest level to top management could "throw in their oar" in conversations about the company's present and future.

The two sections that follow put the spotlight on two of the communication challenges articulated in the short, high-impact messages of the GE employee value card:

- The role of Work-Out, a New England village-style forum for communication that Welch initiated in late 1980,[14] in supporting and extending communications throughout the firm
- The creation of a leaner organization, better prepared to respond to threats and implement new ideas

Work-Out: Extending Communication More Deeply into the Organization.
"GE Leaders...Always with Unyielding Integrity Are Open to Ideas from

Anywhere...and Committed to Work-Out," says the GE employee value card. Although "Work-Out" may sound like an aerobics exercise routine from the 1980s, it was, in fact, one of the premier communication processes at GE. Initiated in the late 1980s, "Work-Out" was a forum for brainstorming and decision making for employees and their bosses that reached down into the organization. The process extended dialogue and debate beyond the very senior ranks, ensuring that GE remained an informal "learning organization." Whereas executives have described the Corporate Executive Council (CEC) meetings as "food fights" and "free-for-alls," the culminating event at Work-Out resembled a grueling oral examination with questions and recommendations hurled at managers by their subordinates.

As described in the early days, Work-Out consisted of three-day sessions where groups of 40 to 100 employees exchanged ideas about their business and how to improve it. At the first session, once the unit boss set up the agenda, he or she departed, and the sessions included only a facilitator and the boss's subordinates, who brainstormed about the unit's problems and possible solutions. When the boss returned on the final day, he or she was subjected to rapid-fire comments and recommendations by subordinates, required to make decisions based on the recommendations, and if necessary, to form a team for follow-up research.[15] Imagine the kind of scrutiny and accountability the bosses faced in this lively public forum. Consider how important their understanding of corporate communication is to holding down their position, and, from a broader perspective, to reaching the best decisions for the organization. As an indication of just how deeply the approach permeated the organization, "by 1992, over 200,000 GE employees—along with customers, suppliers, and others—had experienced Work-Out in contrast to 10,000 managers annually attending programs at Crotonville [GE's management training center]."[16] Early on, Work-Outs focused on streamlining the stodgy, slow-moving bureaucratic processes at the firm, but later sessions dealt with how to improve productivity, quality, and customer and supplier relationships.[17]

Cut Through Bureaucracy!   When he assumed leadership of GE in the 1980s, Welch inherited a huge bureaucracy with communication processes and procedures that slowed down strategic decision making. The business heads spent endless hours compiling thick written documentation about strategy, an activity that deflected their attention from purposeful work. To create an organizational context for growth, Welch had his business heads replace these tomes with short "playbooks" that identified important strategies, and used these documents as the spring-board for his strategic discussions with management.[18] Increasingly, face-to-face talk replaced time-consuming written procedures.

By the late 1990s, the company had all but removed old-fashioned written communication. GE is practically a paperless organization. With the exception of the annual report in which Welch liked to spell out to investors his map and vision of the company, communication at GE means face-to-face meetings, videos, and Web-based communications. Everything that used to be on paper is now on the Web, allowing for instantaneous communication across the business units and 120 countries in which GE operates. What better way to connect a sprawling, diversified company, to reach everyone in real time, and to connect with lots of people on the road located in eight separate businesses that span the globe. No longer encumbered by tons of paper, GE increasingly relies on e-mail and face-to-face discussions, communication channels that allow for the informal exchange of ideas. Many senior-level managers applauded his initiatives:

> "I still remember him [Welch] coming to Louisville, Ky, and saying, 'Lemme tell you how I'm going to get rid of all this bureaucracy,'" says Bruce Albertson, formerly an executive at GE Appliances in Louisville, Ky. "Everyone is sitting there saying, 'Yeah, right.' But he ripped the bureaucracy right out of the middle of that company. All that churn we used to do, preparing internal charts for people who gave them to someone else who gave them to someone else who gave them to Jack, did go away."[19]

To spread and invigorate the exchange of ideas, Welch dispensed with layers of management early in his tenure. From the early 1980s to the early 1990s, he reduced the number of management levels between himself and those in the field from nine to between four and six.[20] A leaner organization meant, in his words, the ability for "GE to develop a big-company body in a small-company soul,"[21] to operate with the agility and nimbleness of a small entrepreneurial firm. Equally important is what he calls the "delayering" of the organization—the reduction of management levels—that has created a climate in which great ideas can be heard, and, for those that pass the rigorous test of scrutiny and debate, implemented. The leaner organization made it easier for employees at GE, in Welch's words, to "Find great ideas, exaggerate them, and spread them like hell around the business with the speed of light."[22]

Welch's assumption of the top leadership position occurred during a time of relative stability at GE. From our perspective, many of the initiatives he championed and the culture he shaped were able to stave off the potential inertia of the more than 100-year-old firm whose command he assumed. When an organization faces the perils of inertia, as in the case of GE, CEOs, armed with a knowledge of corporate communication, can work wonders in leading their organizations through change to renewed health and vitality. Upon taking the reins and throughout his tenure, Welch recognized the need to target important constituencies and to keep communicating key ideas simply and with passion. He knew he had to use face-to-face communications to build credibility and then to maintain relationships with internal constituencies—employees and senior management—who are potentially the most powerful goodwill ambassadors for a firm as it reaches outside its walls. Welch made communication a core value and included it as part of every senior manager's performance review to ensure that this value permeated the organization. And he did not do this all alone. Support came from, among other venues, the corporate communication function. In the next section, we look at the role of these managers in ensuring that corporate communication works successfully in support of their organizations.

GETTING HELP TO BROADCAST THE COMPANY'S STORY

Even the best CEOs need counsel and support to get their company's messages out to important constituencies and to ensure that their strategic decisions are implemented. Corporate communication can't be a solo act. In turn, those who support the CEO—be they corporate communication directors and their departments, pubic relations firms, or some combination of the two—need, as a minimal requirement for success, to be championed by the CEO. As directors of corporate communication have told us, whether a company is an established old-economy firm like Sears or a new-economy company like Dell, the CEO's stamp of approval is essential. From Ron Culp, senior vice president of public relations and government affairs for Sears, Roebuck and Company, we heard:

> It all starts with the CEO. You need commitment on his or her part. When you report to the CEO, this gives the [corporate communication] function emphasis and credibility. Everyone listens to you if you report to the CEO. It's as though the CEO puts his arm around you and says, "This is my guy."[23]

From Elizabeth Heller Allen, vice president of corporate communication for Dell Computer Corporation, we learned:

There's an interesting point about the CEO's understanding of corporate communication. Michael Dell understands the function and supports me. He is an integral part of the brand, a leading component of the brand, and he's very cooperative and easy to deal with. When we make a recommendation, he generally follows then.[24]

A long-time communications expert in the auto industry, GM's vice president for communications Steven A. Harris, explained to us:

When I took the job, I needed the CEO's support, especially with an organization of this size and complexity. It is critical for the Vice President of Communications to be at the table with the CEO and to be involved in strategy development. In this way, he or she can make sure that communication is not an afterthought. It's upfront in decision making. Firms are now aware that so much of corporate reputation depends on how well you communicate where you are going as a company.[25]

The assessment of these experts is backed up by broader survey data and analysis conducted by Heyman Consulting, a division of that executive search firm. In their recent study of corporate communication at over 200 companies (many of which are *Fortune* 500 corporations, representing a range of industries from banking to media and entertainment), Heyman found that "one of the characteristics which seems to distinguish companies with the most effective public affairs departments [called corporate communication departments at most firms] is the consistency of and resultant credibility that comes from having unimpeded access to a CEO, not just a reporting line."[26]

The strong commitment of the CEO to the corporate communication function and the working partnerships between CEOs and directors of corporate communication can spell the difference between the success and failure of the function and, more broadly, can enhance the company's ability to build its reputation and get its strategic objectives implemented. According to David R. Drobis, senior partner and chairman at the public relations firm Ketchum, the head of corporate communication has moved into the top ranks of management. "The most exciting thing that's happening is the elevation of the corporate communication person, moving into a more strategic role on providing direction for all phases of communications—internal and external—and how it affects the company's business. This is way beyond the role of media relations traditionally assigned the public relations function."[27]

Corporate communication has arrived rather late at the CEO's table, long after strategy and more traditional functions like accounting, marketing, and finance. Certainly since the Hooker crisis in the 1970s and the Tylenol scandal in the early 1980s, business has become aware of the importance of the company's voice in times of crisis. In addition, CEO heroes of the 1980s and 1990s like Jack Welch of GE and Lou Gerstner of IBM, who reached celebrity status in this country, have valued the power of communication in formulating and implementing strategy and in supporting the continuous renewal of their companies. They and other corporate leaders have been outspoken about the importance of communication.

But what do we mean when we say that corporate communication directors now have a seat at the CEO's table? Having a seat implies several things, but, most of all, it means having a voice in conversations about strategy formulation and implementation. Such directors can initiate and answer questions like these:

- Will key constituencies be receptive to top management's proposals? If so, why? If not, why not?
- What are the best approaches for persuading these constituencies? For example, what communication channels will work best? Who should be the spokesperson for carrying the initiative to a specific group?
- What are the possible negative and positive ramifications of changes in the company's strategy, vision, and mission to the company's relationship to key constituencies?
- How will we know if we have succeeded? What constitutes measurable results?

With the ascendancy of the corporate communication function to the top ranks of management, the director has come to need expertise and experience common at the senior ranks, like bottom-line responsibility and knowledge of the business from a strategic perspective. Peter Fleischer, managing director and a senior partner at Ketchum, has singled out earlier experiences in profit and loss and in performing favorably against measurable results as extremely important to the credibility of the director and to the companywide impact of the department:

> The corporate communication person needs to contribute to the bottom line of an organization, for instance, start with corporate reputation. Where is the company on *Fortune*'s Most Admired List, the gold standard? What are analysts saying about the com-

pany? Have particular corporate communication initiatives moved the reputation needle? How is reputation linked to share price? The corporate communication person needs to show measurable results.[28]

The importance of business knowledge and experience suggests that corporate communication experts should come more and more from the various business functions, which are usually run by people with degrees in business rather than in journalism or communication, the typical background of corporate communication experts in the past. Companies also have begun to realize that different skills are needed at corporate headquarters than in the operating units. Whereas those at headquarters need to adopt a strategic companywide perspective on communications, "personnel 'in the field' are ever more likely to focus the bulk of their time and other resources on tactical implementation. In addition, they are often perceived inside organizations to have a more intimate knowledge of the company's product lines and capabilities as well as to be closer to the marketplace when compared with colleagues at headquarters."[29]

When to Look for Outside Expertise

Every organization needs to build internal expertise in communications—everything from incorporating it in the strategic-planning process to preparing the CEO for an interview on *60 Minutes*. But there are times when seeking outside counsel makes the most sense. A corporate crisis is one of those times.

Let's say hypothetically that your company produces a drug to enhance longevity—an effort that research scientists are engaged in today—and has produced a series of ads with testimonials by centenarians claiming to have extended their lives through the use of the drug. Meanwhile, a consumer watchdog group decides to spread rumors that the drug is merely an expensive placebo, that, in fact, the old-timers live long because they have inherited great genes. With today's rapid communications, the rumor—whether ill-founded or a legitimate claim—spreads instantaneously and, before you know it, your company is being lambasted in print, on television, and on the Web. What do you do?

In this all-too-frequent type of situation, your company is likely to suffer from several organizational hits at once. The media storm descends suddenly and unexpectedly. Employees at all levels feel anxious, insecure, and under tremendous pressure: "What's true? What's not? What will be the costs to the company and to my own livelihood?" During the crisis, employees have to muster the necessary self-discipline to continue doing business and think rationally while the organization's reputation and bottom line are in jeopardy.

Crises are situations in which a company may want to seek outside expertise. An experienced public-relations firm can do wonders to mitigate a crisis. Among other things, such a firm can provide objective analysis of how the company should proceed, data-gathering capabilities needed to track constituencies' reactions as the crisis evolves, special knowledge about how to manage relations with the press, supplemental staff that can free regular employees to carry on business during the crisis, and a knowledge of best practices in crisis management.

Moreover, during dramatic internal upheavals like layoffs or mergers, expert outsiders can provide the cool-headed perspective and impartiality needed when internal politics heat up and steer decisions in ways that benefit the interests of particular factions or individuals at the expense of the overall good to the company. As Jack Bergen, former director of communications at CBS and now the senior vice president of corporate affairs and marketing at Siemens, has told us, "objective outside counsel's advice is not colored by having to live with the people affected by change. Among other things, outsiders are better able to give 'unwelcome' news."[30] In addition, Bergen notes that public relations agencies can "draw on best practices experience in world-class companies across a company's industry."[31] This is a capability that most companies can ill afford to support on their own.

Since our focus in this chapter is on the companywide role of corporate communication, the stories that follow target three fundamental talents that corporate communication experts should possess: the ability to align corporate communication with major strategic initiatives, to be in tune with both the strategy and the corporate culture in the department's work with others, and to harness the power of communication during times of crisis. We look first at FedEx and its director of communication's leadership in bringing the corporate communication function in to support high-impact strategic initiatives. At FedEx, communication works in tandem with strategy formulation and implementation. Then we turn to Johnson & Johnson's director of communication and his ability to "read" Johnson & Johnson's culture and to adjust his style of leadership and his department's operations to the company's decentralized culture while focusing on ways to promote Johnson & Johnson's strategic objectives. Finally, we turn to Honeywell's director of corporate communication and his involvement in facilitating the company's turnaround in the 1990s, showing how communication experts can help launch and steer communications during downturns and times of "do-or-die" change.

Strategy and Corporate Communication:
A Powerful Partnership

In *Castaway*, Tom Hanks plays a FedEx efficiency expert and plane crash survivor who, upon returning to the United States after years stranded on a deserted island, remains an unfailingly loyal FedEx employee. Within days of his return, Hanks delivers a FedEx package, which had survived the crash and island ordeal with him, to a customer in the American heartland. FedEx, an international company that provides shipping by air and ground and a range of logistics and trade consulting services, must provide speed and dependability globally not only for its core businesses with customers but also in its communications with constituencies about key business objectives. Employees at FedEx work in 200 countries 7 days a week, 24 hours a day. The corporate communication function must operate in as broad a landscape with speed, high impact, and precision.

Given the company's core businesses, communication challenges can arise in many quarters—in anything from crisis management, such as managing communications in the aftermath of a plane crash or computer outage, to e-commerce initiatives, to the rapid implementation of a new business model.

According to corporate vice president Bill Margaritis,[32] the corporate communication function needs to add significant value to the business and must be fully aligned with those making high-impact strategic decisions for the company. But how has he accomplished this at FedEx? First, Margaritis conducts annual audits with executives to find out what they are trying to accomplish and to establish a scorecard for success. Among these are the company's new "customer-facing go-to-market" strategies to improve growth and profit. This structure allows the team to devote complete attention to proactive opportunities rather than getting bogged down by a plethora of operational issues, which are important to manage but uniquely different. Since the company formed cross-functional groups to address these strategies, which are at the heart of FedEx's business, Margaritis assigns corporate communication people to each of the cross-functional groups dedicated to a "go-to-market" strategy. In this way, the perspective of corporate communication on issues like messaging about a new product launch, sending out news about mergers and acquisitions, pitching to the media, and assisting in the management of government relations in the highly regulated environments in which FedEx operates, are voiced alongside concerns about finance, operations, information systems, and long-term strategic goals.

By segmenting corporate communication staff in "go-to-market" groups, that is, customer-facing functions like sales, customer service,

and information technology, Margaritis achieves a significant side benefit. He has developed a multitalented group of communication professionals who can help solve strategic-level problems that cut across
functional areas like marketing, finance, sales, technology, and strategy.
His team members do not just fill a narrow niche, like writing a newsletter for pilots or drafting speeches for senior executives. Instead, his staff
can rotate through projects to build broader knowledge of the business
and to contribute value-added counsel to those decisions.

Senior management at FedEx realizes that when the company
embarks on a new strategy, such as offering new services, and makes
commitments to the marketplace, the company's brand is on the line
with multiple constituencies—opinion leaders, the media, investors,
employees, as well as customers. For the strategy to work, the company's
culture must also migrate in the new strategic direction; employee
behavior, motivation, and emotions must change accordingly.

Using the example of a company's need to get buy-in for a new customer initiative, Margaritis summed up the potential partnership
between corporate communication and a company's larger strategic
decision making in this way:

> When companies are considering transformation of their busi-
> ness strategies or business models at a rapid pace, the corporate
> communication group should play a vital role in the planning
> and execution process. To transform quickly, the company needs
> to get this news out in a compelling, multi-faceted manner
> quickly to key constituencies and has to get buy-in from them. If,
> for instance, the company makes a new pledge to customers, the
> organization must have a program that links employees to this
> new objective. A company wants the loyalty of employees to be
> linked with the new value proposition and to translate the new
> pledge into shareholder value. Employees need to deliver on the
> new strategy. If not, the company's brand and reputation can suf-
> fer. One of the things corporate communication can do is corre-
> late research between employee behavior and actions with
> customer service and, hence address performance gaps with
> actionable communication programs. Corporate communication
> must play a leadership role in a change environment.[33]

FedEx takes a holistic approach to corporate communication across
all channels and audiences: from the workplace to the marketplace and
from planning and executing new strategy to measuring attempts to link
employee behaviors and attitudes to marketplace impact.

Creating the Right Fit between Corporate Communication and Organizational Culture

Early in Bill Nielsen's tenure as the director of corporate communication for Johnson & Johnson, Ralph S. Larsen, the CEO to whom he reported, told him, "I believe in sunlight about everything."[34] Larsen wanted to know the truth about company activities, whether good or bad, in an open way and without embellishment, and offered his assistance to Nielsen. From the start, then, Nielsen knew that the CEO would support him as long as he, Nielsen, was honest and direct.

New to the company in the late 1980s, Nielsen soon discovered that none of the benchmarking studies about corporate communication could provide a model for Johnson & Johnson's corporate communication function, because its culture is unique. As he explained to us: "Johnson & Johnson is a consensus management organization, a culture of shared understanding about how to run the business, not a culture of elaborate rules."[35] Building consensus—rather than imposing one's formal authority and evoking rules—characterizes the way that work is done even at the most senior level of the organization.

Along with a culture of consensus building, Johnson & Johnson has a decentralized structure on which it places a very high value. Decentralization is so important a value that it is inscribed in one of the company's rare written statements about the company's strategic direction and is held in high regard as a primary source of productivity and innovative ideas.[36] As further indication of the importance of this value, all strategic planning occurs at the operations level where senior managers make financial forecasts that are then rolled into an overarching corporate plan. How, then, is Nielsen able to help craft a cohesive voice for the company while he has no control over its parts and pieces, nearly 200 autonomous operating companies? To build consensus, Nielsen chairs a monthly Public Affairs Advisory Group. The group is composed of everyone at headquarters who has responsibility for external constituencies, the heads of the public relations groups at the major operating units and such corporate staff functions as regulatory actions, investor relations, legal, advertising, and environmental safety and health. Discussion ranges from what's in the news that may concern Johnson & Johnson's reputation to investor relations, corporate philanthropy, and new legislation.

In addition, despite the large number of operating companies, Johnson & Johnson has created a climate of understanding and cohesiveness among internal constituencies around a set of values stated in the Credo, including the importance of reputation. As Nielsen has described this, "The key to Johnson & Johnson's global standing is the strength of its reputation in the United States."[37] He, then, gives this value a central place in the work of the division he runs. The division is in charge of tracking issues that make up corporate reputation, such as the company's core messages about the quality and integrity of its management, products, and services; its use of corporate assets, financial soundness, and value as a long-term investment; its innovation; its community and environmental responsibility; and its ability to attract, develop, and keep the brightest and most talented people.[38] Operating managers are encouraged to contact the corporate communication group when issues arise in the operating unit that can potentially affect how people regard the corporation. For any issue below that on the radar screen, Nielsen's group does not have to be contacted; rather, the individual companies decide on their own about such matters. As he explained to us, "If we put out a rule, the whole organization would come to a crawl. It comes down to individual judgment, lots of one-on-one talk, and meetings between me and other managers."[39] Johnson and Johnson has taken first place in the annual reputation survey conducted by the market research firm of Harris Interactive and the Reputation Institute since the inception of the survey in 1999.[40] In other words, Johnson & Johnson is the most highly regarded company in the United States.

Building relationships with senior management also facilitates the work of Nielsen's group. Of the 100,000 employees at Johnson & Johnson, about 18,000 are managers. When a new operating manager comes on board, Nielsen will send a note, phone, or send an e-mail, saying, "Please stop by next time you're in New Brunswick." The manager soon learns that Nielsen has the ear of the CEO and can lobby for ideas internally. In addition to face-to-face communications with senior managers, Nielsen has revamped the management magazine, *Worldwide News Digest*, to reflect senior management's concerns with business issues of strategic importance. Rather than presenting "show-and-tell" anecdotal information, he places emphasis on stories that affect business development.

Harnessing the Power of Corporate Communication During Times of Change

In 1992, Dennis Signorovitch joined Honeywell Aerospace (then known as Allied Signal Aerospace) as vice president of corporate communication. At that time, Honeywell, a company with businesses in aerospace and related industries, consisted of an array of businesses acquired at different times, 26 in all. The company was a welter of names and lacked common purpose and identity. It had over 14 different ad agencies and over 40 publications. To address these and other problems, then president and CEO Dan Burnham brought in a new cadre of managers. In particular, he wanted them to help him take on two major challenges: a depressed market for the company's products and a need to build the morale and commitment of employees.

The market for Honeywell's products in the early 1990s faced two major obstacles: a decline in demand caused by the end of the Cold War threat of the Soviet Union—the "Evil Empire" had collapsed in the late 1980s—and a decline in commercial passenger travel in the early 1990s caused by international threats and instability during the Gulf War. In fact, in 1991, commercial airline traffic declined for the first time in the history of commercial flight.

Facing a collapsing market and a demoralized, much reduced employee base, Signorovitch sized up the situation in 1992 like this: "The company was a 'burning platform.' We thought of our work across the company as a kind of campaign. If you want change, you're on a campaign—town meetings, employee meetings, videos."[41] Using the language of a political campaign, the company's senior management stressed the need for immediate, fundamental change.

When Signorovitch came on board in 1992, he immediately proceeded to size up his team and determine the CEO's goals.

> Fortunately, Burnham was quite open. Communication with the CEO is the sine qua non. I had complete access to the strategy. At that point, Burnham was less concerned about the company's marketing communications than about internal communications and the involvement of his executive management team in supporting the company's communication efforts. He felt that to make money he needed people who focused on high performance and high energy.[42]

Both the CEO and the vice president of corporate communication had, then, realized that employee communication was important *at all times*, but especially during times of major change when companies need to get buy-in from the troops before seeking outside approval and support. Forward thinkers, they recognized in the early 1990s what many other companies have just begun to see today. According to David R. Drobis, senior partner and chairman at Ketchum, a leading international public relations firm, the big change that has recently occurred in corporate communication is a new emphasis on employees: "Companies are understanding that employees are at the heart of brand and reputation.

Employees are needed as the nucleus, the constituency through which we get to all the other constituencies."[43]

Along with the need to boost morale and improve internal communications at Honeywell, Signorovitch immediately recognized that the corporate communication activities were not working well. He needed new leaders of internal communications, marketing communications, and media relations. To find the best candidates, he decided to go outside the industry: "The industry was too self-referential. To create change, I needed to get people from a different place."[44]

The newly hired communications managers, the increased face-to-face communications between the CEO and senior managers, and improved upward communication all came into play in moving the company forward. To increase communication between employees and senior management, Signorovitch also instituted a process called UPWORDS that is still in place and quite successful. Employees can fax or use an 800 number for comments or questions, and then Signorovitch's group gets back to them after checking with senior management for answers.

Signorovitch attributes the credibility of the corporate communication function to the communication campaign of the 1990s, but he also stresses the importance of continuing to sell the function and using a metrics system to gauge the performance of the function. The metrics system, as he described it, "allows me to test the organization's pulse, to see whether we're having an impact. Also, by having numbers to give to the CEO, we increase our credibility with him and with other functions. For instance, if someone from HR says 'employees believe such and such,' we can counter with metrics that refute this anecdotal statement if we think they're wrong."[45] Moreover, just as he is aware that the function must sell the company to its key constituencies, he values the importance of selling the function within the company: "As soon as I define a program, I need to talk about how it will work, tell leadership the results I've gotten and how I may need to modify the program. I have to keep selling the program to senior management. That's my job."[46]

Thus far in this chapter, we have looked at several dimensions of corporate communication. We looked first at corporate communication as the voice of the company and the images it projects as these are shaped, especially by the CEO but also by directors of corporate communication. We then saw, in the case of GE, how the importance of corporate communication can be internalized by members of an organization, and how this process is initiated at the very top of the organization. We've also considered the different choices companies make about corporate communication—when to use face-to-face communication, e-mail, or written documentation. By and large, when CEOs are in the process of spearheading major change, face-to-face communication—as costly and inefficient as it is—needs a central place in a company's corporate communication to instill trust and build relationships. Finally, we looked at the role that experts in corporate communication play in extending the impact of a company's communications. Among these experts are directors of corporate communication who head the corporate communication function in their organizations.

We now turn to the fourth dimension of corporate communication—as an organizational function—be it a department with branches, a single unit, or just a small group—and the scope and placement of the function.

A Map of the Territory

A Conference Board Study of hundreds of the nation's largest firms showed that close to 80 percent have corporate communication functions that include media relations, speechwriting, employee communications, corporate advertising, and community relations. Over 70 percent also control philanthropic efforts and over 20 percent now handle investor relations. (See Table 3-1 for more details of this study.)[47]

Not surprisingly, the different parts of a modern corporate communication function perform companywide, global activities such as corporate advertising, and the management of corporate identity and image

Table 3-1 *Activities reporting to Senior Communications Executive*

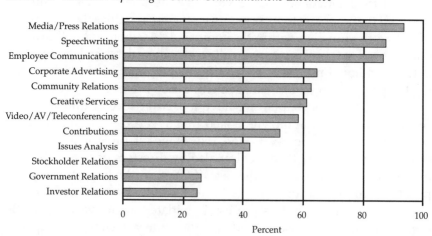

and reputation, as well as communications issues targeted more narrowly to a particular constituency important to the company as a whole, such as employees, investors, or government.

Each of the activities or subfunctions in Table 3-1 is taken up in some detail in one or more chapters in this book. At this point, we offer just a brief explanation of those activities or subfunctions that may not be obvious to you. *Corporate advertising*, unlike advertising for individual products or services, consists of advertising that portrays the company as a whole. By *corporate identity*, we mean the many physical attributes of a company, including names, brands, and symbols. A related concept, *corporate image*, is a reflection of that *corporate identity*. In other words, your corporate image is how each constituency views your organization. *Reputation*, the third of the three concepts, represents the cumulative impact of the images all constituencies have of your organization. Both reputation management and corporate advertising should be handled in the corporate communication function because they have a direct bearing on how the corporation is perceived by its most important constituencies. Taken together, corporate advertising and reputation say, "This is who we are and where we're going." Not every company will be able to include all of the activities identified in Table 3-2 under one umbrella, but a majority of these functions must be included for the function to operate best. Indeed, the activities must be connected in some way for an organization to speak with a single voice.

As the FedEx example presented earlier in this chapter illustrates, the activities of strategy formulation and implementation—though not a formally labeled unit within the corporate communication department—may be the overarching, most vital set of activities that a department participates in. Of course, strategy formulation and implementation are not the sole province of corporate communication—not by any means; however, when communication experts have a seat at the CEO's table or on company teams dedicated to high-level strategic issues, the concerns of corporate communication (and the constituencies it in turn represents) get a hearing. As a result, how a company's various constituencies will react to new strategic initiatives is taken into account in the decision-making process, and, ultimately, in the strategic direction a company chooses to take.

As an example of the positive influence corporate communication can exert on strategy formulation, consider what we learned from one senior communication expert who worked for a large multinational corporation that decided to give away to the local community an expensive facility the company had acquired in a merger. In the absence of the

Table 3-2   *Activities of the Corporate Communication Function*

Strategy formulation and implementation

Corporate identity, image, and reputation

Corporate advertising and advocacy

Customer relations

Employee communications

Investor relations

Government affairs

Community relations

Media relations

Crisis communication

Management of new communication technologies

expert's counsel, the firm initially decided to sell the property. But when the corporate communication expert was brought into the discussion, he alerted his colleagues to the needs and influence of two constituencies: the government and the local community. The senator who represented the state in which the facility was located held powerful seats on committees that dealt with corporate tax and trade relations. In that capacity, he could either champion or block key legislation that would strongly favor the company. The senator's constituents who lived in the community where the facility was located had made an urgent plea to him to help them acquire the company's physical plant which the community wanted to use for youth and recreation programs. Had the communications expert been excluded from the strategic decision-making process, the company would have made the wrong choice, realizing modest gains from the sale and sacrificing long-term profits of a substantial size by alienating the local community and their representative in Congress.

Managing Communication Technology

Along with a role in strategy formulation and implementation, corporate communication has recently expanded its scope of responsibilities to include a say in the use of communication technologies. The most visible change in communication in the last decade is the rise of the Internet, the Intranet, and the Web. With the technology's ubiquity in corporate life has come the increased responsibility of the corporate communication department for many of the communication functions that technology allows companies to perform. According to a Heyman survey, "Most corporate public affairs [sic] executives and staff...in recent years perceived the Internet to have significant present as well as potential impact on their work and activities."[48]

At first glance, you may think that communication technologies most logically fall under the exclusive purview of an information systems manager. Moreover, according to the Heyman report, "a number of studies confirm that a majority of professionals approach the Web as little more than a new, cheaper and faster communications tool or channel, not as a fundamentally new or different framework for conducting business into the future."[49] Nonetheless, many of the functions the technology allows companies to perform have a direct bearing on the voice and image that a company projects to major constituencies, and a few companies are pioneering innovative ways to use the technology to enhance communications. Let's look at Sears as an example.[50]

In the late 1990s, every department at Sears and some of its stores were setting up Internets and Intranets. When employees went on-line, they might find 60 to 70 sites for Sears. So would customers. To create a consistent, single image for the company it was then logical for the corporate communication department to take charge of developing a single point of entry for all constituents, and they have done just that.

The need for efficient use of the technology also led to increased responsibilities on the part of Sears' corporate communication department. This change occurred rather dramatically. To demonstrate the need for an intelligent approach to the use of technology, the corporate communication department set up a fictitious store in the late 1990s, one that received all the e-mail that an actual store would have received. The department then began collecting everything sent to the fictitious store manager, a quantity of messages that filled a closet. As Ron Culp, the director of corporate communication at Sears, described the demonstration, "the e-mail alone—if the store manager were to read it all—would be equivalent to reading *War and Peace* twice each month."[51] Culp presented these findings at a management retreat and, as a result, his group is now in charge of improving communication efficiency.

In this enhanced role for corporate communication, the department at Sears now provides corporate content for both the Internet and the Intranet. In addition, the group also studied the uses of print and on-line communications, and, by shifting some of the print material on-line, reduced the cost of print production by 20 to 30 percent. Here is a measurable benefit that expertise in corporate communication can produce.

Improved use of technology, guided in part by the corporate communication department, can even help in a company turnaround. John

Iwata, the vice president of corporate communication for IBM, has described the multiple ways that IBM learned to use technology creatively to enhance employee communications in the late 1990s as the company struggled its way out of a major decline.[52] The company created a personalized news service, a tool to facilitate the work of cross-functional teams, and a virtual space for discussion of topics important to specific internal groups. For the personalized news service, "each employee created a profile of work-related interests and based on that profile, 'My News' [the name of the new Intranet service] filtered news feeds from inside and outside the company. Several times a day, it created a news page for the employees with information they specifically wanted."[53] To facilitate the work of cross-functional teams, the Intranet allows team members from diverse units in the organization to connect seamlessly with one another on-line. Finally, for those employees wanting to exchange ideas about specific topics, the company has launched a feature called "World Jam" that lists key topics and invites employees to share ideas and best practices. As evidence of the technology's success, a survey of employees in 2000 identified the Intranet as one of the two most important channels of communication, a leap ahead of the Intranet's sixth position in 1997.

Not only has the corporate communication function expanded at some firms to include responsibility for communication technology as it affects corporate communication, but the expansion of technology use in the broader society has given greater visibility and importance to the function of corporate communication. Company activities are increasingly transparent to multiple constituencies worldwide over the Internet. As David R. Drobis, senior partner and chairman at the public relations firm of Ketchum, explained: "Even a local community event can't be contained. Company issues of greater import also cannot be isolated. We can't isolate issues by country with the Internet working as it does. There is no such thing as U.S. versus an Asian audience. Everyone has quick access."[54] The Internet is, then, a destabilizing force. Steven J. Harris, vice president of communications at General Motors, reflected: "The Internet is invasive and so companies need to be proactive. To do nothing is not the answer. Results won't speak for themselves. You will be pummeled. Especially with the advent of the Internet, if you don't mold your image, someone will mold it for you."[55] Companies can't control who sends or receives messages online, nor can they control the content of messages. Much of the content is decidedly antibusiness, and the expansion of anticorporate Web sites makes the corporate communication department's vigilance and responsiveness all the more important. Dissatisfied constituents of every stripe—

employees, investors, consumers—now have ample virtual space to air their grievances against companies. Among the sites dedicated to getting back at corporate America are thirdvoice.com, planetfeedback.com, peta-online.org, vault.com, gripenet.com, epinions.com, bitchaboutit.com, and wordofmouth.com.[56] Especially in light of the ease with which criticism can be showered on an organization, companies need a powerful, integrative corporate communication function.

Design and Placement of the Corporate Communication Function

One of the first problems in designing a corporate communication department is whether to keep all communications focused by centralizing the activity under one senior officer at a corporation's headquarters or to decentralize activities and allow individual business units to decide how best to handle communications. The more centralized function provides a much easier way for companies to gain consistency and control for all communication activities at the top of the organization. The decentralized function, however, gives individual business units an opportunity to adapt the function to their own needs rather than to the needs of the organization as a whole. According to the Heyman study, "After some two decades of gradually dismantling centralized capabilities and experimenting with a range of decentralized models, many of America's leading corporations seem to have come full circle."[57] The move toward centralization may reflect the increasing need of companies to respond quickly with a single voice to issues that affect the whole company.

On the other hand, the need to centralize or decentralize usually comes down to weighing the considerations of company size, product or service diversity, and geographic spread. For a company as diverse and large as General Electric, for example, the question was moot. Such a huge, diverse organization involved in activities as different as aerospace and network television cannot possibly remain completely centralized in all of its communication activities. The same was true for other organizations in different industries like RJR-Nabisco, which had to integrate units selling cigarettes with others selling cookies.

Perhaps, then, the best structure for large companies is some combination of a strong, centralized, functional area (with all of the relevant activities mentioned earlier in this chapter) plus a network of decentralized operatives helping to keep communications consistent throughout the organization while adapting the function to the special needs of the independent business unit. For example, Champion International (now part of International Paper), a forest products company, operated this way with a strong centralized communication function at its corporate headquarters in Stamford, Connecticut, and a network of communications professionals at each of its paper mills.

Despite its advantages, the mix of centralized and decentralized activities presents problems for organizations in terms of reporting relationships. If the communications operatives report to their local managers, as they inevitably would, they will run into problems when the manager from headquarters disagrees with an action taken at the local level. On the other hand, if they report to headquarters, the operatives may not fit in with the rest of the organization at the local level.

These problems can often be handled creatively using some combination of both a strong centralized control for all affairs related to communications throughout the company and the participation of local operatives who, as in the case of General Electric, act as "reporters" back at headquarters. The problem of centralization versus decentralization across business units will be more or less important depending on company size, geographic dispersion, and the diversity of a company's products and services.

Companies have also begun to recognize the need for different talents in communication experts at the corporate and operations levels:

> The former increasingly brings more of a strategic perspective to planning, goal setting, recruitment and development, issues and crisis management, and evaluation of activities across the organization....personnel "in the field" are ever more likely to focus the bulk of their time and other resources on tactical implementation. In addition, they are often perceived inside organizations to have a more intimate knowledge of the company's product lines and capabilities as well as to be closer to the marketplace when compared with colleagues at headquarters.[58]

One final issue of centralization versus decentralization needs to be addressed as well. In addition to the communication challenges of companies with multiple business units spread throughout the world, companies looking to build their corporate communication function need to worry about how decentralized communication activities are at the corporate level. Often, some of these activities are already handled through another functional area. For example, the employee relations function could be handled within the human resources department and the investor relations function could be included in the treasury department, even though all of these activities require communication strategies connected to the central mission of the firm.

Recent surveys of major companies have shown that most of the top corporations in the United States place the responsibility for employee communications in the corporate communication function. This trend suggests that companies today realize that the internal constituency is not very different from external ones in terms of the need for sophisticated communications techniques. To ensure that messages sent to employees are closely aligned with those sent to external constituencies, employee communications should be tied very closely to an overall corporate communication strategy.

Increasingly, the corporate communication department gets involved in employee communications that pertain to the company's overall mission and strategy, and the human resources department deals exclusively with employee issues, such as information about training programs or complicated health and benefits packages. For example, if employees read in the press about increased competition from foreign competitors, the corporate communication department should get involved in giving employees an idea of how senior management sees the problem and plans to respond to meet the challenge. This kind of communication helps employees feel more like insiders and can motivate them to serve as goodwill ambassadors of the firm to its outside constituencies.

Ideally, both the corporate communication and the human resources departments would have someone in charge of communications to employees. The person in the corporate communication department would obviously report to the vice president in charge of that area, while the person in the human resources department would report to his or her respective vice president. Both should have a dotted-line relationship with the vice president in the other area to ensure that each department's goals are fully met in all communications and to keep the lines of communication open between these two critical functional areas in a firm.[59]

Financial communications, which is also called investor or shareholder relations, has emerged as the fastest-growing subset of the corporate communication function and an area of intense interest at all companies. (See Chapter 7 for more on investor relations.) Traditionally, financial communications has been handled by the finance or treasury department, but the focus today has moved away from just the numbers to the way the numbers are actually communicated to various constituencies. For this reason, although financial communications usually "reports to the Chief Financial Officer at most firms...this function has closer ties to corporate public affairs in many cases today than it did 10 years ago, especially in shareholder communications and media relations."[60]

Financial communications deals with securities analysts on both the buy and sell side who are often also a direct source for the financial press, which this subfunction cultivates, as do the company's experts in the media relations area. This area also involves direct contact with investors. Every public firm must produce financial statements and annual reports, which are produced by financial communications professionals. Given the highly quantitative message involved in all of these activities, as well as the need for individuals to choose their words carefully to avoid any semblance of transferring inside information, investor relations should be a coordinated effort between communications professionals and the chief financial officer, comptroller, or vice president for finance.

Where Should the Corporate Communication Function Report?

We come full circle in this chapter when we consider the question, "Where should corporate communication report?" Our answer is "as high as possible." Ideally, the head of corporate communication reports to the CEO, because this reporting relationship can confirm the importance of the function to the organization and allows corporate communication directors to lend their expertise to the most vital decision-making processes of a firm—those that determine strategy, vision, and mission—and to the implementation of those decisions through gaining buy-in from key constituencies.

Many polls taken over the last decade have consistently shown that a huge percentage of a chief executive officer's time is spent communicating with one or another of the company's constituencies. Estimates from research conducted at the Tuck School of Business suggest that between 50 and 80 percent of a CEO's time, on average, across all CEOs at the *Fortune* 500 companies, is spent communicating to constituencies. As an example, in the early 1980s, Johnson & Johnson's CEO, James Burke, estimated that he spent over 40 percent of his time as CEO communicating the J&J credo.[61] The CEO, the person most involved with developing the overall strategy for communications, is usually the person to deliver those messages to constituencies. As Gary Ames, CEO of US West. has said, "It's not clear to me what else my job is other than communications."[62] It should come as no surprise then, that for most companies, the CEO should have a direct line to the corporate communication function. Without this connection, the communication function will be far less effective and far less powerful. Figure 3-1 presents the ideal structure for the corporate communication function, one that places the director of corporate communication in a direct reporting relationship to the CEO.

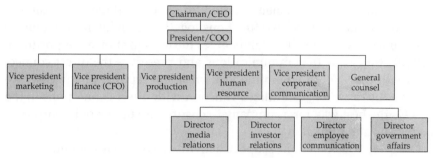

Figure 3-1   *Ideal structure for corporate communication function.*

In many cases, however, we find the function, such as it is, reporting to the catch-all executive vice president (EVP) in charge of administration, often someone who is also responsible for personnel, security, and buildings and grounds, for example. This reporting relationship, split off from top-level decision making, presents tremendous problems for the communication function—especially if the EVP has little interest in or knowledge of communications. In these instances, corporate communication becomes something tagged on to decision making as an afterthought or a reactive response to crises.

In other companies, we find corporate communication reporting to a strategic planning function. Given the importance of linking communications to the overall strategy of the firm, we can see that this might benefit the growing corporate communication function.

In the early 1990s when Union Carbide Corporation was still dealing with the fallout from the accident in Bhopal, India, it transferred its communications responsibilities to the vice president of strategic planning. In a letter to executives, the chairman and CEO of the company, Robert Kennedy, said:

> The Corporation's strategic direction is a key element of our communication to shareholders, employees and the public at large....It is therefore more important than ever to be open and consistent in our communications to all of these groups, to keep them informed of our progress as we implement strategy, and to make sure that we address the special concerns and interests of all the groups and constituencies with a stake in Union Carbide's future....To ensure the closest possible alignment of our communications with management directed at strategic planning developments, the management of those functions is being consolidated under...[the] Vice President of Strategic Planning and Public Affairs.[63]

Whether this arrangement worked for Union Carbide is unclear, but the idea of linking these two functions together is an interesting one for companies to consider. It certainly gives the organization an opportunity to link strategy with communications and preserves the direct connection with the CEO to whom the vice president reports. In any case, we believe that a strong, centralized function with direct connections to the CEO is the best way for a company to ensure the success of its corporate communication function.

Having considered the scope of activities a corporate communication department should participate in and the ideal reporting structure for that department, we would, however, be remiss if we did not underscore the following important caveat: Emphasizing the department's scope of activities and ideal placement on an organizational chart can lead to a false sense of security and accomplishment. As John Onoda, the vice president of communications at Charles Schwab, has said, "There is too much focus on structure and title and reporting relationships and not enough on how to be impactful."[64] Much more important than the structure of the department and the scope of its responsibilities is the credibility of corporate communication professionals—their insights during crises, their ability to be heard at the big table, the respect they garner from the CEO, their track records of success, and their ability to substantiate that success with measurable results.

CONCLUSION

If we could draw a map of the scope and placement of the corporate communication function, then a company's CEO needs to provide direction for the map-making. Successful CEOs who are themselves effective communicators set the tone for communications in their businesses and turn to communications experts within and outside their organizations to achieve major impact with key constituencies. Directors of corporate communication stand at the top of the list of experts from whom they seek counsel. When CEOs, directors of corporate communication, and corporate communication departments work together harmoniously, companies have a great opportunity to create a cohesive voice and project convincing images of themselves to their key constituencies.

Increasingly, departments of corporate communication have extended their responsibility beyond traditional areas like media relations to work on strategy and on communications technology. We anticipate that growth in the function's power will continue in these two areas.

4

IDENTITY, IMAGE, AND REPUTATION: FROM VISION TO REALITY

FOR 250 YEARS, IMMIGRANTS TO America have believed in and celebrated a story titled the "American Dream." This story codifies the best
America has to offer: freedom, prosperity, and justice.[1] Business often
plays a central role in these rags-to-riches tales, by propelling innovators
from humble beginnings to the loftiest heights of wealth and success.

Henry Ford embodied the proverbial rags-to-riches story; he
dropped out of school at the age of 16, yet managed to build the biggest
industrial organization of the early twentieth century and to accumulate
a personal fortune of $36 billion.[2] However, Ford wasn't just building
cars to make a profit. He boldly placed people before profits, vowing: "I
don't believe we should make such an awful profit on our cars...I hold
that it is better to sell a large number of cars at a reasonably small
profit...I hold this because it enables a larger number of people to buy
and enjoy the use of a car and because it gives a larger number of men
employment at good wages."[3] These priorities, combined with Henry
Ford's vision of cars for every man, enchanted millions of Americans. In
turn, after he shared this vision—and joined with close friend Harvey
Firestone to convey it—the nation saw the car transformed into the unof-
ficial American symbol of freedom, status, and mobility.[4]

When Ford approached Firestone and asked him to sell tires for Ford
motorcars, one of the oldest partnerships in American business history

was born. The marriage of their grandchildren, William Clay Ford and Martha Parke Firestone, made the business relationship a personal one, reiterating how both companies literally invested their lives in the partnership.[5] Given such historic and personal roots, you'll be hard-pressed to think of a company that built a stronger reputation than Ford and Firestone over the last century.

THE BUILDING BLOCKS OF REPUTATION

Today, long after Henry Ford established his cultural legacy in America, the tradition he launched continues with significant momentum in the corporate realm. With globalization breaking down national borders, people are turning to omnipresent companies to provide the direction previously offered by culture, community, and inspirational narratives. As a result, similar to Ford's effect on American culture, corporations' identities, images, and resulting reputations are determined by how well their corporate visions are crafted, maintained, and conveyed to the public.

What allows successful companies to create strong, enduring images? Several factors determine how well your company conveys its vision to constituencies and, in turn, what kind of reputation you have. The three chief contributors to your organization's reputation are

- The identity it shapes
- The overall coherence of the images the public perceives
- The alignment of your organization's identity with the images held by its constituencies

A few concrete definitions of these terms, with the help of a chart, will be useful in distinguishing how identity and image contribute to your organization's reputation and success in communicating to both internal and external constituencies (see Figure 4-1).

Simply stated, your company's identity is the concrete, often visual, manifestation of its reality, including names, brands, symbols, self-presentations, corporate sponsorships, and, most significantly, your company's vision. How you build this reality determines if your company successfully engages all of its constituencies. The company's vision is supported by its core values that should transcend leadership and external circumstances. Henry Ford's vision of cars for all Americans serves as a perfect example of this sort of core value. A company's vision is the source of inspiration for internal and external constituencies, fostering loyalty, and distinguishing the great companies from the mediocre ones.[6]

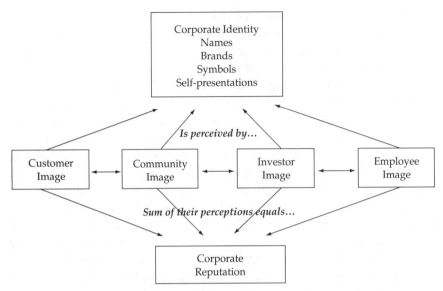

Figure 4.1   *What are identity, image, and reputation?*

By contrast, the company's image is a reflection of an organization's identity. In other words, it is how each constituency views your organization. And, in all likelihood, each constituency—be it customers, the community at large, investors, or your own employees—has a different image of your organization. The associations and impressions that linger after an interaction with the company come together to constitute your corporate image. The tone and demeanor of employees, the type of publicity generated by the media, and even the company's activism within the community all contribute to your company's image as well.[7]

How do image and identity relate to building a reputation and constructing a cultural institution like Ford? If the images of your company (that is, the perceived notions of all your constituencies) all align with the organization's reality, your reputation management program is a success. If constituencies' perceptions differ dramatically from the reality—which often happens when companies do not analyze whether a match actually exists—then either your strategy for aligning identity and image is ineffective or your corporation's reality (that is, its identity and self-understanding) needs modification. An organization can get a much better sense of its image (as conveyed through visual identity) by conducting research with constituents. Both qualitative and quantitative research can help determine how consistent your corporate reality is perceived across constituencies.

But how exactly do you begin to manage the alignment between identity and image that produces a strong reputation? Your company must invest its efforts in building a corporate identity and managing people's perceptions of *who* and *what* it is.

Because identity-building is the only part of reputation management you can completely control, we will first discuss what contributes positively to corporate identity—an inspirational corporate vision, consistent self-presentation, effective names and logos, memorable symbols and brands, and the delivery of a powerful multisensory experience. Second, we will examine how various constituencies—consumers, the community at large, investors, and even your employees—formulate images of your organization. In turn, you will learn how building the strong corporate identity you desire provides the only way to influence the kinds of images you are generating in the minds of all constituencies. Finally, we will discuss how a strict alignment between your company's identity and image can generate a positive reputation, and the kind of competitive advantage that can bring. We will then provide you with a step-by-step approach to how you can start your journey down the path of strong reputation-building.

Before offering you solutions, however, think about how you would define your company's identity as it stands now. What do you think are its tangible entities like logos, physical structure, and employee uniforms? With your own impressions in mind, think about how you feel your company's various constituencies perceive the organization. Do their sentiments align with your own? Does their image correspond to your understanding of what the company is all about? The approaches outlined in this chapter will help ensure this crucial harmonizing of image and identity.

YOUR COMPANY'S IDENTITY

Before you can expect constituencies to comprehend your company, you need to understand what the organization is really about and where it is headed. This is often hard for anyone except the chief executive officer (CEO) or president to grasp. What, for example, is the identity of an organization as large as ExxonMobil, as diversified as Mitsubishi, or as monolithic as General Electric? Although there are inevitable differences in how the elements are perceived by different constituencies, it is this cluster of "facts" that provides your organization with a starting point for creating its corporate identity. In concrete terms, identity is conveyed by an organization's logos, products, services, buildings, stationery, uniforms, and any other tangible bit of evidence created by your organization to communicate with a variety of constituencies.

Identity—A Vision That Inspires

Most central to your corporate identity, however, is the vision that encompasses your company's core values, philosophies, standards, and goals. Corporate vision is a common thread that all employees, and ideally all other constituencies, as well, can relate to. Thinking about this vision in terms of a narrative or story approach may help ensure the overall coherence and continuity of your company's vision and the collective messages you are sending constituencies. In the most successful of corporate stories, the company will transform itself into a hero, and competitors, in some cases, into adversaries. As a result, customers get caught up in your company's drama, novelty, or romance, rooting you all the way to a happy ending.[8]

Cees B. M. van Riel, a professor at Erasmus University in the Netherlands, links the importance of narratives to successful corporate reputations. He explains that "communication will be more effective if organizations rely on a…sustainable corporate story as a source of inspiration for all internal and external communication programs. Stories are hard to imitate, and they promote consistency in all corporate messages."[9] This story can be told through official mission statements, declarations of identity, and any other means of communication with all constituencies. In particular, the main sources that external constituencies will rely on for information about your company and the story you are telling include articles in publications, television ads, discussions about the company with other people (for example, family, friends, and colleagues), and direct interaction with company employees.

The most appealing stories, literary and corporate, often involve an underdog—an unsung hero that audiences can admire and rally behind enthusiastically. Going against the grain can instill a sense of noble purpose in the actions of a hero, or entrepreneur, hoping to do things differently. Just think about Steve Jobs, the founder of Apple Computer. His total unwillingness to succumb to IBM and Microsoft had such a heroic appeal for countless individuals that it effectively launched Apple into the coveted megabrand stratosphere, where it still remains today.[10] Consider how powerful a corporate story could be if it combined an approach as heroically novel as Jobs' with a politically and environmentally conscious product that could tap into an increasingly aware global consumer. Anita Roddick crafted a story that managed to do just that with her founding of The Body Shop.

Business as Unusual

The Body Shop story begins in 1976 in Brighton, England. The reputation of the cosmetic industry that Roddick was humbly entering was consistently negative; the identity of most competitor cosmetic companies, such as Estee Lauder and Revlon, was vacuous. They were seen to be selling superficial image as opposed to anything of substance. In essence, the industry was selling hopes and dreams, often extraneous to products, and packaging and advertising constituted an average of 85 percent of cosmetics companies' costs.[11] Ironically, founder Anita Roddick's minimal-hype approach to the promotion of her new company was so unconventional that it attracted a tremendous amount of attention. Her "profits with principle" philosophy helped Roddick differentiate her skin and hair products from the many heavily advertised competitors on the market. Minimalist, refillable packaging replaced glamorized labels, and a social and environmental consciousness supplemented the standard promotion of the products' attributes. The Body Shop charter spells out these differences to employees loud and clear, stating that "goals and values are as important as our products and profits...The Body Shop has soul—don't lose it," echoing Ford's insistence on profits taking a back seat to people.[12] Roddick carries this creed so far, in fact, that her product sales seem merely to be means to achieve a greater social end, not vice versa.

Roddick recognized from the beginning that she needed to instill a sense of purpose, removed from profits, in both employees and customers—a theme she continuously weaves into the corporate story that The Body Shop still adheres to today. Customers sense this continuity: the dark green walls, committed salespeople, as well as posters displaying socially conscious themes and products that create an atmosphere where social awareness, and not superficialities, rule.

Although survival prompted Roddick to adopt money-saving tactics initially, through remarkable luck they coincided with emerging social trends in environmentalism and consumer choice. The Body Shop has never promised miraculous remedies, only the ability to clean, polish, and help guard against hair and skin ailments. Adhering to these founding principles enabled The Body Shop to take off throughout the 1980s, with sales skyrocketing at a rate of 50 percent yearly. As Roddick explains, "It turned out that my instinctive trading values were dramatically opposed to the standard practices in the cosmetics industry. I look at what they are doing and walk in the opposite direction."[13]

Fittingly, a heading in The Body Shop's 1996 Annual Report read: "Business as Unusual: The Body Shop—definitely not an Olympic

Games sponsor." The back cover thanked the reader for "resisting the ordinary."[14] Roddick's unusual approach includes contrarian marketing—giving the customer detailed product information, establishing lasting credibility by educating customers about products and issues, and, above all, pushing her social agenda. These tactics have enabled The Body Shop's story to cut through an impressive amount of corporate cynicism, while differentiating itself from the often-stereotyped cosmetic industry and fulfilling the need for environmental activism. Everything at The Body Shop coincides with Roddick's overarching vision and story. It is thus no coincidence that, speaking at the Tuck School of Business at Dartmouth in 1996, Roddick reiterated the importance of myth in this day and age, when people are increasingly distanced from their natural affinity for storytelling.

However, even such a success story is not safe from critics, or an unhappy ending, for that matter. Dangers arise when some constituencies begin to doubt the honesty that is essential to a company's narrative. Doubts have circulated about The Body Shop's no-animal testing claims, its sincerity, and its ability to be both green and globally competitive in the long run. Others have opposed the intermingling of business with a social agenda. As a Price Waterhouse report noted: "Some customers may be willing to pay $3.00 for a bar of soap, knowing that some of the money is going to a worthy cause. Others will be turned off to a company that uses its profits to support such a bold political agenda."[15]

Another niche-threatening development has been the introduction of Bath and Body Works, which opened 412 stores between 1991 and 1996, seriously eroding The Body Shop's dominance in the marketplace.[16] In 1999, Estee Lauder also responded to The Body Shop's success by producing a stand-alone chain of natural cosmetics—Origins—that was not openly connected to the Lauder name. The emergence of such stores, mimicking Roddick's original vision, continues to erode the uniqueness, and as a result the dominance, of The Body Shop in today's cosmetic industry. Even the most innovative corporate visions are not immune to imitation. Companies, therefore, need to reassess frequently who they are to ensure they are exactly who they want to be.

As a leader in your company, you must consistently ask questions that go beyond short-term goals and probe deeply into issues of long-term strategy. After taking over Kimberly-Clark in 1971, for example, Darwin Smith asked the right questions: "What could Kimberly-Clark be best at in the world? What would ignite its passions?" By asking these fundamental questions, Smith instigated a lot of internal discussion, revealing every employee's individual understanding of the organization's future. Such discussion within an organization can help eliminate misunderstandings and establish a common vision of where the company is indeed heading. Two years after Smith's questioning began, he sold Kimberly-Clark's mills and channeled all proceeds into their consumer-products business. Fast-forward to 25 years later in 1998 and Kimberly-Clark was ahead of Procter and Gamble in six of eight paper-product categories.[17] Unless you and your employees know who your company is and what vision propels it forward, you cannot expect any of your constituencies to understand the corporate reality you are working to create. Kimberly-Clark's sustained self-interrogation proved effective—*Fortune* ranked Kimberly-Clark as number one in the forest and paper products industry for the nineteenth year in a row in their 2001 survey of the most admired companies.[18]

The difference between companies experiencing a temporary reputation upsurge and those enjoying a long-term growth in reputation also seems to lie in the former's dangerous reliance on external events and trends. Hush Puppies footwear made a phenomenal revival in the mid-1990s as Manhattan trendsetters rediscovered the comfortable brushed suede footwear line. In 1995, sales leaped from 30,000 pairs to a startling 430,000.[19] However, the phenomenon did not result from internal questioning. Rather, it relied on the unpredictable fashion whims of New York trendsetters. In contrast to this externally dependent approach, Walgreen—which consistently beat Intel in year-end stock price from 1975 to 2000—looked inward, questioned its vision, and *proactively* invested its efforts and resources into its drugstores, instead of its failing restaurant chain, to become a market leader.

All the while, however, it refused to merely jump on any bandwagon and react to unpredictable external events, particularly the Internet revolution of the 1990s. Instead, Walgreen adhered to its original corporate credo of "Crawl, walk, run." Warren Buffett's Berkshire Hathaway, topping *Fortune*'s list of the most admired companies of 2001, maintains a similar philosophy. Buffett invests in businesses that will not be susceptible to major changes. For this reason, he has avoided tech investments, which are subject to extreme volatility due to rapid changes in technology.

Preserving a core, long-term vision that will evolve over time, proves much more beneficial in attempting to construct a strong reputation. Your corporate vision should be consistent, but should also be responsive to rapidly changing conditions. It must be re-envisioned, flexible, and responsive to changing opportunities and threats in the competitive environment. Broadcasting this vision in the form of a clear-cut story has become all the more important today as companies face greater pressure and accountability from constituencies such as the media and investors. The popularity of business news due to private investing, the requirement for companies to publish an annual report, and increased governmental intervention and control in the corporate world have all contributed to a marked increase in corporate transparency over the last decade.[20] Recognizing these developments is one of the first steps in building a strong and enduring reputation.

The fragmented state of today's media poses yet another challenge as your company attempts to send its story to all constituencies. Public relations (PR) departments, both internal and external to a company, face an increasingly difficult time disseminating clear and concise messages to the ever-expanding number of media outlets.[21] In the 1980s, PR officers could limit their focus to the top-tier business magazines and the top two or three television outlets. The number of business newspapers, business magazines, and Web sites that exist today has broadened this narrow focus substantially. More ears are listening to corporate stories today, meaning that even greater care needs to be taken in what you say.

Cutting through the Clutter

Several other new challenges and opportunities have emerged since the mid-1980s to increase the importance of creating a distinct and compelling corporate vision in today's marketplace. While today's proliferation of brands offers customers a wealth of purchasing options, increased choice has not been entirely positive for many businesses. They now must place greater emphasis on marketing. Gone are the days when your company could be the only branded product of its kind on the market. If ten products sit side-by-side on a shelf with identical attributes, then it is the company's credibility and overall reputation that could very well make the difference in which product the consumer picks up to purchase.

When a consumer decides between two gas stations to buy gasoline, for example, aside from the location of the gas station, only intangible factors influence the buying decision (given similar pump prices). Gas from either station will keep the car going, gas from either station has approximately the same octane rating, and both service stations will offer a similar level of service. But if you watch public broadcasting (PBS) and like the notion that ExxonMobil supports certain programming on that network, you might want to buy gasoline from the company because of the image you hold in your mind about the company. If, however, you are an opera fan and listen to the Metropolitan Opera broadcast that Texaco supports regularly, this might actually convince you to buy your gasoline at its stations. Consumers are only now beginning to make the kinds of distinctions that we are talking about, based on notions other than the product itself, and this reliance on nothing more than identity and image will become the norm as products become increasingly homogenized across the globe.

Not Just the Product, But the People, Too

As the gasoline example above reveals, advertising campaigns and product attributes are hardly the only contributors to your company's distinct identity. In fact, the human element—the people running your company and selling your products—can have an even greater effect on the positive or negative perceptions of your company's constituencies. For example, the self-presentation of your most visible employees, especially the CEO, can affect overall reputation significantly. A March 2001 survey of 600 business leaders conducted by Yankelovich and Partners in Norwalk, Connecticut, revealed that at least half of a company's corporate reputation is attributed to the public image of its CEO.[22] In accordance with this statistic, Rich Karlgaard of *Forbes* magazine points to the reputation of Steve Jobs, Apple's chief executive, as the source of Apple's undervalued worth of $3.5 billion. Inconsistent CEO self-presentations can tarnish the trust an organization steadily builds with external constituencies, generating feelings of suspicion and sometimes even betrayal. Karlgaard observes that "the man who invented the PC industry and liberated 'the rest of us' in an act of manic heroism 25 years ago has now become just another self-possessed artist who parks his Mercedes 500 in the handicapped zone."[23]

Names and Logos: What's in a Name?

In addition to the positive self-presentation of leaders, your company can also differentiate itself through names and logos. McDonald's logo, for example, has built itself up so powerfully over the years that the golden arches speak volumes by themselves, without even the mention of the company name. On the other hand, you can also lose very quickly whatever image you have built up with constituencies through impetuous changes in the use of names and logos. Nissan in Japan is a good example of this phenomenon. To consolidate the company's brands worldwide, an edict from Nissan's Japanese headquarters in the 1980s eliminated the well-known Datsun brand name from the U.S. market in favor of the company name Nissan. This name change took over five years to complete because dealers refused to pay for new signs and resisted the change. In addition, customers became confused. Virtually everyone in the late 1960s and early 1970s knew about the Datsun 240Z, and the company's line of small cars helped Americans get through the first oil crisis. After the name change, however, customers thought that Nissan was a subsidiary of Toyota, its arch-rival. Only after two decades has the Nissan name become about as well-known in America as the old Datsun name.

Symbols and the Modern Brand

Brands are the manifestations of your company in a person's life. As such, individual brands that appear on the shelves are much more in touch with the everyday lives and routines of millions of consumers worldwide than the everyday routines of CEOs. Large corporate brands and more minor individual brands generate a vast number of associations and impressions that customers link to organizations to help determine their overall images. In this way, brands act as an additional means that your company uses to affect the minds and emotions of customers, deliberately—or unintentionally—promoting certain product attributes, relationships, credibility, and values.[24] Brands, often incorporating symbols to emphasize certain attributes of a product, provide cohesion and structure to an identity and make it easier for the company to gain recognition.[25]

Brands thus provide the symbolism and vivid imagery necessary to convey to constituencies a good sense of who and what you are. In the case of large-scale companies, such as GE, consumers' impressions of a number of brands can contribute to the company's overall multibrand reputation. Regardless of your organization's size, brands demonstrate how much power intangibles have on your company's image and bottom line.

Branding and corporate identity may appear to be recent trends—ones gaining impressive momentum in the new millennium—emerging from the need for concrete definition in a complicated world, but, in fact, identity programs can be traced back to ancient civilizations. In ancient Egypt, the Pharaohs used their signatures as a symbol of their administration. Anyone who has been to Luxor can attest to the fascination Ramses IV had with his "logo." It appears virtually everywhere and is especially noticeable because his cartouche—the nameplates ancient Egyptians used for kings, queens, and other high-ranking people—primitive and bold, stole the thunder from earlier symbols on columns and buildings.

When the Symbol Says It All

The U.S. and French revolutions provide more recent historical examples of corporate identity and the power of symbols to inspire and engage people. As part of those upheavals, both countries changed their identities with the development of new flags, national anthems, uniforms, and, in the case of France, with a new execution device: the guillotine. In the 1930s and 1940s, Nazi Germany terrified the world with its identity program. Although we regard the swastika today as abhorrent and probably the most negative logo imaginable, the same symbol had strong, positive connotations to earlier generations of German nationalists. In all of these cases, impressions ride on what story individuals read into various identity cues and images communicated by the organization.

Symbols constitute a powerful dimension of the identity picture. These visual manifestations receive an inordinate amount of attention because of our increasing focus on the visual and the exposure this type of shorthand receives on television and in magazines, annual reports, and brochures we see at work and at home.

In a world in which consumers depend on brands to simplify what would otherwise be an overwhelming purchase decision, many executives fail to grasp the importance of logos and all other parts of identity in their quest for success in corporate communication. Despite a general awareness of the importance of reputation, a surprisingly small number of executives actually understand how to create a coherent corporate identity and exploit constituencies' perceptions as an essential organizational asset.

The Modern Obsession with Brands

The modern obsession with visuals and, more specifically, brands may force many executives to open their eyes to the overall importance of brands when attempting to create a coherent corporate identity. In fact, society's preoccupation with branding means that brands are crucial vehicles for speaking to customers and telling your story, whether your company offers products, services, or a mix of both. In the wake of the IT revolution, multimedia innovations, and the rapid expansion of brands, brands are not only associated with products but also with services. Wally Olins, cofounder of the branding and identity consulting firm Wolff Olins in the United Kingdom, explains that "in fact, service brands are more innovative and becoming more dominant than ever before."[26] And, as the marketing of Martha Stewart and Oprah has shown, brands can be people, too.

Before considering what branding qualities will help your company build a distinct identity and reputation, let's think about what has caused brands to reach an unprecedented level of importance today. The answers reveal trends in public values your company may want to take advantage of. Olins offers three chief reasons to account for the branding craze: competition, consistency, and empathy. The heightened levels of competition in today's marketplace have made brands the primary way to differentiate one product from a host of others. Brands can also provide the comfort of consistency in today's quick-paced society. As Olins describes, "[brands] give us the reassurance that what we have today is the same as we had yesterday and the same as we will have tomorrow." If your company offers diverse products all packaged under a consistent brand, a sense of trust and cohesion is often generated in the minds of customers, building a greater sense of loyalty toward the tried-and-true brand. Disney is a great example, keeping its brand in a consistent format but supplementing it with sub-brands on an annual basis, such as *Aladdin* and *The Lion King*, to add innovative spice to a formula that clearly works.[27]

Americans, in particular, place a high value on material wealth and often judge others by the brands they use. In a society dominated by markers of wealth, where a person's worth is often equated with his or her net worth, brands increasingly act as global measuring tools of universally recognized standards and symbols against which we rank ourselves and others. Consider the following two examples: A gray-haired man sits in a Mercedes E320, dressed in a blue Zegna suit, wearing a gold Patek Philippe watch. Across the street sits another man in a Toyota Camry, wearing blue jeans and a black turtleneck, who tells time with a Timex digital watch. Even for people with very little understanding of American culture, these quick glimpses into the lives of these two men speak volumes about what they are like.

In the same way, brands can forcefully evoke in the user's or observer's mind an unspoken corporate story. In fact, as part of the most powerful of corporate stories, brands have the ability to enchant people in an American Dream–like manner—convincing them that wearing a pair of Nikes means they can "Just Do It" or anything their heart desires. In 1997, Internet entrepreneur Carmine Colettion made the command decision to have the trademark Nike swoosh tattooed on his navel. He explains: "I wake up every morning, jump in the shower, look down at the symbol, and that pumps me up for the day. It's to remind me every day what I have to do, which is, 'Just Do It'."[28] Colettion's anecdote illustrates how a powerful corporate story can become a personal mantra. The rest of the world will recognize and understand this mantra because brands are turning into an increasingly global shorthand.

Just as our society demands top-ten lists and rejects the full story in favor of a summary of highlights, it prizes brands as identification tags that can allow us to quickly and effortlessly gauge everything around us. Given this branding phenomenon, the capital value of your company can be significantly influenced by the success of your branding strategy and resulting reputation. Coca-Cola, for example, has a value that far exceeds its total tangible assets because of its strong branding.

Don't Just Buy It, *Live* It

In this branding bonanza, how can your company stand out from the rest? How do you actually distinguish yourself? Amidst all the marketing static and noise hurled at the public today, the most successful companies come alive by creating a conspicuous corporate personality. The winning personality will successfully engage consumers with the promise of inter-action and experience—"It's the Starbucks Experience...the Nike Experience... the Caterpillar Experience...the Levi's Experience...the Absolut Experience...the marketing of sensory experiences that con-tribute to the organization's or brand's identity."[29] In his book *The Circle of Innovation*, business consultant Tom Peters explains that the companies able to captivate consumers promise them unique experiences that people will associate with that company alone. Because today's sophisticated technology enables companies to bombard consumers with images, videos, text, and increasingly, sounds, smells, and even touch, your com-pany has to dazzle consumers with an experience that stands out from the rest, which they will automatically associate with your company, product, or service.[30]

Affording consumers such an experience can give your organization many tangible benefits. In fact, when a company's product cannot be dif-ferentiated from its competitors in terms of attributes, "intangibles like experiences become the key selling points." The thematic associations of Absolut vodka's magazine ads (discussed in Chapter 5), and the distinc-tive names of Ralph Lauren's home collection of paints are good exam-ples of ordinary products made a cut-above by image and connotations. Well-respected companies with strong reputations can also get away with charging more for their products, which explains Starbucks's abil-ity to charge upward of $3 for their coffee and milk concoctions. Most importantly, a strong identity achieves the highest communication impact possible and increases the memorability of a product or company in the easily distracted minds of consumers by cutting through the clut-ter of today's multimedia.[31]

Using an approach that appeals to all the senses emphasizes novelty and credibility as the two most important parts of the unified message you are sending to all your company's constituencies. Not only do constituen-cies need to be enticed by innovation, but they also need to wholeheart-edly believe in it. Moreover, the use of multisensory communications that aesthetically engage constituencies can make all the difference, determining whether your product or service will be worth remembering.[32]

Building a distinct corporate identity, however, is only half of the story. Just as critically, your organization must be acutely aware of how all constituencies perceive you, in addition to how you perceive yourself. Let's first consider how constituents formulate images of your organization in their minds before we analyze how these images can help or hinder your company's reputation management, determining your ultimate success.

WHEN IMAGE IS EVERYTHING

Constituencies form perceptions based on all of the messages that your company sends out through names and logos, and through self-presentations, including expressions of your corporate vision. As a result, products or services alone are not the only parts of your company that are attracting attention. The relationship your company hones with employees, shareholders, and the local community will also directly affect how your company is perceived, and thus, the kind of image you're generating. As former CEO of Procter and Gamble, Ed Artz observed, "Consumers now want to know about the company, not just the products."[33] Day-to-day behavior of employees, especially high-level executives, can rank just as high as quality of products as the source of a strong corporate image that is aligned with the company's identity.

But another challenge has recently arisen. No longer do individuals fall neatly into a single constituency group; rather, they can belong to multiple constituencies at the same time. In the past, constituents were easy to differentiate, but now they assume multiple roles. A consumer can easily be a member of a larger community-based organization, just as employees frequently invest in the companies for which they work. How does this make communicating to constituents more difficult? As an example, no longer can your company assume that messages communicated to shareholders will not be seen by employees—since often shareholders and employees are one and the same.

As a result of this trend, the clarity of your corporate identity is the chief determinant of how consistent constituencies' perceptions of the company will be. Unclear identities can easily hurt your company's success with certain constituencies, particularly in the case of changes in packaging and labels or new advertising campaigns. If your company doesn't seem to understand the new message it is conveying, you can hardly expect your constituencies to do the same. For example, after

Miller Genuine Draft generated momentum in draft beer sales, Adolph Coors altered its cans and bottles to read "Original Draft" instead of its previous "Banquet Beer." Because Coors did not clearly indicate that the beer itself had not changed, merely the labels, constituencies were left speculating. Soon after, Coors lost a substantial number of older customers in loyal regions such as California and Texas who were displeased with what they believed to be a change in the composition of the beer they knew and loved.[34]

Consumer Perceptions: Walking the Walk and Talking the Talk

As the speed of everyday life in the new millennium quickens, many consumers will be seeking clarity and stability more frequently in the brands and companies they know and admire. As a result, confidently constructing a solid identity for your company will become increasingly important.

Identity can help companies get through crises, as discussed in our chapter on crisis communication (Chapter 10). Because Johnson & Johnson had such a clear identity and image as an ethical company, it was able to weather the Tylenol crisis in a way that other organizations of lesser stature could not have. Constituencies not only find a solid image to be attractive, but they are also influenced by your company's credibility, a sense that the story your company tells is one they can believe in. Social-power theorists discuss the importance of credibility on a personal level, but clearly these ideas can apply to corporations as well. Constituents have certain perceptions about your organization before they even begin to interact with it, based on everyday life experiences, which gradually add or detract from this sense of credibility. These images stem from what they have read about your organization, what interactions others have had, and what visual symbols they recognize. Even if you have never eaten a hamburger at McDonald's, you have certain perceptions about the organization and its products through vicarious experience. If constituents have a high regard for the organization based on an initial impression, they are more likely to give you the benefit of the doubt in difficult times.

Don't forget that constituents may have a different perception of the organization after a single interaction. One bad interaction with a Verizon operator can destroy a relationship for a lifetime with a customer. One aloof salesperson at Bergdorf Goodman in New York could turn a shopper off to a line of clothing forever. That's why your organization must be so concerned about the quality of each and every communication. The goodwill and credibility that your company acquires through the repeated application of consistently excellent behavior will determine its image in the minds of constituents in a much more profound way than a one-shot corporate advertising campaign.

Taming the Corporate Beasts

In 1961, David Ogilvy, the founder of the Ogilvy & Mather advertising agency—a company that exists on brand proliferation alone—confessed his animosity toward the brand craze and omnipresent marketing in his classic book *Confessions of an Advertising Man*: "When I retire from Madison Avenue, I am going to start a secret society of masked vigilantes who will travel around the world on silent motor bicycles, chopping down posters at the dark of the moon. How many juries will convict us when we are caught in these acts of beneficent citizenship?" Ogilvy, embodying the principles most under attack by the antibrand movement, here boldly equates the demise of marketing with the liberation of society.[35]

The burgeoning antibrand movement, which picked up significant steam in the late-1990s, provides compelling evidence for you to invest significant time and effort in monitoring constituencies' images of your organization and its reputation. In recent years, global companies have replaced government bodies as the primary target of many staunch activists across the globe. As a result, your company must be extremely careful about the types of messages it is sending and, in turn, the kinds of images it generates. The new focus of attack on corporations speaks of the enormous political power many large corporations wield today. This is hardly surprising when one considers that out of the top 100 economies, 51 are global corporations and the remaining 49 are countries. Activism extends well beyond traditional union bodies and includes the young and old alike, concerned parents, and student activists. Anticorporate protests reached such a pitch throughout the 1990s that by October 1997, Earth First! produced a calendar listing important anticorporate protest dates, announcing the first "End Corporate Dominance Month." Horrific sweatshop images began appearing with increasing frequency and candidness in magazines such as *Life* and television shows such as ABC's *20/20*. The shock hit American consumers in June 1996 when *Life* depicted photos of Pakistani children toiling over Nike soccer balls for six cents an hour.[36] Mainstream notions of "political correctness" have prompted more people to criticize the disturbing and amoral elements of corporations and the global economy as a whole.[37]

Vancouver-based *Adbusters* magazine devotes itself to mocking brand giants—a practice generally referred to as *culture jamming*—in an attempt to cut them down to size. As editor Kalle Lasn explains: "In one simple deft move you slap the giant on its back. We use the momentum of the enemy." Plastering the image of Charles Manson's face over a Levi's jeans billboard, holding up meager pay slips to giant price tags at public presentations, pie-ing Bill Gates's face, and dumping garbage bags full of shoes outside Nike Town, are some of the routine tactics culture-jamming activists are boldly employing to make a conspicuous anti-corporate statement. This activism took a technological spin in 2000, when antiglobalization protests came to Seattle. Thousands of antiglobalization protestors convened in Seattle at the World Trade Organization (WTO) meeting, coordinated by extensive Web planning. John Delicath, a University of Cincinnati expert on antiglobalization protests, explains that "Starting with the protests against the WTO in Seattle, so-called 'anti-globalization' activists have used the Internet to build relationships and create networks for sharing ideas, information and resources."[38] Culture-jammers' use of the Internet gives them impressive force, potentially enough to severely damage corporations across the globe.[39]

Investor Perceptions: Beyond the Fanfare

While being acutely aware of how culture jammers and the masses of consumers are perceiving your organization, be sure not to neglect the individuals who are your monetary stakeholders—investors. During the upsurge of dot.coms at the close of the last century, investors became so preoccupied with thinking "outside the box" that they forgot about the necessity of a tangible box—a corporate reality—for a company to succeed. Did the company have a product or service that could be successful? Did it have a substantial business proposition in the competitive climate they faced? Did it have seasoned management that could run the business? These were questions that were not asked frequently enough...until recently.

Enchanted by the prospect of the radically new way of conducting business over the Internet in the mid- and late-1990s, many investors were in a hurry to do away with all traces of the old. Thus, when the dot.com craze first took off, investors bought into a hypothetically bright future. In this rapidly growing tech bubble, investors were enchanted by the convincing corporate stories dot.com start-ups were telling. This "story" focused on "what a company's potential market was, how it was going to continue growing exponentially. Tech utopians could see the future, so short-term problems didn't matter. (Sure, Amazon was losing money hand-over-fist, but once everybody started shopping online, it would turn big profits)."[40]

These stories of the mid- and late-1990s were so compelling and so heavily backed by the media that nobody stopped to question their validity. As a matter of fact, the more grandiose the Internet dream and the more money a company burned to fuel the illusion, the higher stock prices soared as investors' eyes were dazzled. As a result, a flashy, eye-catching Web site alone seemed enough for most dot.com companies to go public.[41]

With such a promising start, why exactly did the dot.com bubble burst? In short, because in many cases, the dot.coms lacked a substantial corporate reality—products and services likely to succeed in the market-place, seasoned management with a solid track record, and a business model supported by evidence . These companies then presented an identity to investors built on an illusion, not a concrete corporate reality. The dot.coms were doomed. A study by Webmergers.com identified over 210 Internet companies that ailed globally in 2000, causing many to dub dot.coms "dot bombs." All too many investors got caught up in the fairy tale of what *might* be instead of the reality of what actually *was*. Not surprisingly, the Pew Internet and American Life Project revealed that two-thirds of American respondents to a survey blamed the "irrational exuberance [of investors] looking for fast money." Some dot.com organizations played on this irrationality by hyping the potential and disguising the actual.[42]

In reality, however, these dot.coms offered no technological or logistical advantage that would effectively transform the promise of profit into reality. Conveniently, the start-ups downplayed this part of their corporate reality in the tales they were telling. As Kanwal Kehki, the "Godfather" of Silicon Valley's Indian Community explains: "The problem was that the dot-com phenomenon was not driven by nerdy engineers like me. Slick MBAs with a get-rich-quick mindset and new theories drove it. There was no technology advantage or logistics advantage. If I had to choose between a dot-com and an old-line, brick-and-mortar business building a Website, I would back the old-line business anytime."[43]

What lessons, in terms of image and identity, should you take away from the dot.com nosedive? Regardless of the business you're in, investors today are quite skeptical. They will scrutinize your company in the aftermath of the dot.com burst bubble. Essentially, the crash should remind you of how essential it is to have a substantial corporate reality that doesn't rely on hype and fantasy. From this reality, a company can then craft an identity. Armed with a substantial corporate reality and a well-crafted identity, an alignment between identity and investors' images is much more likely. Today, most investors have learned the hard way that "if it seems too good to be true, it probably is."[44] And today, the smart approach that careful investors are taking when being wooed by a company is: "Don't show me the money; show me the business plan."[45]

Many current dot.coms have answered the call and have built substantial corporate realities, involving products and services that are potentially successful because of the strong business framework upon which they are founded. Most importantly, however, many new dot.coms have strong management. In fact, the best management, like Meg Whitman of eBay, carries old-economy credentials, thus avoiding the hype so heavily relied on by dot.coms. The industry was so tainted by the dot.com collapse that technology-based companies coming forward today cannot afford to exaggerate their claims. Instead, they must strip all hype or flippancy from communications with investors.

At the outset of the twenty-first century, business reality is prevailing once again, and your organization must be prepared to have a bona fide reality to have any possibility of building a positive and lasting reputation on Wall Street and beyond.

Employee Perceptions
Aligning corporate identity with the images that external constituencies such as consumers and investors have of your organization requires keeping inside people on track. The perception employees have of your company and its vision determines the caliber of work they will do. Ensuring that all employees firmly grasp the company's mission statement and vision helps foster a sense of attachment that can spill over from this internal constituency to external ones, like consumers, investors, and even the community at large. Affording devoted employees the opportunity to become shareholders in the company can help reinforce that sense of trust that they will, in turn, convey to the world around them.

Be sure not to focus so heavily on the images held by external constituencies that you ignore the importance of those held by your own employees. Starbucks Coffee, for example, has built one of the strongest brands and reputations in America by creating an equally powerful and unified story and culture—beginning inside and working out. CEO Howard Schultz explains the philosophy: "We built the Starbucks brand first with our people, not with consumers, the opposite approach from that of the crackers-and-cereal companies…Because we believed this was the best way to meet and extend the expectations of employees who were zealous about good coffee." Every *barista* plays such a key role in inspiring a customer to come back again that Starbucks refers to each one as a partner, the official name for a Starbucks employee.[46]

Starbucks makes this commitment to inspiring customers tangible through Bean Stock and the discounted stock incentive purchases plan (SIP), of which 30,000 Starbucks "partners" take advantage. This stocks-for-everyone approach gives employees a vested interest in the company's success, creates even more incentive to provide quality service, and instills in employees a sense that the company values them in more ways than one. PepsiCo uses a similar strategy of offering stock options to most of its 140,000 employees, hoping to bolster loyalty to the company. Starbucks' employees have used holdings to pay for down payments on houses, motorcycles, vacations, and tuition, enabling the company to weave itself into the everyday lives and successes of the employees who implement its vision daily. The strategy has proved to be a winning one, to say the least. In *Fortune* magazine's February 2001 ranking of the most admired companies, Starbucks even beat McDonald's to earn the top spot on the list of the most admired food service organizations.[47]

In addition to the commitment of employees, Starbucks's innovation also depends on their creation of a multisensory experience in their coffeehouses that was unique to the U.S. market when the company began to expand beyond its original Seattle location in 1987. The Starbucks "coffeehouse" is consistent worldwide: *Baristas* are attentive and enthusiastic; the green and brown tables, counters, and walls echo the color of coffee beans; the brown bags and Starbucks logo send a modern message. Together, these aesthetic elements invite consumers not only to enjoy the coffee Starbucks is selling but also the experience, as they receive an unfailing smile from a *barista* and sink into a cushioned armchair before the warmth of a lit fireplace.[48]

This common experience, in which Starbucks employees are the *producers* of the in-store experience, helps ensure an identity coinciding with the images held by consumers across the country and around the world. While Starbucks locations in California may not offer the lit fireplaces of East Coast locations, the friendliness and attentiveness of employees are the common element that ties the decorative and aesthetic elements of each store together, bringing them to life. Despite many imitators, Starbucks is still the leading brand because the company got such a great head start by being the first to implement this unique model.

Concentrating on your corporate identity—the names, brands, symbols, self-presentation, and most of all, vision—to create a personality will enable your company's image to come alive and engage your constituencies. Just like animated and memorable people you encounter in your everyday life, such organizations will live on in the minds and hearts of all constituencies, earmarking these organizations as *different*.

After you gauge the impressions all constituencies have of your organization, consider how you view yourself. Is there a large disparity between your company's self-image and the images held in the minds of all those around you? Where do the differences lie: in perceptions of employee demeanor or in your company's overall vision and direction? Identifying these perception gaps will determine where you need to channel your efforts in aligning your company's identity and image to produce an overall sturdy reputation.

Why Reputation Counts

Why do you need to care so much about the cumulative effect of the messages and stories that you are delivering to your constituencies? You need to care for two related reasons. All these messages and stories contribute directly to the overall impressions any given person—a consumer, an investor, an employee—has of your organization. And these impressions, depending on how well they align with your company's reality, can result in a positive or negative reputation for your firm.

Companies face consumer backlash if they don't live up to the expectations they create in the minds of their constituencies. Companies and brands live in the imagination of consumers, and in this imaginary world, even the smallest shortcomings or misalignments are seen as premeditated and an attempt to dupe the consumer. A strong reputation generally makes constituencies more willing to forgive the flaws that your company may develop over time.

But what kind of effect can something as intangible as *reputation* have on your company's bottom line? Reputation expert Charles Fombrun discusses the value of an organization's reputation as the primary way people are informed about what products to buy, what companies they should try to work for, or what stocks to invest in. In general, large differences exist between the book values and market values of highly valued brands. A strong reputation also has important strategic consequences for a firm, because, as Fombrun notes, "it calls attention to a company's attractive features and widens the options available to its managers, for instance, whether to charge higher or lower prices for products and services or to implement innovative programs."[49] As a result, the intangible entity of reputation is undoubtedly a source of competitive advantage.[50] Just ask the companies ranked high in *Fortune's* "Most Admired," and *Business Week's* Global Brand ranking, or the *Wall Street Journal's* reputation survey.[51]

Even if your company sells a more unconventional, less tangible product, for example, business schools offering students knowledge and a coveted degree, the benefits of a strong reputation are clear. Business schools that are successful at reputation management as measured by ranking in the *Wall Street Journal* and *Business Week* can charge a premium price, pay less to suppliers, entice the best recruits and faculty, experience fewer crises, and can more successfully weather the crises that do hit. To build such a valuable reputation, however, you must remember that you can only create and manage your organization's identity, not your reputation. Burberry's overhaul of its structure and organizational reality, which resulted in changes to its identity, ushered in huge changes in its overall reputation worldwide.

Burberry—Dressing Up a Down-and-Out Reputation

Your company's story and the personality it projects are crucial not only when introducing your product or service to the marketplace but also when trying to revive your company and bring a faltering brand back to life. Brand revival has much less to do with a CEO's personality than with what he or she does with the personality of the company and brand he or she is trying to build back. In analyzing how mediocre companies were able to ascend to greatness in his latest book *Good to Great*, Jim Collins explains that "it wasn't the leader's personality that mattered so much as the organization's personality…[and] to make those personalities seem as palpable…as human ones."[52] Rubbermaid achieved great reputational success in the late 1980s through the mid-1990s, but experienced a decline after the departure of CEO Stanley Gault. Collins cites Gault's mistake as making his personality the focal point of his strategy, not the personality of Rubbermaid itself. As a result, he prevented the company from succeeding without him.

The hallmark of a solid corporate identity, therefore, is one that finds strength beyond temporal parts, such as its present management or external environment. Establishing your organization's distinct identity, and figuring out what story it wants to tell all of its constituencies, is the most crucial step on the path to enduring success. Let's now look at the comeback of the designer label Burberry under the leadership of Rose Marie Bravo, who brought cohesiveness and a refreshing breath of contemporary fresh air to a stodgy brand that couldn't decide what story it wanted to tell the world.[53] Since its founding in 1856, Burberry told a distinct story with its gabardine, plaid-lined raincoats that exuded British upper-crust tradition. One hundred and forty years later, the same type of 50-plus crowd maintained respectful appreciation for the brand, and the famous Burberry plaid was still equated with the coat granddad wore on rainy days. By the late 1990s, however, Burberry watched its sales begin to plummet, with 1997 profits dropping a devastating 60 percent, from $106 to $43 million.[54]

What was Burberry doing wrong in the late 1990s to cause such a sudden drop? A number of factors contributed to the general disarray and inconsistency in Burberry's story, management, and strategy, all leading to a fatally stagnant reputation. First, before 1997, instead of proactively developing a cohesive Burberry brand across the globe, Burberry's pre-Bravo management adopted a laissez-faire approach and allowed each country's management team to develop the brand as they wanted. The result was an incoherent identity, and an even more confused image in the minds of customers. When customers thought of Burberry, what came to mind depended on their geographic location—in the United States, it meant $900 raincoats and $200 scarves, in Korea it meant whiskey, and in Switzerland it meant watches. Current CEO Rose Marie Bravo explains that before her arrival on the scene as Burberry's new CEO in 1997, "[Burberry] had a disparate network of licensees marketing Burberry around the globe. It wasn't a coherent business. Each country was representing its own version of Burberry. Demand slowed. The business needed a clean up. The brand was over-exposed and over-distributed."[55]

Second, not only did Burberry seem confused about what it was selling, it also seemed confused about who it was selling to. Burberry's inability to decide whether it was targeting upper- or lower-end consumers caused massive problems in the Asian market. Burberry products were being sold in bulk to discount retailers, undermining the image that the exclusive, high-end Burberry boutiques were trying to generate. The conflicting messages of both types of retailers tarnished the previously pristine Burberry brand. Bravo took one look at the Asian market and realized that Burberry had to sharpen its focus and concentrate on high-end retailing alone to send a consistent message to consumers. Similarly, a poor choice of products caused Burberry to miss the boat entirely on the clothing consumer group that matters most: women. The Burberry story, by speaking to older males as a high-end men's raincoat retailer, was missing out on the lucrative female clothing audience. Amidst all this confusion, Burberry began to focus too heavily on the Asian region, in which it seemed to find success, ignoring all its problem areas. Since the late 1980s, Burberry had relied heavily on its brand's popularity in Asia and neglected its marked lack of popularity elsewhere around the globe. By 1996, Asians generated two-thirds of the company's revenue, whether at home or traveling.

This spelled disaster for the brand when Asia's economies began to tumble in the mid-1990s.[56]

When did the reputation revival really take off? The most visible turning point in the revamping of the Burberry brand was a daring, and altogether unexpected, advertising campaign that threw supermodel Kate Moss into a signature plaid bikini. The ads caused sales to sky-rocket, and the average age of the Burberry consumer to plunge. Being a high-end label since the brand's inception in 1856 gave the brand a degree of credibility with consumers that facilitated the turnaround. Bravo recognized the need to have the Burberry store portfolio reflect this luxurious label, upgrading the flagship store in London, doubling the size of the New York store, and expanding from there. Even more importantly, Burberry began to take a firm grasp of its detached network of franchises. The company purchased its Spanish licensee in 2000, and plans to take control of licensing and distribution in Asia in January 2002, to give Burberry a greater share of profits.[57] All of Bravo's initiatives, from store renovations to a more unified product focus across all franchises, moved toward overall brand cohesiveness, making constituencies equate the signature plaid with a blend of both traditional and innovative fashion. To tap into the female fashion market, Bravo says she "got [the brand] into the right kind of stores and developed an expertise in a variety of new products beyond just raincoats. Rainwear was the bulk of the business. We wanted to get our share of womenswear. Accessories have the highest margin potential."[58]

What was the tangible result of these identity changes? After the makeover in 1998, Burberry's revenues increased approximately 156 percent in the following 2 to 3 years. The danger this newfound popularity has caused is overexposure, and turning off high-end consumers should the Burberry plaid be pirated by street corner vendors everywhere.[59] Bravo dubs this danger "check management," which Burberry must always keep at the forefront of its strategy, to maintain its air of elitism and luxury. Her efforts to abolish the discount retailing of the brand in Asian markets is helping keep plaid proliferation in check. Similarly, Burberry personnel are infiltrating vintage clothing stores and flea markets to snag old Burberry raincoats to update and resell them in their boutiques.[60]

In addition to worries about overexposure, the main threat to Burberry's future is whether the brand will keep its strength and appeal. Some already claim that the brand is approaching the dreaded fashion status of "passé." Bravo has taken a crucial step in recognizing the possibility of becoming outdated and recognizes the need to take preventive measures to ensure that this does not occur. She acknowledges that "one has to constantly innovate. You can't rest on your laurels and you can't be predictable." In this way, the world of high fashion mirrors the Darwinian world of reputation—evolve or face the inevitability of extinction.[61]

How is Bravo managing to evolve while keeping Burberry's crucial tenets of Britishness and traditionalism to maintain its older segment of loyal consumers? Diversifying the product line to include prams, dog sweaters, and minikilts targets a younger demographic group, while the traditional cashmere scarves and gabardine trenches are still available for the older crowd. As the Burberry story evolves and appeals to a more youthful audience, it maintains consistency by putting quality and luxury at the top of its priority list. "As long as we deliver the quality for the price," Bravo says with confidence, "then I believe there will always be people willing to pay for something that is well made and well done. People love well-designed clothes. And the Britishness is something we like to hang our hat on." With Burberry valued at $280 million in 2000 and an anticipated value of $2.8 billion when Burberry's IPO launches in mid-2002, that's one valuable plaid hat. All credit goes to Bravo's successful management of the company's reputation.

As the Burberry case reveals, the key to mastering reputation is determining what each of your constituencies wants, and ensuring that the cohesive story you are telling responds to those desires. Analyzing your key constituencies' needs and wants will allow you to think strategically about every communication you send to constituents and to measure the success of each communication. In addition, developing a convincing story for your company to follow will help ensure that communications to all constituencies are cohesive and consistent, generating a sense of trustworthiness that constituencies will appreciate and admire.

Ford and Firestone—The Crumbling of Cultural and Corporate Pillars

But what happens when a company destroys that sense of trust? As we discussed at the beginning of this chapter, Ford and its tire counterpart Firestone were two pillars of the American Dream as founders of the car industry, the product that came to define American culture in the twentieth century. The ease with which the reputation of two widely respected corporate giants, with roots in the very fibers of the nation, collapsed in the year 2000 reveals how delicate matters of reputation are. As David D'Alessandro, president of John Hancock Mutual Life Insurance, said in 1999, "It can take 100 years to build up a good brand and 30 days to knock it down."[62] This comment applies literally to the Firestone tire tragedies of 2000. Harvey S. Firestone founded the Firestone Tire and Rubber Company in 1900, which grew to generate revenues of $20 billion in the 1999 fiscal year following the 1990 merger with Bridgestone Corporation of Japan.[63] Yet a hundred years of conscientiously building the company, as well as its relationship with Ford, seemed to vanish instantaneously under a black cloud of scandal in July 2000. Almost overnight, Firestone was transformed from the hero of its own corporate story to a villain abandoning consumer welfare in the relentless pursuit of profit.

Despite their close marriage, the year 2000 saw these two American pillars turn against one another to pin blame for 203 deaths linked to Firestone tread separations on Ford Explorers. The majority of the 6.5 million tires recalled because of the tragic accidents were on popular Ford models—the Explorer and Mercury Mountaineer SUVs, Ranger, and F-150 pickups, from which Ford derives 90 percent of its profits, along with other big trucks such as the Ford Expedition.[64] Clearly, since both companies feared they would suffer enormous losses if they assumed total blame for the incidents, each of these long-term business associates had ample reason to pin the blame for the accidents on the other. Ultimately, Ford's greater credibility with consumers and Firestone's failure to create emotional ties with its buyers caused Firestone to suffer the most significant, and potentially fatal, blows to its reputation.

As we take a closer look at the crisis of Firestone's massive tire recall of 2000, notice how the company failed to construct close personal ties with its consumers and other constituencies, giving the company no safety net to fall back on when the public realized their earlier perceptions of Firestone as a company with integrity no longer matched the reality. Also, take note of Firestone's failure to construct a cohesive corporate narrative to convey to consumers; instead, the company aired its internal disputes about the crisis in front of a public outraged by the company's conduct and the loss of life. In fact, the Firestone debacle serves as a model of how *not* to be admired. Not surprisingly the company experienced the biggest drop in *Fortune*'s 2001 survey of the most admired companies, assuming the bottom spot on the list of rubber and plastics companies.[65]

The public at large lost a substantial amount of faith in Firestone based on its tardy reaction to the tire tragedies. Many came to categorize the company as apathetic, unconcerned, and generally disorganized. Not until the October following the scandal's outbreak did the first signs of a distinct Firestone PR strategy became discernable. Even then, the strategy was completely off base. Firestone mistakenly targeted one constituency—dealers—when it should have targeted the public—potential buyers and the group most outraged by the company's conduct. Because dealers build customer satisfaction in the tire industry and manufacturers are largely removed from buyers, Firestone distributed ads to local dealers to be cosigned by both the company and the dealers. Under a headline of "We Believe in Firestone," the copy reads: "I've sold Firestone products for over 25 years to our customers in Jonesville. We've found the quality to be excellent. We decide what we sell based strictly on how it performs. We deal with tires daily, so we know. Our confidence in Firestone does not come from a brochure, but from experience...As an independent dealer, I have a choice."[66] The ads used local dealers as a seemingly neutral third party to help reassure buyers that the confidence they had lost in Firestone should be restored based on the amount of faith the dealers themselves have in the company. In making this strategic move, Firestone assumed that local dealers had fostered strong relationships with their buyers, giving the company a solid reputation as a tire retailer in their local community. Using such a voice to convey a corporate message meant Firestone attempted to ride on the buyers' reputations to help build back its own. Instead the company should have channeled effort and resources into targeting consumers *directly* to bolster their view of the company.

It was not until February 2001, months after the news of the tire recall raged across media channels, that Firestone began to speak to consumers directly by moving its safety efforts on-line. The company launched the Web site TireSafety.com, containing pertinent information about daily tire maintenance while prominently displaying the Firestone name. Since Firestone labeled improper tire inflation as one possible cause of the Ford Explorer accidents, the site offered free tire gauges to those people who registered, and provided e-mail alerts upon request to warn customers when to check tire pressure to ensure safety. Woody McMillin, manager of motor sports and consumer products PR at Firestone hoped that the site would convey to the public the notion that Firestone cares. He explained: "Bottom line: you have to have the highest regard for customer safety. We and other tire manufacturers probably have not done a good enough job of telling people how to maintain their tires."[67]

Leaving consumer safety out of Firestone's corporate narrative until months after the scandal exploded with the unveiling of the TireSafety.com Web site left many consumers with a sense of betrayal.

Acting so late, and so inadequately as many argue, showed the public that Firestone only paid attention to consumer safety when backed into a corner in the heat of a crisis, not because it is a notion fundamentally built into their corporate philosophy. This is a far cry from Johnson & Johnson, which cites family and consumer safety as its most important priority in its Credo, listing profits last. Johnson & Johnson lived up to its Credo in the way the company responded to the public's needs first during the Tylenol cyanide crisis—as discussed in detail in Chapter 10 on crisis communication.

By contrast to Johnson & Johnson's responsiveness to consumers during the Tylenol poisonings, one of McMillin's responses to the media's demands for answers about the accidents seemed more focused on obligatory restitution than legitimate concern for the 119 lives lost in the Ford Explorer accidents: "We've had some rocks thrown at us...I don't think we've done a good enough job in talking about tire safety."[68] It seems it did not do a good enough job fostering relationships with buyers either, relying too heavily on the credible images of local retailers. Richard Johnson, president and CEO of Heafner Tire Group Inc. in Charlotte, explains: "Firestone has no problem with the dealers...Their problem is with the consumer."[69] Instead of standing on its own two feet, it seemed to rely on third-party validation.

The power of reaching out directly to consumers should not be underestimated in brand-building and reputation management. Sam I. Hill of Booz-Allen & Hamilton notes that "the strategic value of brand equity is consistently underestimated and often slighted in favor of more tangible competitive advantages, such as technological superiority or lower pricing. This is a fundamental mistake."[70] In fact, the faulty tires on the Ford Explorer caused the accidents, but consumers' feelings of betrayal, disbelief, and outrage are responsible for Firestone's loss of reputation. Had the company acted swiftly and compassionately, assuming responsibility for the mishaps, consumers might have felt more valued and thus more willing to forgive a company that made a mistake. Instead, people felt betrayed and outraged by the company's apparent lack of concern for loss of life and its contribution to that loss.

Did any of Firestone's belated PR moves actually work? What happened to the Firestone story? And is a happy ending even possible after such tumultuous plot twists? While the company no longer occupies the front page of the daily paper or headline the nightly news, its reputation is in sorry shape. In March 2001, Total Research Corp., a market researcher in Princeton, New Jersey, surveyed consumers about the reliability of various brands and rated Firestone at less than 4 on a 0 to 10 scale, a drop of

40 percent from its rankings a year ago, prior to the crisis. On top of those disheartening numbers, the $754 million recall and litigation caused Firestone's North American business to lose $510 million from $7.5 billion in 2000 sales, with a projected loss of $200 million for 2001.[71] GM announced that it would drop Firestone tires from several of its SUV and car models in the next year, in reaction to consumers' lingering fears and concerns. It's no wonder that Jay Leno dubbed the company "Tombstone" during a spring 2001 show.[72]

What seemed to hammer the most decisive nail in the Firestone coffin, however, was its divorce from its long-time partner in the car industry—Ford. Ford's public statement that it could no longer believe in Firestone was a massive blow to Firestone's credibility. For example, as CEO Jacques Nasser bluntly put it: "We don't want to be out there every year with another Firestone recall." When the crisis exploded in the summer of 2000, Ford headquarters in Michigan posted a large sign in the main meeting room, reading: "Protect Our Customers, Protect Our Business, Protect Firestone." By May 2001, after communication between the two companies had dwindled substantially in the chaos of the crisis and the frantic desire of each to save its own skin, the laminated index cards that Ford handed out to its employees to outline their primary goals made no mention of Firestone.[73]

If Firestone's strongest ally could no longer maintain faith in the company, other constituencies understandably could not either. When Ford and Firestone met on May 21, 2001, to discuss the future of their relationship together in the wake of the crisis, each still blamed the other for the hundreds of deaths caused by tire tread separation, degrading the tragedy into a finger-pointing feud. Firestone handed Ford a letter explaining its viewpoint and desire for a corporate divorce, thus ending the 96-year partnership founded when Harvey Firestone, as we mentioned at the beginning of the chapter, started selling Henry Ford tires for his new Model T vehicle. The next day Ford announced it would replace 13 million Firestone tires—at a cost of $3 billion. In the realm of reputation, even when dealing with cultural legends, the larger you are the harder you may fall in the case of poor crisis management.[74]

HOW TO BUILD A REPUTATION TO LAST

After analyzing a number of cases—The Body Shop, Starbucks, Burberry, and Firestone—and highlighting the individual corporate identity and image components that contribute to either a positive or negative reputation, where do you begin with your own organization? And how can you ensure that the reputation you are investing substantial time and effort into building is, in fact, a positive one? Let's take a look at a framework that you can use as a step-by-step approach to building a reputation that will endure and ward off the inevitable fickleness of human nature.

Who Are You, Actually?

Despite the rapidly changing world around you, resist the temptation to ask yourself "How should my company change?" and instead ask "What do we stand for and why do we exist?" To begin, your organization needs to assess its current picture. How does the public currently view your organization? What do your company's various symbols represent to different constituents? Does your identity accurately reflect the company's underlying reality or is the identity simply a leftover from days gone by? Your company should start finding answers to these questions by conducting research and surveying customers and members of other constituencies. Conducting broad surveys from a random sampling of individuals, however, might not be the best solution. When conducting research to uncover relationships and inconsistencies, concentrate on being thorough and then use the audit as a basis for potential identity changes. In this process, you should be looking for red flags.

When conducting research, anything outdated or inconsistent should leap out at you if you are looking hard enough. Typical identity problems you might stumble upon include symbols that conjure up images of earlier days at the company or just generally incorrect impressions. Once you have compiled the facts, you can move to create a new identity or institute a communication program to share the correct and most up-to-date profile.

While an identity audit seems to be a fairly straightforward and simple process, it usually is not. Often the symbols that exist and the impressions that result are not how your organization sees itself at all. Companies that are trying to change their identity are particularly difficult to audit because the vision that top executives imagine for what the company will be in the future is so different from what the current reality is. And often executives disregard the best research that tells them how constituents' perceptions about the organization differ from their own. Such cognitive dissonance is a company's first challenge in managing its identity. The change in identity of your organization must be far enough along so that the new image the company is trying to adopt will actually make sense, some day at least, to those who will encounter the company in the years ahead.

A Purposeful Plan

Having clear goals and an even clearer vision is essential to the identity process. Goals should be set by your company's senior management and understood by employees at all levels. Effective goals explain how each constituency is supposed to react to specific identity proposals. For instance: "As a result of this name change, analysts will recognize our organization as more than just a one-product company" or "By putting a new logo on the outside of our stores, customers will be more aware of dramatic transformations that are going on inside."

Problems in establishing effective goals arise because most managers are more likely to formulate issues from their own perspectives—particularly senior managers—and have great difficulty seeing things from the viewpoint of constituents. Consultants can help clarify the main issues you are facing, but your organization as a whole must be motivated to change and willing to accept the truth about the new image, even if it hurts.

In addition, companies need to avoid the syndrome of "change for change sake." To meet some kind of standardization worldwide is not the kind of objective that is likely to meet with success. Usually, such arbitrary changes result from a CEO wanting to leave his or her mark on the organization rather than as a necessary step in the evolution of the company's identity.

Careful analysis of the company's situation should guide change, as in the case of Kentucky Fried Chicken in the mid 1990s and its desire to change its image and menu in response to changes in American dietary habits. The strong corporate identity of this company worldwide (it has one of its biggest restaurants on Tiananmen Square in Beijing and can be found in remote corners of Japan) conjures up images of Colonel Sanders's white beard, buckets of fried chicken, salty biscuits, and gravy. To an earlier generation, these were all positive images closely connected with home and hearth. Today, health-conscious Americans are more likely to think of the intense cholesterol, the explosion of sodium, and gobs of fat in every bucket of the Colonel's chicken. Thus, the company has recently tried to reposition itself with the growing population of health-conscious Americans by offering broiled chicken and chicken salad sandwiches. The company's goal was to change the old image and adopt a position in tune with Americans' greater awareness of health and nutrition.

To do so, executives decided to gradually change the name of the 5000 restaurants to just "KFC." The obvious point was to eliminate the word *fried*. While most identity experts would agree that it is very difficult to create an identity for a restaurant out of initials alone, this one has the well-known Colonel as a symbol to go along with the change. While this change is still going on and cannot be evaluated yet as either a success or failure, the objective for this particular change makes a lot of sense and puts KFC in a better position for the more nutrition-conscious consumers of the twenty-first century.

Painting a New Picture

Once the identity audit is complete and clear objectives established, the next phase in the identity process is the actual design. If a name change is necessary, consultants must search for alternatives. Because so many names have already been used, this is a step that simply cannot be taken without the help of consultants to avoid any possibilities of trademark and name infringement. But options for change can still number in the hundreds. Usually, certain ones stand out as more appropriate. The criteria for selection depend on several variables. For example, if the company is undergoing a global expansion, the addition of the word *international* might be the best alternative. If a firm has a lot of equity built into one product, changing the name of the corporation to that of the product might be the answer, as happened when Consolidated Foods changed its name to Sara Lee.

The process of designing a new look or logo is an artistic one, but so many times executives can't help getting involved in the process, which can sometimes complicate matters. Everyone has an opinion about designs and usually the choice is a matter of taste coupled with the excellent work of a professional designer. Despite the reliance on professionals to develop designs, many CEOs rely on their own instincts rather than the work of someone who may have spent an entire career thinking about design solutions.

Consider the CEO who designed what he thought would be the perfect logo for his company on a napkin. After several weeks of design exploration by a reputable design firm, he kept coming back to that same napkin design over and over again. Until the designer finally caught on and came up with an exploration that resembled the napkin design, each of the suggestions was rejected. When the CEO saw his own idea come back at him, he was happy. Everyone agreed that it was not the best design, but it was adopted and is in use today.

In another story, a CEO took the favorite exploration of everyone on the design team out on the road for a couple of weeks to show it around. The designer warned him not to do this because it would only complicate matters with everyone thinking he or she is an expert in logo design. When the team met again, the favorite design was scrapped because of the candid comments of a first-grade teacher who felt that the lopsided positioning of the letters in the design would affect young children's perceptions of correct lettering. One person made the difference, but had no knowledge of design and no sense of the company's goals.

Obviously, there has to be a balance between the professional opinion of a designer and instincts of senior management at the firm. Both need to participate in the final decision whether a name change is involved or just a new logo. In some cases, designers and identity consultants are perfectionists or idealistic, presenting ideas that are unrealistic or too avant-garde for typically conservative large corporations. In the end, your senior management must exert strong leadership to effect the change, no matter what it is, for it to succeed.

Develop Powerful Prototypes

Once the final design is selected and approved, hire consultants to develop models using the new symbols or name. For products, prototype packaging shows how the brand image may be used in advertising. If a retail operation is involved, a model of the store might be built. In other situations, the identity is applied to everything, including ties, t-shirts, business cards, and stationery to see how it works in practice.

During this process, you may very well experience cold feet. As the reality of the change sinks in, criticism mounts (as in the case of the schoolteacher) from some if they have not been involved in the process and from others because they do not have a good sense of the evolution and meaning of the design. At times, negative reactions from constituents can be so strong that proposals have to be abandoned and work started all over again. Recognize that these obstacles are possible and try not to be discouraged.

Your company can take several steps to ease the identity-building process. First, involve a diverse range of people and viewpoints. The one caveat is to avoid accommodating different ideas by diluting key concepts. You should never accept an identity that is simply the lowest common denominator. Two ways to deal with the task are either to let a strong leader champion the new design or set up a strong committee to work on the program. In either approach, everyone has to be informed. Try to actively involve a variety of employees, even if only to receive feedback along the way. The more people involved in the process from its inception, the less work necessary to sell the idea once it's formulated.

Build Emotional Bridges

Once you have developed prototypes, consider how well you are engaging the emotions of your company's constituencies—in particular, consumers. In a *Design Management Journal* article, consultant Tom Peters writes that the design and aesthetics that attract and maintain consumer loyalty are "about love and hate, not like and dislike (research shows that long-term consumer attachment is tied to an emotional reaction to a product or service)—'like' does not a long-term relationship cement."[75] When you consider the power of consumer sentiments toward your company, building emotional ties with consumers and all your constituencies becomes a crucial step to long-term success in reputation management.

Whenever you consider issues of identity, image, and reputation don't forget that since constituencies are human beings, they sometimes act on the basis of capricious feelings. Much like relationships on a personal level, the relationships companies forge with their constituencies can breed a sense of trust that will keep them loyal, or a sense of uncertainty or distrust which may push them away. For example, Scott Bedbury, Starbucks's vice president of marketing, oversaw the "Just Do It!" campaign launch when heading up Nike marketing before moving to the coffee giant. With both companies Bedbury emphasized the necessity of building strong emotional ties with customers. He explains, "Nike, for example, is leveraging the deep emotional connection that people have with sports and fitness. With Starbucks, we see how coffee has woven itself into the fabric of people's lives, and that's our opportunity for emotional leverage..."[76] Personality, intimacy, and direct incorporation into a customer's daily life breed reputational strength.

Branding expert David Aaker describes these sorts of challenges and affirmations as the *emotional benefits* a company or brand can afford a consumer, adding richness and depth to ownership and use of a particular brand. This emotional connection is what causes one to feel in control of time and the aging process when applying Oil of Olay night cream, rugged when sporting a pair of Levi's, excited when tuning into MTV, a rush of adrenaline when winding a BMW along a mountain road. The emotional appeal of brand identification draws people to cult brands:"...they want to belong to something, and if religion doesn't fill the role, then something more materialistic takes its place."[77] Brands are a cultural means to belong. In light of the materialistic values of American culture, some may even argue that the most powerful companies and brands are even able to help define who you are as a person, offering what Aaker refers to as *self-expressive benefits*. In this way, wearing Ralph Lauren gives one a sense of sophistication and strapping on a pair of Rossignol powder skis makes one feel daring and adventurous.[78]

Offering an Identity-in-a-Box

Pulitzer-Prize–winning author Daniel Boorstein says that in Western society products and brands today often serve the function once served by religious and fraternal organizations—effectively helping people define who they are as individuals, and then helping them communicate that desired definition to the world around them. Such emotional connections can be so powerful that they literally shape the lives of consumers worldwide, telling them who they are and what they one day can be. Tom Hanks's character Joe Fox in the movie *You've Got Mail* humorously remarks that thousands flock to their local Starbucks daily to achieve a sense of personal autonomy and confidence in decision making. Fox writes: "The whole purpose of places like Starbucks is for people with no decision-making ability whatsoever to make six decisions just to buy one cup of coffee. Short, tall, light, dark, caf, decaf, low-fat, non-fat, etc....so people who don't know what the hell they're doing or who on earth they are can, for only $2.95, get not just a cup of coffee but an absolutely defining sense of self." The scene hits the mark perfectly. As Scott Bedbury of Starbucks reiterates, "A great brand raises the bar— it adds a greater sense of purpose to the experience, whether it's the challenge to do your best in sports and fitness or the affirmation that the cup of coffee you're drinking really matters."[79]

Et Tu, Brute? The Fickleness of Human Emotion

Just as you should recognize the erratic nature of human emotions, you should also, according to cultural critic Naomi Klein, be aware of the precariousness of the corporate-consumer relationship. "...This connection is a volatile one: it is not the old-style loyalty between lifelong employee and corporate boss; rather, this is a connection more akin to the relationship of fan and celebrity: emotionally intense but shallow enough to turn on a dime." If a company has established itself as an integral part of consumers' everyday lives, as in the case of Ford, it must tread very carefully. Strong consumer attachment means people are placing an enormous amount of trust in a company. This can lead to feelings of intense betrayal if widely believed perceptions of the company fail to align with the corporate reality. As Klein describes:

> For the past decade, multinationals like Nike, Microsoft, and Starbucks have sought to become the chief communicators of all that is good and cherished in our culture: art, sports, community, connection, equality. But the more successful this project is, the more vulnerable these companies become: if brands are indeed

intimately entangled with our culture and our identities, when they do wrong, their crimes are not dismissed as merely the misdemeanors of another corporation trying to make a buck. Instead, many of the people who inhabit their branded worlds feel complicit in their wrongs, both guilty and connected.[80]

There can be a high price to pay for the high visibility and public expectations generated by a strong reputation.

Recognize the Apostles of Your Vision

As you think about your corporate reputation, particularly in crafting and conveying your corporate vision, remember that if your employees are not telling a consistent story, external constituencies cannot be expected to have consistently favorable images of your company. Klein points to what she deems a major source of this volatility of consumers' loyalty toward a company: Companies forging intimate relationships with consumers but forgetting to do the same with their workforce, create an all-too-dangerous discrepancy. Empowering employees by instilling a sense of responsibility in them—through a call to activism as with The Body Shop employees, or through shares in the company as with Starbucks' partners Bean Stock—gives them an even greater incentive to convey your company's vision loud and clear, and with an even more contagious smile on their faces.

CONCLUSION

Most managers who have not thought about corporate reputation tend to underestimate its value. On the financial side of the organization, for example, all too many people think it is silly and trivial. Some of this hesitation emerges from a lack of understanding about what the alignment of corporate identity and image is all about and what it does for an organization. But such skeptics should understand that an inappropriate or outdated identity can be as damaging to a firm as a weak financial performance. In fact, a weak reputation can cut into your bottom line drastically. People seek consistency amidst all the flux around them, and if perceptions about a corporation fail to mesh with reality, constituents take their business elsewhere.

As a result, you need to be fully aware of the tremendous effect of identity and image and must learn how to manage this crucial resource effectively. Success in this area is a catalyst for and a symbol of change and for the dynamic process that will keep your company thriving.

Success also matures into pride and commitment—among employees, consumers, and the general public—irreplaceable assets in our intensely competitive business environment.

Einstein once claimed that imagination is more important than knowledge. In the realm of corporate reputation, this statement rings true. What constituencies imagine or believe about your company—the image they hold in their minds—may prove more important than what it actually is and the corporate identity you have fostered. As a result, you need to build a solid organization with a clear corporate identity that represents the underlying reality, and work to align these with the images held by all of your constituencies to create a strong, coherent reputation.

5

CORPORATE ADVERTISING: WHY AND HOW COMPANIES USE IT

YOUR WORK RESPONSIBILITIES probably take you far from the offices where corporate advertising is created to promote your company's reputation. So, why, then, should you spend any time learning something that's apparently so far afield from your own work? What impact, if any, do corporate ads have on your ability to get work done, on your organization's current success, and on the likelihood of its prospering in the future?

In essence, what corporate ads say about your firm is "This is who we are and where we're going." So, at a bare minimum, your company's corporate ads should tell you something about how senior management views the company's identity and strategic direction. But, in addition, the successful portrayal of your organization as a whole can increase your ability to get work done more efficiently in your corner of the business. An effective corporate ad campaign can solidify a company's reputation with constituents, help secure new business, encourage job applicants to join the firm, and increase the overall value of a company's products and services.

It's easy to imagine a few likely outcomes of a successful corporate ad campaign. A customer may comment favorably on the ad campaign you have launched to mark a merger or acquisition. Because of the advertising, the customer really understands why the company made the strategic decision, thinks it's a good one, and looks forward to doing business with you. A new recruit lets you know that she decided to sign on with your firm rather than with a competitor because of your company's aggressive support of the environment, a position displayed prominently in the firm's ad campaign. An investor alerted to good news about your company's strategic partnerships in its latest ads looks more favorably on the stock's potential. In a sense, then, an effective corporate ad campaign may pull you along in its wake, allowing you to enjoy the positive branding the ads create as you deal with the constituencies you work with most—be they suppliers, distributors, customers, other employees, government, or the media.

In this chapter, we will first explain what corporate advertising is. Then we will consider the functions it can perform for an organization and the challenges to achieving successful outcomes through such advertising. Before going any further, though, we urge you to take stock of the state of your firm's current corporate advertising by considering these questions:

- What's the purpose of your company's corporate advertisements—in print, on TV, on billboards, on the Web?
- What story do the ads tell about your company? Is it the right story to tell now? Why? Why not?
- What constituencies are the ads aimed at? Does this choice make sense?
- Is the ad campaign likely to succeed or will it backfire?

Try to keep these questions in mind during the discussion that follows. Perhaps more challenging, try to identify the impact a corporate ad campaign has on your own work. This might mean tracking anything from remarks about an ad made by a customer, employee, or another important constituent, to gauging the ad's impact on sales and the bottom line, quantitative measurements that many companies use to determine whether they are spending their advertising dollars wisely.

WHAT IS CORPORATE ADVERTISING?

Corporate advertising is the paid use of media that attempts to benefit the reputation of the corporation *as a whole* rather than promote its *specific products* or *services*. Such advertising should brand a company the way that product advertising brands a product. As we'll see later in this chapter, the distinction between corporate and product advertising blurs, however, in the case of a one-product company such as Absolut, the Swedish producer of a single product line, vodka.

Because good corporate advertising acts as an umbrella covering all the products and services associated with a company, any corporate advertising campaign should be both *strategic*, looking toward the future of the company and aligned with its mission, and *consistent*, aligning with the products and services that the company sells. An effective corporate advertising campaign also needs to be part of an overall communication strategy designed to establish and build corporate reputation, presenting the company's identity in a way that reinforces other company-initiated messages (for example, analyst reports, CEO presentations, employee communications). In the absence of such coordination, an ad campaign may be at odds with other company communications, leaving constituents with a confused image of who the company is and where it's headed. Moreover, since constituents are exposed to corporate ads alongside potentially competing messages about the company from sources outside the firm, the ads need to speak to constituents with greater volume, clarity, and punch than do the streams of messages about the firm originating on the outside.

Since the early 1900s, corporate advertising has had a place in the corporate communication strategies of major U.S. companies. AT&T was the first company to engage in large-scale corporate advertising. The company embarked on an advertising campaign in 1908 to convince the American people, who were repeatedly exposed to the opinions of muckrakers and trust busters, that private monopolies have virtues and should not be subject to massive governmental regulation.[1] Confident that the company could convince the public of its point of view, then AT&T president Theodore Vail supported ads that combined advocacy for the company's position with employee morale building and enhancement of the company's prestige. To make the case against government regulation, the corporate ads stressed the quality and service that AT&T provided its customers, emphasizing that bigness—rather than resulting in a huge impersonal institution impervious to the needs of customers—actually helped to create customer-friendly qualities.

Although initially AT&T's ads were defensive responses to public criticism, they quickly gave way to messages about user empowerment: "Under headlines such as 'The Multiplication of Power,' 'In Touch with His World,' 'Annihilator of Space,' and 'Your Telephone Horizon,' AT&T consistently placed the subscriber…in a position of command."[2]

By 1914 the ads struck a new theme, the dedication of employees to customer service, by placing telephone operators and linemen at the

The Multiplication of Power

There is no higher efficiency in the world than that of the American business man.

The multiplication of *power* in a business man—if he has the ability within him—depends upon the *increased number* of people whom he can, *by personal contact*, interest in his purposes.

He does this by telephone, and the multiplication of *the telephone's* usefulness depends on the *increased number* of persons whom he can reach.

Has the vast development of industries since 1890—the greatest period of advance in the world's history—*when America has advanced faster than all the rest of the world*, been the force that has built up this great, unified, efficient telephone service; or

Has the increased ability of the American business man to bring people to him from every locality, far and near, *over the Bell Telephone System*, been the cause of the multiplication of his power and his principality?

... whever ... se and

Figure 5-1   *The empowered AT&T subscriber.*

center of the ads.[3] The campaign also focused on the telephone's contribution to progress.

The most persistent "advertising motifs" combined personal service and political messages. AT&T promoted the idea that the telephone and democracy were linked, and by 1920 the company characterized itself as an "investment in democracy," adding slogans such as " Democracy—'of the people, by the people, for the people,' " and stating outright that its huge number of stockholders made the company a democracy.[4] The ads ask the public to believe that the customer constituency was, in effect, also the investor constituency. Thanks to AT&T's sustained use of a corporate advertising campaign that responded to changing times, the company enjoyed public support even during the wave of governmental scrutiny in the mid-1930s.[5] Since that era, corporate advertising has been seen as the easiest and fastest way to communicate about an organization's image, and that is why corporate advertising is used by most of the large corporations in the United States.

The continent that became a neighborhood

An Advertisement of the American Telephone and Telegraph Company

THROUGH slim wires etched against the sky . . . through cables laid in the earth under cities and fields . . . millions of Americans, miles' or days' journeys apart, speak to each other as readily as though they stood face to face.

Over her telephone, a housewife in a Wis-

System is the vital one of making it possible to maintain social and business contacts in cities that contain many times more people than this nation once boasted . . . in a neighborhood which the Census reports to hold 127 million people. Year after year from its beginning, the Bell System has inc

Figure 5-2   *AT&T as a force for democracy and community.*

In the absence of a strong function in a company, we often find that corporate advertising is paid for by the chairman or CEO's office. Not surprisingly, the CEO is sometimes featured in corporate ads as the spokesperson delivering the company's central message. For instance, Hitachi's president and director, E. Shoynana, appeared in a full-page ad pledging his company's leadership in twenty-first-century information relations.

As another example, the head of Edison International addressed TV audiences during the fall 2000 energy crisis in California to assure them that Edison would act as a good corporate citizen to mitigate the impact of the crisis on southern California consumers, underscoring by his pres-

Figure 5-3   *The CEO as corporate spokesperson.*

ence the seriousness of the company's engagement during the crisis. The CEO who stands at the helm of an organization can project *through his or her person alone* a company's commitment to goals, a commitment that would be less credible if voiced by anyone else.

Whether funding for ads comes directly from the CEO's office and—in some cases—features the CEO as spokesperson, senior management needs to confirm that corporate ads extend and support the identity and strategic direction of the firm. Obviously, the firm must have an agreed-upon identity and strategic direction. If the firm does not, an ad campaign can be damaging in two ways. First, anything created by the group charged with producing the ads will be muddled or inaccurate, and, second, it will be costly in terms of both dollars and the effects of miscommunication. More a symptom than an underlying problem, an ad's lack of clarity in these instances stems from lack of agreement at the highest levels of the organization about the company's identity rather than from an inherent deficiency in the ad team's ability to create good copy.

With a long history and a place at the highest levels of the corporation, corporate ads can perform a variety of functions for an organization. Let's take a look at just what ads can do.

THE FUNCTIONS OF CORPORATE ADVERTISING

Generally, corporate advertising can perform one or more of four functions. It can

- Create a new company image or rejuvenate an old one
- Put forward a company's position on an issue significant to the company's welfare
- Enhance a company's status through linking the organization to a cause
- Strengthen a company financially

Let's consider each of the four functions to get a better understanding of what this kind of advertising is all about.

Advertising to Create or Renew an Organization's Image

How does a company announce a name change, especially when the old name was well known? How does the company explain itself to constituents who may have known the company quite well in an earlier incarnation but may be struggling to figure out what the new organization stands for? How can the company create a new image while retaining the strengths of the old one? And what role might corporate advertising play in all this? These were some of the challenges faced in 2000–2001 by Accenture, formerly known as Andersen Consulting.

In August of 2000, an international arbitrator finally put to rest the struggle between Andersen Consulting—a $10 billion global management technology organization—and its parent organization, Andersen Worldwide. According to the settlement, Andersen Consulting had 147 days to change its name; that was the price the firm had to pay to break from its parent organization and its rival sister organization, Arthur Andersen, which was competing with Andersen Consulting for some of the same business.[6]

As Jim Murphy, global managing director for marketing and communications for the new company, Accenture, explained to us:

> The need to change the name gave us a good opportunity to position ourselves differently. Two years ago in the fall of '99, the CEO initiated "Horizon 2010," an examination of our future strategic direction, so we were already in the throws of a new business strategy prior to the arbitration discussion. The work started in '99 was fortuitous. We were ready [by January 1, 2001] to launch the new name and the new positioning of ourselves as a network of businesses built around our core of consulting and outsourcing, and expanded to include venture capitalism, joint ventures, equity investment in technology companies, and alliance relationships. There were, then, several reasons for the launch of the new name: to reposition the firm, to transfer the brand equity, to raise awareness of the name, and to separate ourselves from Arthur Andersen.[7]

The name change to Accenture signaled the birth of a new company with expanded services (consulting, technology, outsourcing, alliances, and venture capital) bridging traditional consulting and the consulting needs of the new economy, which is rooted in technological innovation, and especially in the Web.

Corporate advertising played a large role in spreading the news about the new organization, including a mid-December pre-announcement of the launch. So, around the time of the court ruling that forced the name change, the company began an aggressive ad campaign announcing the name change and using the occasion to alert constituencies about a shift in strategic focus to Internet-related consulting. One ad stated, "Why change your name if it's the only thing you change?" Another ad covering two full pages used just a few phrases, set off by lots of white space, to tell readers: "In a Bid to Seize the Future, Andersen Consulting Redefines Its Field as Accenture." On page two the ad tells us parenthetically, "{You might say our name was one of the smaller things we changed.}", driving home the ad campaign's key message that the change in name heralded an even greater change—in strategic direction. The phrase, bracketed parenthetically, "{Now it gets interesting}" appears in several ads that pique the readers' interest by providing startling facts about the new digital

Figure 5-4 *Accenture's playful ad to publicize the new company name and strategic focus.*

age—"Bacteria Tested as Digital Circuit: Use in Chips May Dwarf Silicon" or "Chinese to Become #1 Web Language by 2007," beautiful visuals that reinforce this fact, and a key repeated message about Accenture: "To see how to harness emerging technologies, visit accenture.com." Our favorite in this series adds a playful note: a field full of rabbits that underscores the point, "Mobile Devices Multiply to 1 Billion by 2003: Mobile Internet Surpasses Wired Internet in 2 years."

Only slightly less dramatic than the creation of a new company like Accenture is the merger of two companies. Especially since increased company size is associated with bloated bureaucracy and slow, stodgy responsiveness to opportunities, the new, larger organization often uses corporate advertising to enhance its image with constituencies. For example, the new Pfizer—a merger of two pharmaceutical giants Pfizer and Warner-Lambert in June of 2000—seems to have anticipated the negative response to its increased size and turned this stereotype on its head by emphasizing the *advantages* of size: the company's larger commitment to R&D, the range and depth of its products, and the growth of its global marketing capabilities.

These changes, the company claimed, were intended to improve the health of the consumer. Notice how the ad manages to achieve several goals at once: it appeals to the consumer, underscores the attractiveness of the new Pfizer to the investor community, and mitigates the criticism that often accompanies growth.

For the merged company composed of Credit Suisse and First Boston, the ad campaign focused on the international reach of the organization. According to Samuel Hayes, a professor of investment banking at the Harvard Business School, the decision to rename the merged company, formerly CS First Boston, reflects the company's desire to wed the idea of "Swiss permanence" to a volatile U.S. business: "The deep pockets of Credit Suisse now are being played up again as the 10-foot-tall giant standing behind the firm."[8] The ad campaigns for both Pfizer and Credit Suisse First Boston underscore a common theme, the additional value that resulted from the mergers, the benefits of size for Pfizer and increased global presence of a European/U.S. merger in the case of Credit Suisse First Boston.

Since corporate advertising can tell a story about a company as a whole, large organizations may need to use corporate ads to simplify their image in the minds of key constituents and to show what unifies the company, despite the geographical spread and variety of its businesses. Given the many stories that might be told, the questions companies must ask are, "Why this story?" and "Why this story now?"

Figure 5-5   *Pfizer's ad to emphasize the benefits of the merger with Warner-Lambert.*

As early as the first forays into advertising by AT&T at the beginning of the twentieth century, companies have been asking these questions and revising their answers as new circumstances or views of their image emerge. Think back on how AT&T's focus on quality and service gave way to a focus on portraying the company as an "investment in democ-

Figure 5-6   *A CSFB ad to announce the expansion of the company's capabilities.*

racy," without losing the earlier message. When we fast-forward nearly 100 years, we can also see the evolution of corporate ads for Siemens, a German-owned multinational company with many joint ventures, diverse businesses, and decentralized operations in the United States from the early 1990s to the new millennium.[9] Because the U.S. organization lacked a unified image, it wanted to use an ad campaign to tell a single story so that the overall corporate brand would not be lost.

In the early 1990s, Siemens chose to tell a "before" ("That was then") and "after" ("This is now") story in print and on TV to stress the company's long-standing involvement in technological innovation and its commitment to having a presence in the United States. Across the ads, the "before" segment stressed the company's participation in the technology of the nineteenth century, such as with the telegraph and x-ray tubes, while the "after" segment updated this picture, showing the x ray replaced by state-of-the art medical imaging, and the telegraph by high-tech products, created in U.S. factories by U.S. workers. The story lines in these ads emphasized the company's commitment to working in high tech as well as to retaining a presence in the United States; at the same time the ads were targeting the company's key constituencies, including its management and employees, government decision makers, medical professionals, and investment analysts.

By the mid-1990s, the company's ad campaign needed to change: It needed to emphasize Siemens' transportation products, a business line that Siemens felt lacked sufficient visibility in the United States; it also needed to focus on the company's image as a high-tech leader and its commitment to U.S. workers, specifically through its apprenticeship programs.[10] By 2000 the company emphasized its growth as a global e-business, and, with its appearance on the New York Stock Exchange in March 2001, its widespread, though rarely acknowledged, influence on our lives.

Advertising for companies, their products and services, gets an extra boost from the many awards given annually for the best ads. For example, the Effie awards are selected by the New York American Marketing Association for ads that exceed their advertising objectives in the marketplace. In 2000 IBM received an award for its 1997 e-commerce commercial that featured those companies IBM had helped to achieve business results through IBM e-commerce solutions. Featuring customers in the ad was a kind of second-party endorsement that motivated prospective e-commerce solutions users to get in touch with IBM and, according to data gathered by IBM, resulted in $35 million in new business for IBM in the three months following release of the ads.

Figure 5-7   *A Siemens ad to emphasize the company's state-of-the-art e-business.*

A corporate ad campaign—and, though rare, even a single advertisement—can have a huge impact on a company's reputation. Consider Apple's now famous 1984 Super Bowl ad, directed by Ridley Scott, who had earlier directed *Blade Runner* and would go on to direct *Gladiator*. The

You got out of bed this morning and the world was still there.

The trains were running.

The lights worked.

And so did everything else you turned on.

But who's making sure it all works?

We are.

All over the world.

We're one of the largest companies in the world.

And if you haven't heard of us,

You will.

On the New York Stock Exchange March 12, 2001.

SIEMENS
Global network of innovation

Figure 5-8   *Siemens' announcement of its appearance on the New York Stock Exchange.*

commercial shows an audience of "true believers," silent and worshipful human drones, seated before a "Big Brother" figure on a huge screen who serves as a stand-in for IBM Big Blue. The screen is then smashed by a woman athlete who runs through the audience wielding a sledgehammer that she hurls at the screen showing Big Brother's message about conformity. The final words of the ad sum up the key message: "Apple computers will introduce Macintosh and you'll see why 1984 won't be like *1984*." Researcher Ted Friedman attributes the impact of the ad to its successful depiction of the PC as a form of personal empowerment and freedom rather than as a tool or commodity: " Steve Jobs [the CEO of Apple at the time] thought he knew what was special about Apple: his people were the underdogs who battled the corporate giants and brought computing power to the masses. What was needed to tell that story, though, wasn't a slice of life, but an allegory. And the best mode would be science fiction."[11] Apple then followed up this commercial with point-of-purchase ads to boost sales of its new Macintosh, but what added significantly to the computer maker's efforts was that the commercial was picked up and rebroadcast on the TV news. The Apple ad was the first example of "event marketing," or "a high visibility commercial [that] garners mountains of extra free publicity."[12]

When we think of "event marketing" for the 1990s and the new millennium, the product that often springs to mind is the Swedish vodka Absolut and the company of the same name. In all our examples thus far, corporate advertising has broadcast what a company as a whole is all about. But in some cases, the company and the product are one and the same, and so corporate advertising also means product advertising.

Creating a New Image When the Company and Product Are One and the Same

We've looked at how large companies with diverse products try to create a consistent, powerful set of messages about the firm's identity that will unify its parts and pieces in the minds of significant constituents. But one-product companies like Absolut also need to create excitement and awareness. Whereas the large, multibusiness firm must communicate unity across disparate products and services, one-product firms must create interest on the part of constituents for what can easily be seen as a "one-note" enterprise with a single—and for that reason alone—dull, repetitive message. Just how much can be said about one product and the company behind it without people tuning out the message?

What greater challenge could there be than a corporate ad campaign for a colorless, odorless, and, some would say, tasteless, liquid like vodka, which is often viewed by consumers as a commodity. After all, since vodka is usually served with a mixer, any distinct taste of a particular brand of vodka would be masked. In fact, one of us did an informal blind-test of vodkas in an executive business class and found, to no one's surprise, that the executives could not distinguish one brand from another. So, when Absolut set out in the early 1980s to expand into the U.S. market, it faced considerable challenges, not the least of which were the obscurity of the brand and the country in which it was produced as well as the general consumer's lack of exposure to vodka as anything more than an uninteresting type of hard liquor.

What, then, has Absolut done to build sales and a positive buzz for the company and product? The company's ad agency has created and sustained an award-winning print media campaign that uses a single image—the distinctive shape of the Absolut bottle—as a powerful symbol for the company and the product, a symbol that has accumulated new meanings as the bottle has been associated with specific cities, seasons, and artists. We have had Absolut Atlanta, Absolut Brooklyn, Absolut Geneva, Absolut Trick or Treat, Absolut Cummings, Absolut Irving, to name a few. Moreover, as the ads became ubiquitous in upscale magazines and developed a following, the bottle was often replaced by the shape of the bottle alone. People could imagine the absent bottle.

Through these ads, the Absolut bottle has become a celebrated icon of American pop culture. Over the years, the company and product have come to represent status, trendiness, artistic expression, fashion, glamour, and urbanity. Not surprisingly, the allure of these ads has been so strong that even the famous American pop visual artist Andy Warhol, known for his "enshrining" of Americana such as the Campbell soup can and Marilyn Monroe, accepted a commission in the mid-1980s to create an Absolut ad. Following his lead, other artists, photographers, and fashion designers got into the act, and the ad concept itself broadened dramatically.

Absolut has commissioned dresses, sweaters, shirts, and even boots, created by top designers, that feature the Absolut bottle and label.[13] Ads in some upscale magazines can sometimes talk, are made up of puzzles, or play music and have been accompanied by attachments like a poncho made by designer Kate Spade or a Nicole Miller scarf.[14] As part of its branding campaign, Absolut held a twentieth anniversary celebration of its artwork at New York City's Grand Central Station, underscoring both the artistic quality of its ads and its financial support of artists. Cities now see having an Absolut ad as a matter of civic pride, a statement that the city has arrived as a player on the world scene. The ads have become so popular in their own right that an ad collectors' group—the Absolut Collectors Society—was founded in the spring of 1999 and has its own Web site (www.absolutsociety.com) and newsletter. Yet the ad campaign has not only created this outbreak of interest but has also helped to increase Absolut sales significantly. Sales have risen from 10,000 cases to the United States when the campaign was launched in the early 1980s to projected sales of 4 million cases 20 years later.[15]

Perhaps the most striking feature of this ad campaign is its appeal to the reader's sense of playfulness. In effect, each ad challenges the reader to "get the joke"—to figure out the play on words, to delight in the visual humor, to find the outline of the Absolut bottle concealed in the picture. For instance, "Absolut attraction" shows a martini glass bending toward an Absolut bottle.

See if you can figure out the joke in the Absolut Chicago ad. For this and most other ads, you can check out the Absolut Web site, which includes a long section devoted exclusively to cataloguing and deciphering the meanings of ads. For Absolut Chicago, they tell us: "This ad shows an Absolut bottle with the letters being blown off to portray Chicago's reputation as the 'Windy City.'"

Figure 5-9   *One of Absolut's many whimsical ads.*

With its focus on play, its imaginative variations on a theme, and its finger on the pulse of whatever is trendy in the culture, the Absolut ad campaign suggests that the product, on the one hand, doesn't take itself too seriously and, on the other, is at the center of whatever is culturally new. By implication, consumers who envision themselves in these ways should buy the product, and many of them do.

Figure 5-10   *The "Windy City" Absolut ad.*

Using Corporate Advertising to Turn
Around a Negative Image

In Chapter 1, we discussed how public sentiment against a few highly visible companies in an industry could spill over to damage the reputation of *all* the companies in that industry whether or not a particular company is really to blame. For this reason, an individual company may sometimes invest in an ad campaign that attempts to build the company's reputation with key constituencies by directly or indirectly evoking the negative reputation of the industry as a whole and then distancing the company from that criticism. For example, E-Trade highlighted its status as a prosperous dot.com organization in its Super Bowl 2001 commercial by reminding viewers of the disastrous year many dot.com companies suffered in 2000 following their dizzying rise in the late 1990s and their dominance of Super Bowl 2000 ads. A survivor of the dot.com debacle of 2000, E-Trade emphasized its ability to survive in the midst of devastation, featuring, in its Super Bowl 2001 ad, the E-Trade cat walking slowly away from a ghost town of former dot.coms.

The investment firm of Dun & Bradstreet made a similar attempt to set itself apart from the negative reputation attached to an industry as a whole. Aware of the financial community's reputation for discriminating against gays and minorities, Dun & Bradstreet featured its open hiring policy and work environment in its corporate ads, its main message that a "company where people feel included and valued is a company that is ready to solve its customers' business challenges."

All corporate advertising serves to enhance the image of a company. But some ads may place other concerns in the forefront: issues that the company supports, philanthropic efforts, or financial performance. The sections that follow take up each of these topics in order.

Advertising to Advocate a Point of View about an Issue

Typically called advocacy or issue advertising, this type of corporate advertising is used by companies to respond to external threats from constituencies, such as the government, special-interest groups, and the community. According to communications expert Annette Shelby, corporate advocacy aims to present a company's position on a specific controversial issue that threatens its livelihood, and, if possible, to build alliances with other constituencies.[16] The ABC television network devised a series of public service ads for the new millennium that condemned the outbreaks of violence in this country as a way for the network to position itself as a good citizen interested in family values at a time when the entertainment industry was being attacked for allegedly exploiting the appeal of violence in films and on television.[17] In a sense, the network was saying, "We're as concerned about violence as are groups advocating family values." At best, such a campaign might turn an old enemy—advocacy groups that want to censure the entertainment industry—into allies who recognize the network's interest in curbing violence.

In the winter of 2001, California Edison and PG&E, the utility companies that supply energy to California, used, among other communication tactics, corporate ads in an attempt to gain public understanding and support for their side of the story as the energy crisis in California turned ugly. In mid-January, northern California experienced rolling blackouts, as well as shutdowns of power in homes, schools, and businesses. By mid-March, southern California was involved as well. To make matters worse, the utilities claimed that, without rate hikes, they would go bankrupt, and consumer advocacy groups insisted that the utilities' cry for help—a rate hike or else—just masked their greed. Indeed, critics argued that California Edison's parent company, Edison International, was "flush with cash."[18]

Amidst the growing anti-utility sentiment, Edison Chairman John Bryson appeared in TV ads stating that the electricity crisis was harming California's economic health and that Edison would do its part to help solve the problem. Then, in what was considered the "most dramatic example of a campaign by the industry to soften public opinion about the utilities' role in the state's electricity crisis,"[19] the utilities enlisted David Horowitz as an advocate in their television ad campaign. Horowitz, known earlier in his career for his groundbreaking advocacy of consumer rights in California, argued—through the force of his own reputation—that those who were against the utilities were actually against California consumers. In his television pitch, Horowitz concluded: "A few activists…think letting utilities fail is part of the solution. They're dead wrong. Letting utilities fail…would cost us more, not less. We've got to fight back and keep the lights on!"[20]

Yet, as is often the case with corporate advocacy ads, the utilities came under attack for their use of the ad. Some claimed that the sponsorship of the Horowitz ad by the Edison Electric Institute, a trade association that represents Edison and PG&E, was "barely perceptible in the ad and not recognized for what it is by most TV viewers."[21] As a result, they claimed, the utilities created the false impression that they had nothing to do with Horowitz's advocacy. Thus Horowitz seemed to be acting as an independent spokesperson, a role viewers were most familiar with, rather than as a hired gun who had betrayed his original principles by promoting big business instead of consumer rights. The Los Angeles Business Advisors, top-level business spokespeople for the energy industry, came under similar attack for deceptive tactics in their corporate ad. They failed to identify Edison Chairman John Bryson as a member of the group, thereby implying that the group's ad—in the form of an open letter to California government officials in support of the utilities—

represented an unbiased opinion on the part of industry experts looking out for the good of the state.[22]

The limited positive impact of the utilities' ads suggests some underlying weaknesses in most advocacy campaigns. First, they must contend with the negative reputation of big business, fostered in the media and films, that leaves companies at a disadvantage whenever they enter the fray to take sides on an issue. For this reason, a company should weigh the costs of taking a highly visible stand versus the possibilities of public and governmental backlash. In addition, since these ads are often launched in the midst of public controversy, they face huge difficulties in being heard above the hue and cry against the companies the ads are seeking to support. The immediacy of the public's negative feeling may overwhelm corporate attempts at fighting back. How much credit are Californians willing to give utilities when their homes and work lives are disrupted by power outages, a persistent intrusion on their lives that has an immediacy that Americans have not experienced since they waited in long gas lines in the 1970s during the oil embargo? Moreover, since these ads need to appeal to the minds as well as the emotions of constituents, companies should consider how open the public will be to reasoned argument and the careful consideration of a corporate point of view when people are caught up in political—and in the case of the California crisis—personal stress?

In his classic study of persuasion, *The Art of Rhetoric*, the Greek philosopher Aristotle argued that audiences could be persuaded in several ways:

- By appealing to the audience's intellect and sense of logic
- By playing on the audience's emotions
- By projecting a sense of trustworthiness

Advocacy ads generally rely at least in part on persuading constituents through intellect and logic. But this appeal can be lost in times of high tension. Just how effective can an ad be when the emotions of the moment are intense and assertions from antibig-business groups are loud, and oftentimes provocative, even if the arguments are devoid of supporting evidence? And what can be achieved by appealing to intellect and logic if a company's reputation for trustworthiness is already damaged?

Despite the problems inherent to issue advertising, companies have been using it for years. Many companies began using these ads in the late 1970s and early 1980s to meet the challenges presented by the antibusiness

sentiment in the media. By taking issues directly to the consumer, companies could compete primarily with print journalists for a share of the
reader's mind. As a result, these corporate advertisements are often pur-
posely placed on op-ed pages in prominent newspapers such as *The New
York Times* and *The Washington Post*. Perhaps the most famous example of
this kind of advertising is Mobil Oil's series of issue advertisements, which
ran for over 30 years and continues to run under the ExxonMobil name.
What began as a dialogue about the oil embargo in the early 1970s
expanded to become a sort of bully pulpit for this powerful organization
as it has tried to advocate positions on a wide variety of topics.

Many other organizations have also adopted an "op-ed'" style for
their advocacy ads. For instance, United Technologies ran several ads
during an unsuccessful takeover attempt in the early 1980s, and Amway
typified the trend of companies taking a positive approach to dealing
with environmental issues. Amway ran a series of ads that tried to position the company as bullish on the environment. One ad had a photo-
graph of five Amway distributors and the headline: "Find the
Environmental Activist." The copy goes on to explain that everyone in
the ad is an environmental activist and that all Amway distributors are
committed to the cause of environmental awareness. The tag line reads:
"And you thought you knew us."

This advertisement also suggests the problem with a lot of issue
advertising. As David Kelley pointed out in an excellent essay on the subject of issue advertising in the *Harvard Business Review*, most companies
"pay too much attention to the form and too little to the content of the
message."[23] Does the tag line in the Amway ad, for example, imply that
"You thought we were a bunch of polluters because we specialize in
detergents that come in huge containers"? Or does it mean "You thought
we were just selling detergents when what we are really doing is protecting the environment"? In either case, the advertisement seems to be playing into the hands of critics rather than setting the terms for the argument.
Since the advertisement is so short, it never gets across the point that this
company is trying to make: that is, the company would like to argue
directly with critics who charge Amway with environmental neglect.

Kelley points out in his *HBR* article that such a modest approach
comes across as arbitrary and leaves the reader more suspicious than he
or she was before. He goes on to say:

> If we can judge by numerous corporate advocacy campaigns,
> speeches by top executives, and discussion in business publica-
> tions, the defenders of business feel constrained to operate

within a framework for discussion that is skewed against the free market system and corporate enterprise. Simply put, the critics of corporations have been allowed to set the terms of the debate in which everything concerning business is argued.

In the current climate, then, the opponents of a free market and corporate enterprise hold the upper hand before the debate over a specific issue even begins. Edison and PG&E must be wrong. They're big business. ExxonMobil is wrong for the same reason. Given this bias against big business, a company should proceed into the world of issue advertising with extreme caution, mindful of the dangers that wait despite, in many cases, the company's ability to put much greater resources into the argument than its adversary can. If the company decides to use issue advertising, top management must have the courage to argue forcefully for its ideas and must not be afraid to alienate certain constituencies in the process. For example, when the major booksellers took on the conservative groups that were advocating a cleansing of their shelves of all "dirty" books, the booksellers won the argument with those advocating first amendment rights, but lost with family-oriented fundamentalist groups.

Cause-Related Ads

Cause-related corporate advertising publicizes a company's commitment to a cause that benefits society, such as ecology, health, or education and is linked to a company's philanthropic program, which we will discuss in Chapter 8. Like all effective corporate advertising, cause-related ads should target a company's key constituencies. According to David Adler of Cone Communications, this kind of advertising represents a company's attempt to associate with a cause or issue that affects the consumer. He calls it "passion branding," and says that it "starts with a true belief structure that involves giving back to the community and creating win win situations for business and causes."[24]

Take Disney's Learning Partnership, a philanthropic effort to support the improvement of elementary school education. The company's efforts are featured in both television and print ads. Here is an initiative that supports a social need while targeting two of Disney's key constituencies: parents and elementary-age children. Consider, too, Weyerhaeuser's ads focusing on its commitment to environmental causes, targeting policy makers at the state and national level. A leader in the forest products industry, Weyerhaeuser developed ads targeted especially for the Washington, D.C., market that display a dreamlike watercolor of a forest

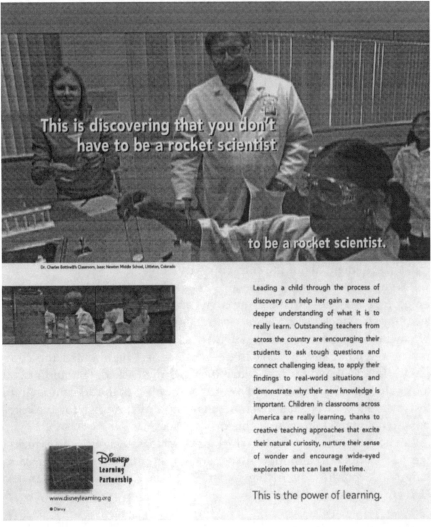

Figure 5-11   *Disney's philanthropic support of a cause valued by the company's customers.*

with actor Jeff Bridges speaking softly about the company's long-term promotion of ecology. Through these ads, the company hoped to influence the national politicians who create forest policy.[25] In another example, the pharmaceutical company Merck took the role of a medical adviser, disseminating vital information to the consumer. One ad targeted older women and their need for bone density testing as protection against broken bones. The lead remarks read: "If you're over 60, you should know the warning signs of osteoporosis. Unfortunately, there aren't any."

Taken as a whole, companies that run cause-related ads portray themselves as good corporate citizens, companies that "cultivate a broad view of their own self-interest while instinctively searching for ways to align self-interest with the larger good."[26]

Advertising to Enhance Investment

Later in this book (Chapter 7) we will look at the importance of a strong investor relations function within the corporate communication department. One of the methods companies use to enhance their image in the financial community, appealing to analysts, investors, and money managers, is financial-relations corporate advertising campaigns. This kind of corporate advertising can stimulate interest among potential investors for a company's stock. Analysts are a particular target of this type of advertising. Given that analysts have to study hundreds of companies, a good corporate advertising campaign can stimulate their interest and make a statement about the company's dynamism.

Some corporate advertisers also assert that a strong financially oriented corporate advertising campaign can actually increase the price of a company's stock. A W. R. Grace campaign that ran in the early 1980s is often cited as evidence of this potential. The television campaign, which ran as the company's "Look into Grace" series, highlighted the company's financial and business attributes and then asked, "Shouldn't you look into Grace?" Attitude and awareness studies of the ad campaign in test markets showed that awareness and approval ratings for the company were much higher after this campaign ran.

In addition, the company's stock price increased significantly during the test campaign, although it did not go any higher with later campaigns. Corporate advertising expert Thomas Garbett, writing in the *Harvard Business Review*, stated:

> I interpret the relationship between corporate campaigns and stock pricing this way: advertising cannot drive up the price of a reasonably priced stock and, indeed, doing so might not be entirely legal; it can, however, work to ensure that a company's shares are not overlooked or undervalued.[27]

Professors at Northwestern University's Kellogg School of Business tried to study this trend using econometric analysis of the link between corporate advertising and stock price. They determined that, indeed, corporate advertising does have a statistically significant positive effect on stock prices. They further determined that the positive influence from such campaigns averaged 2 percent and was particularly strong when the market was in a bull phase as in the mid- to late-1990s.

The implications of this study, if true, are very exciting for companies that may consider their stock to be undervalued. Even a 1-point increase in the stock price can add up to tens or hundreds of millions of dollars for large companies with many shares of stock outstanding. In addition, an increase in stock prices that improves the company's price-earnings ratio can present opportunities for stock options and dividends for employees. And the effect on bonds is equally impressive considering the impact even a slight improvement in a company's rating can have on a large bond offering.

Although financially oriented corporate advertising campaigns are really just a subset of image-oriented ads, they can usually be identified by the presence of a chief financial officer's name and address appearing with the ad or a mention at the end of the ad for interested parties to write for copies of the company's annual report.

WHO USES CORPORATE ADVERTISING?

According to recent studies, over half of the largest companies in the United States have corporate advertising programs of one sort or another. Usually a direct correlation exists between size and the use of corporate advertising—the bigger the company is, the more likely it is to have a corporate advertising program. Since big companies tend to have more discretionary income, this makes sense. In addition, larger companies tend to be more diversified and thus have a greater need to establish a coherent image out of disparate activities.

In addition to size, we can see trends in the kinds of industries that are most likely to use corporate advertising. Typically, the more problematic the industry, the more likely we are to find corporate advertising widely used. This explains the heavy use of corporate advertising among cigarette companies, which have health-related issues to deal with; among oil companies, which have environmental issues and the issue of excessive profits to face; among insurance companies, which are seen as charging too much for too little and face regulation such as we have seen develop in California and other states over the last few years; among utilities that are basically monopolies; and among all large industrial companies as a result of the by-products that tend to come from the manufacturing process.

Overall, heavy industry spends more on corporate advertising, while consumer-packaged goods firms lead all other industries in terms of product advertising. In the latter case, a company with a strong market-ing focus may tend to scoff at the importance of developing a strong cor-porate image rather than focusing on the four "Ps"—product, price, promotion, and place (distribution).

It is surprising that companies in certain industries shun corporate advertising given the potential threats that exist. For example, one can imagine that cable and telecom companies will encounter a hostile envi-ronment if they ever become part of a controversy. Most people already have a negative impression of the industries and their poor service. More extensive use of corporate advertising could help the industry change its poor image and at the same time build a reservoir of goodwill for the tough times ahead.

Although we can see that many different kinds of companies use cor-porate advertising, many more do not. There are several challenges to achieving a successful corporate advertising campaign. Let's take a look at these now.

CHALLENGES TO SUCCESS

Simply stated, corporate advertising should strive to present a clear and convincing image of your organization to key constituencies. At first glance, this goal appears to be simple enough to achieve, but several challenges can stand in the way:

- The appropriate placement of the ad
- The desire to exercise creativity in an ad campaign at the expense of delivering a powerful message
- The tenacity of a poor reputation, even in the face of positive news backed up by a corporate ad campaign to publicize the news

    Let's see how companies can address these challenges.

Find the Right Fit between Message and Communication Outlet

Even though a corporate ad may be your company's best opportunity to explain who it is directly to a target audience, a corporate ad can never present an unobstructed view; rather, the newspaper, magazine, televi-sion or radio show where the ad appears influences the message. At best, the reputation of the magazine with the target audiences you want to reach is a great fit for your message, and the circulation is large. *Readers Digest* has mass appeal; specialized magazines such as *Aviation Week* have a specific target audience of key corporate players and industry analysts in the aerospace business.

With the proliferation of video outlets, the Internet, and niche magazines, it's easier than ever before for companies to target their ads more carefully. But the sheer number of outlets means that messages must be spread farther and more widely. A TV spot can bring the viewer a vividly portrayed and animated vision of a company, but it cannot convey detailed information about the company effectively, a strength of print ads. Web sites present another option, combining the opportunity to display written text and animation. The largest Internet sites are using new techniques, "letting advertisers occupy a much larger portion of their pages, as well as create ads that move, make noise, and otherwise do whatever is necessary to attract attention."[28] Web portals like About.com are inviting companies to post bigger ads and 5- to 15-second video clips.[29]

The choice of the communication outlet needs to be a good fit. Even if the fit between the ad and communication outlet is good, however, the impact of the ad depends on factors that are sometimes out of the company's control. What news article or editorial is adjacent to the ad? Where does the TV or radio ad appear over the course of a particular program? And, in the case of television, will the ad be seen at all, or will viewers use their remote controls to "channel surf" as soon as the ad begins? Do they hit the "mute" button or skip right through the commercial of a taped show—tactics most of us have used?

Make the Central Message about the Company Your Top Priority

Time and again, ads fail to put forward a clear value proposition for the company as a whole. An ad may be clever, it may be funny, but it may leave us clueless about the firm. People may remember the message tactic, created to gain attention, such as humor, state-of-the-art computer animation, or a well-known spokesperson, but they may forget, or even fail to recognize, the content of the message itself. For example, EDS—a company that sells a portfolio of services including management consulting, e-business, and information technology services—launched commercials featuring animals in two successive Super Bowls: Super Bowl 2000 and 2001. The TV commercial debuting in Super Bowl 2000 featured rugged cowboys of the West, figures of mythic stature applauded for their stoic individualism, herding *cats* over streams and across the open range. The parody implies, we would guess, that the cats are like parts and pieces of an information network, and the cowboys are like the committed workforce and technological know-how of EDS, capable of keeping all the parts under control. But coming up with this analogy is a big stretch. Most viewers will remain fixed on the clever, humorous image of the impossible task of cat-herding and have no awareness of what EDS does, or even what company was being promoted by the ad. In Super Bowl 2001, the company shifted from the American West to a small Spanish town with an equally mythical motif, the running of the bulls, in a spoof showing EDS's version of the running of the *squirrels*. The ad concludes with a focus on EDS's "squirrel-like" agility in staying ahead of the competition by responding to the needs of its clients.

According to EDS, "the day after [the Superbowl ad featuring cats] traffic surged at EDS's Web site."[30] Moreover, according to EDS senior vice president Donald Uzzi, the commercials were a success: "Our target audience is chief executives, chief financial officers and chief information officers and we wanted to hit them in a more relaxed atmosphere."[31] So the ad attracted enough attention to motivate viewers to check out EDS's Web site. In an effort to gain attention, though, a creative strategy can inadvertently sacrifice the message. What is the point being made about EDS? Do the ads really convey a clear image of the firm? Do we even remember the name of the company? The attention of Super Bowl viewers of both ads may have been grabbed more by the cleverness of the ads than by anything else. After all, the Super Bowl ad has become a genre all its own with companies vying for the best ads based on creativity, and CEOs enjoying the ego satisfaction that comes simply from being able to afford an ad. Moreover, the price of playing in this arena is steep and rising all the time. A 30-second Super Bowl slot, which went for $42,000 in 1967, cost $2.3 million in 2001.

Super Bowl I, 1967	$42,000
Super Bowl V, 1971	$72,000
Super Bowl X, 1976	$110,000
Super Bowl XV, 1981	$275,000
Super Bowl XXV, 1991	$800,000
Super Bowl XXX, 1996	$1.085 million
Super Bowl XXXV, 2001	$2.3 million

Source: Michael McCarthy and Theresa Howard, "Traditional Heavy Hitters return to Super Bowl lineup." *USA Today*, January 8, 2001, page 13 B.

Figure 5.14   *Price of Super Bowl 30-second ads from 1967 to 2001.*

Can Positive News Offset a Poor Reputation?

Companies that suffer from a poor reputation built by a host of negative messages from the outside face a steep uphill battle as they consider using corporate advertising to improve their image. When Chevron, or another company with a questionable environmental record, launches a series of print ads featuring endangered species and a pristine but fragile landscape, pitching their commitment to the environment, not everyone will be convinced of the company's commitment to ecology. For some, Chevron's attempt to create a positive image may be overshadowed by the public perception of the entire oil industry as a menace to the environment, a reputation intensified by graphic displays of oil spills and dead wildlife in print and on the screen. Almost a quarter of a century of bad press for the oil industry—fueled by the Exxon *Valdez* oil spill and the crises of the 1970s when oil companies were suspected of holding back supplies to boost prices—is hard to overcome. Yet Chevron continues to target the consumer and the general public, a growing proportion of whom look positively on companies that are pro-environment. The company's intent with these ads may be to establish a climate that would allow for dialogue with environmentalists and for a more receptive hearing from the public when an environmental crisis arises.

Even more than the oil and gas industry, tobacco faces substantial challenges in building a positive reputation. Take Philip Morris, for example. A company that has been engaged in philanthropic efforts for years, Philip Morris uses corporate ads to present its activities to combat hunger and provide for teen shelters, among other things. But its ads featuring the company's philanthropic efforts to combat hunger can fall flat. One television ad features an elderly woman, a "shut-in" who waits for food delivered by a cheerful singing volunteer for "City Meals on Wheels," an organization supported by the company. Both the names of Philip Morris and Kraft appear in this ad (Philip Morris is the majority shareholder in Kraft Foods, Inc.). For some viewers, the ad may be the first time they become aware of the Kraft–Philip Morris connection and of the parent firm's efforts to be a good corporate citizen. The explicit link made in the ad between Kraft and Philip Morris may end up tarnishing Kraft by association with the tobacco firm rather than improving the public's perception of Philip Morris. The difficulty Philip Morris confronts in building reputation through this and similar ads is that its reputation has been long since tarnished by the public's perception of the company as a manufacturer of a cancer-killing product. For some people—cynics or realists depending on your point of view—the company engages in philanthropy only to improve the bottom line.

How can a single ad—or even a whole campaign—turn around a bad image if the company's history is marked by negative behavior in the minds of constituents? The short answer is "not very well." Aware of these challenges, Steven Parrish, senior vice president for corporate affairs for Philip Morris Companies, explained to us that because of the public's hostility to the company, the corporate ad campaign must be a long-term effort: "Ads must talk about the history of our *actions*, not our *promises*. I know that the more people know about the diversity of the products we make and our history of giving back to the community, the more likely they are to have a favorable opinion."[32] Along with a focus on philanthropy, the company has also begun to advertise its efforts to achieve "responsible marketing of cigarettes" by participating in efforts to stop kids from smoking. Parrish believes that the multifaceted view of the company that such advertising conveys can open up dialogue with those members of the society who are not totally closed off to discussion with the company.

The Philip Morris ads underscore another important point: The attitudes of constituents toward corporate ads are influenced by past experience with the company and industry as a whole as well as the constituents' values and biases. Rather than presenting a "blank slate" willingly receptive to the identity the company puts forward in its corporate ads, people judge the company from their own vantage point. A stockholder in Philip Morris may approve of the ad, but many citizens will remain resistant to anything that the company says because of the products it sells.

Even when companies enjoy a good reputation, the impact of corporate advertising may be limited by a cultural bias: The American public is skeptical about truth in advertising. We have been raised on commercials, and we are less likely to believe what we see and hear when the message is paid for by a company than we would be if the communications came from a third party like the press.

Should Your Company Use Corporate Advertising?

Given what corporate advertising can offer large companies, most of them should certainly use it. Through such advertising, companies can build goodwill, help recruit and retain employees, enhance the financial situation of the company, and increase sales of products and services. Yet the decision to invest money in corporate ads is difficult, especially since ad campaigns can be costly.

The debate about whether to invest time and money in corporate advertising and, if so, how much, will continue, particularly during difficult economic times. But corporate advertising remains one of the most efficient ways to get a corporation's message out in the best possible light without any distortion.

CONCLUSION

Although many companies may decide against a corporate advertising campaign simply because no one can prove that it will work to the company's advantage, many others will leap into the fray simply to enhance the egos of senior managers. Both are wrong in their approach. Corporate advertising can help companies get their message out to a mass audience and to specific constituencies quickly and efficiently. Though costly, such advertising can help position an organization for future success when that advertising is part of a larger corporate communication effort, especially when the company has targeted some key areas for improvement, such as enhancing its image, taking a stand on a crucial issue, broadcasting its good citizenship, or increasing its financial performance.

6

COMMUNICATING INTERNALLY: THE "EMPLOYEE CARE" REVOLUTION

MANAGERS HAVE FOCUSED FOR decades on customer care. But only recently have they realized that employees who work with those customers have more to do with the success of a business than does virtually any other corporate constituency. For example, Gary Ames, CEO of U.S. WEST Communications in Colorado, recognized the potential power of his employees as he faced a dilemma many CEOs share. Despite the company's success, U.S. WEST needed to improve its efficiency to meet ever-increasing competitive demands. Ames sought to engage employees to achieve even higher levels of excellence in a company that already was performing well but needed to do even better. To realize his goal, he did a lot of listening, which constantly reinforced what he described as the "incredible power of frontline employees at solving business issues."[1] CEOs are beginning to realize the importance of internal communications with employees to harness their organization's human capabilities.

Today anyone in a supervisory or managerial role needs to understand how to care for the corporation's most valuable asset—the employee. With the cost of hiring and training new employees rising, and negative feelings about big business already high, organizations need to find ways to satisfy, nurture, and educate employees to succeed in this highly competitive global environment. Companies need to use the power of internal communications to differentiate themselves, and they need to shed the stereotype that all corporations are "bureaucratic" and "stodgy" so that they can attract and retain fresh, young minds. Companies also must learn how to retain the highly educated workforce exemplified by the "baby boomer" generation.

In terms of values and needs, today's employee is a different person compared with the employee in earlier decades of the last century. A CBS news report showed that 25 percent of today's workforce is unhappy and 25 percent is angry.[2] Another report in *The Wall Street Journal* showed that almost two-thirds of employees want more open communications with managers.[3] In addition, the workplace is different for employees who now face tighter staffing, longer hours, a greater workload, more emphasis on performance, and, in many cases, greater autonomy than ever before.

Employee care means creating a lasting, flexible partnership with employees. As we will see in examples from Navistar, Colgate-Palmolive, and RCN, each of these companies has found successful methods for creating this sort of caring relationship with its employees. Rather than looking at employees as liabilities on their balance sheet, companies need to see their workers as assets to be nurtured and cared for in the same way that companies care for customers.

As you read the chapter, consider these questions:

- What sort of attention does your company give the problem of caring for and retaining employees?
- How do you, as an employee, want to be treated? Like a disenfranchised servant or like an empowered partner?
- What strategies can your company implement to realize the potential of its workforce?

John Horne, stepping in as CEO of crisis-laden Navistar in 1993, understood that for a company to weather change successfully, its employees needed to be brought on board first. Robert Frazier, plant manager for Colgate-Palmolive's Mennen plant in Morristown, New Jersey, intuitively understands the need for and the approach to a new type of employee communications. Through his experience as an entre-preneur, David McCourt, CEO of RCN in Princeton, New Jersey, under-stands both the power of his employees, whom he considers the "builders" of his company, and the even greater importance of commu-nicating with them.

If we could observe the work life of these three employee-care pioneers, what useful information would we find in their experience to guide us as we try to manage employees through the power of communication? Before visiting with Frazier and McCourt, let's get a better understanding of Horne's philosophy—recognizing employees as the crucial ambassadors of your company's vision and identity.

INSTILLING THE IMPORTANCE OF COMMUNICATION IN EMPLOYEES

Not so long ago communications was a field only delved into when damage control was in order and fences needed to be mended. Take Navistar, which you may recognize as the old name for International Harvester, a heavy truck manufacturer headquartered in Chicago. Navistar was a company in crisis when John Horne became CEO in 1993. Before he was appointed, the company's idea of communications—like that of many other companies—was confined to the realm of "crisis communication." Once on the scene, however, Horne immediately grasped the magnitude and depth of the company's problems with both its internal and external constituencies—employees, unions, senior management, the financial community, and the media. And, not surprisingly, the problems were rooted in the company's failure to make everyday communication, both inside and outside of its doors, a priority.

When Horne analyzed the company, he saw that a precedent of poor communication had been set years earlier. A long strike in the 1970s and a history of union conflict had scarred the company's reputation and little had been done to rectify the situation. To make matters worse, the general discontent of Navistar's workforce has shaken investors' confidence in the company.

Employee Communications to Spearhead a Turnaround[4]
In confronting these problems, however, Horne believed—in the words of the director of corporate communication, Maril McDonald—that the company "couldn't muscle our way out [of the problems]. We had to sell our way out."[5] Change had to begin with Navistar's parochial view of internal communication, which aggravated all of the company's existing problems. While the company's newsletters and videos distributed to employees were efficient communication channels for conveying information, they were remarkably ineffective in establishing the human contact that is so necessary for building employee trust.

Horne knew that to complete the much-needed turnaround, Navistar's employees would first have to be mobilized. Believing that he had to bring his employees on board before he could raise the confidence of the financial community, he supported initiatives to find out what problems concerned employees. To accomplish this, he used a three-pronged approach: extensive plant visits, an employee survey with follow up, and direct involvement of union representatives in employee issues.

At the start, Horne and a group of senior managers began visiting Navistar's plants. Initially, plant managers didn't want senior management around, fearing that the managers would meet with employee hostility. Horne persisted, reiterating his "rule of three." His rule dictated that because employees distrusted senior management he would be unable to communicate successfully with them until his third visit to a plant. And in fact, the first meetings tended to be gripe sessions, but, by the third visit, management and employees were seriously discussing how to beat the competition.

The discussions between senior management and plant employees were so successful in raising morale and in generating ideas about corporate strategy that the plant visits were formalized by the fall of 1996. Subsequently, a senior manager began visiting every plant each month. The meetings included the senior manager and about 30 to 40 employees, representing a cross-section of the plant. Before the meeting, the employees spoke with co-workers to learn of the larger constituency's concerns. After the meeting, the senior manager published management's response to employees' concerns in the plant publication and got back to the plant with answers to questions that the manager had not provided at the session. From these beginnings, senior management's responsiveness to employee concerns has gone so far as to include inviting assembly plant workers to visit headquarters and discuss work-related problems directly and informally.[6]

Soon, the monthly meetings reached far beyond their initial goal of gauging employee concerns. Senior management recognized that employees, the people who are most intimate with the challenges of manufacturing or dealing with customers, had a special knowledge. And so management brought what they learned to corporate headquarters. In this way, the employees' voices are now brought into top management's discussions of strategy.

Horne also used a survey to identify employee concerns. The surveys, based on one-on-one interviews with a cross-section of employees, were presented jointly by management and union leaders at every plant and published in the plant newsletter. In turn, the survey results became the basis for action plans the plant management developed to address employee concerns and to establish deadlines for completion of these plans. Plant management is held accountable for these goals.

To strengthen the relationship between senior management and plant employees, Horne also initiated and maintains discussions with another constituency—union representatives. Union members have been invited to recommend changes in the education and training of employees. Believing that employees can be dealt with directly, Horne has also collaborated with the UAW on wage and other employment issues.

But plant employees were not the only key internal constituency with whom Horne improved communications. He also targeted senior management, and to do so, he instituted a "leadership conference" in 1995—a three-day conference for the top 550 managers in the firm. Horne's overriding goal at the first conference was to "pump life back" into the leadership, who were, in general, risk-averse survivors of the old Navistar. He used skits and humor—including rap performances by the most senior members of the management team to the accompaniment of boom-box music—to illustrate new strategic initiatives and to poke fun at the old ones.

On the first day of the first conference, Horne learned that only 24 percent of the top executives were even aware the company had a strategy. By the end of the conference, 98 percent knew and understood this strategy. These leadership conferences are now a permanent component of the company's approach to internal communication.

From Inside to Out

Once Horne began implementing his internal communication initiatives, he could turn his attention to the outside world, and the customers who are, of course, his first external concern. Since Horne became CEO, the company has focused on customers: doing research on customers' overall experience and expectations of the brand, rethinking each target market group, holding press conferences and giving speeches at industry events in order to project Navistar as an industry leader in its product lines. The company is working to extend its brand image beyond that of "reliability" and "durability"—qualities that its customers identified—to include technological leadership and excellence for its extensive distribution network. Imprinting this revamped brand image in the minds of employees through Navistar's bolstered communication programs helped ensure that these same messages would be conveyed clearly to the customers with whom employees interact regularly.

To address the skepticism of the financial community about Navistar's ability to resolve its union problems, Horne and the rest of Navistar's senior management developed a powerful, consistent story about how the company was going to resolve its difficulties. Although senior management would take the blame for the company's problems, Horne emphasized his philosophy that all employees needed to work together to solve them. Practicing exactly what he preached to employees, Horne persisted in communicating with the media, even in the face of negative stories surrounding union strife. Despite initial lack of trust on both sides, Horne's willingness to respond to questions and his ability to present a consistent company strategy—just as he had done with employees internally—bolstered relations.

As a result of Horne's putting communications at the heart of the turnaround he led, he has been able to change the image of the company, raise employee morale, and improve Navistar's reputation and financial status. In accomplishing these goals, he was ably assisted by his corporate communications vice president, Maril McDonald, who considered that her role was to "help John understand where all of our publics are relative to what we're trying to accomplish."[7]

Whatever the monumental change facing an organization, be it the threat of rapid decline, as in the case of Navistar, or stagnancy, employees instilled with the knowledge of corporate communication can increase the possibility that any transition is painless and successful. Despite the importance of good relationships with external constituencies, Horne's success serves as a reminder that employees and senior management are your firm's most influential apostles reaching the world beyond company doors. Making communication a core value and including it as an integral part of any performance review will guarantee that this value permeates all levels of your organization.

Keeping Horne's philosophy in mind as a valuable framework, let's now visit with Rob Frazier of Colgate-Palmolive and David McCourt of RCN to take a look at their respective approaches to employee communications. As we learn about each executive's communication doctrine, we'll stop along the way to review the contributions each has made to our understanding of the employee care revolution.

USING COMMUNICATION TO CREATE CHANGE AT COLGATE-PALMOLIVE

"When I arrived at the Mennen plant in 1996, most of the key people were unhappy that we weren't meeting our KPIs [key performance indicators]," said Rob Frazier. "There was no communication going on in the plant, and what was being sent across the transom was inaccurate. We were losing over $10 million a day, and morale was at an all-time low."[8]

Prior to the 1992 sale of the plant to Colgate-Palmolive, the Mennen family had built a sizeable business in underarm deodorants. The highly mechanized Morristown facility was run in a patriarchal manner befitting a business that had been family run throughout its history. Faced with demands to increase volume, to pick up the slack from other plant closings, Colgate-Palmolive asked Frazier to turn Mennen into a profitable enterprise within a year. When he took over in 1996, Frazier found himself in an environment of disenfranchised employees floundering under a top-down organizational structure.

Although he had no formal training in communication, Frazier, an engineer, intuitively knew that communication was the right tool to use to repair the damage his predecessors and the Mennen family had done to the organization. To garner a clear understanding of the situation at the plants, he met with all employees in groups of ten. Then he began an internal marketing campaign dedicated solely to creating a clear vision in employees' minds about where the plant was headed and what he expected the plant to achieve. His mantra became "Here's where we are; here's where we want to be." Frazier decided the only way to ensure a turnaround was to make employees recognize their roles as the keys to success; they were to see themselves as the solution bearers, if you will. Finally, in another attempt to inspire involvement and interaction, he decided to teach his employees about the business: finance, gain-sharing, industrial pressures, and competition were among the topics taught.

"It never occurred to me that I was involved in any kind of employee communication activity," said Frazier. "My goal was to turn Colgate-Palmolive's Morristown facility into a global business. In fact, my presentation on this subject is called 'Variety, Innovation and Speed to Market through Flexibility and Low-Cost Production.' I don't see it as just communication, but rather as a whole philosophy about how to run a business."

To put his philosophy into action, Frazier began with a daily morning "check-in" routine. In a small asymmetrical room with no windows, few chairs, and furniture in odd places, people line up against the wall all the way around the room, making a circle. This is Frazier's first innovation—the stand-up forum. Employees talk about what happened yesterday and what is likely to happen today. No one looks up at Frazier as he enters the room.

Short conversations take place, questions are answered, problems solved. Aware that their voices have been heard and their concerns have been recognized, the 20 employees file out of the room ready to get to work, to contribute to the plant's success, as they do 5 days a week, 50 weeks a year. Their words, actions, and expressions reveal their awareness that their contributions count. Even on the plant floor, the workers seem content and satisfied with the jobs they are doing. White boards chock-full of information reveal details about breakdowns, goals, sick leaves, birthdays, vacation schedules, and numbers of units coming off each line. A special racecar billboard depicts the productivity of each line relative to the others. It is a visual measure of success; every employee can see the placement of her or his racecar. This board is also accompanied by handwritten remarks concerning the outcome of the race. Banners hang from the ceiling extolling the virtues of open communication; along the walls are pictures with inspirational messages encouraging employees to push toward their next goal.

Frazier's Assessment of His Efforts

The energy in this plant appears dynamic next to the fixtures of the old approach to employee communication. Frazier explains how he engineered this transformation:

> I started out believing that communications could drive any of our key performance indicators if we could only share the right information. For instance, if everyone knew the real value of lost material in terms they could understand, they would never allow the top from a stick of deodorant to lay on the floor until the janitors came around to pick it up before the next shift.
>
> So I started talking to line workers about creating an image in their minds of a nickel sitting on the floor every time they saw a cap. The visual imagery stuck, and over the last three years we cut material losses at Morristown by 86 percent.

Similarly, Frazier believes that communication is the best tool to focus employees on issues that management believes are crucial to the success of a business:

> The people who work for us aren't stupid. Very soon they could see a direct connection between what they were doing and success for the business as a whole.
>
> The key to our success throughout this three-year period from 1996 to 1999, however, was making everyone at this facility strive for the best and receive recognition for what they were doing. It's really quite simple when you think about it. Look, most of the

times our employees are going to understand our actions if they have the same information we do. If they understand our actions and feel like they are a part of the solution, our only other duty is to recognize their performance, day to day, week to week, month to month, etc.

Frazier's open, straightforward communication style and the level of credibility he built for himself have helped him to achieve his goals. He personally took over the company's internal newsletter to communicate directly with his employees. His front-page articles in the plant's internal newsletter became the most valuable source of information for those motivated to attain greater success for the company and themselves. A few months after his arrival in Morristown, Frazier decided to write about the 12 characteristics of an excellent manufacturing operation. Number 4 on his list (after zero accidents, neat and orderly at all times, and people are important) was excellent communication.

Excellent communication is very difficult and will not be achieved unless we work very hard to make it happen. I am referring to communication between functions (planning, manufacturing, finishing, warehouse, engineering, etc.), communication on our results, communication on jobs well done, communication on how we can improve our performance and communication on how the business is doing.

Please make a note to yourself to do something to improve communication this week. I will be installing a white board near the entrance and writing a piece of information on that board each day in an effort to improve communication. What will each of you do?

Over and over again, Frazier communicated to employees about where they were and where they were going in terms of asset utilization, the quality of products, material losses, financial results, and even teamwork. Years later the success is obvious.

In numerical terms, asset utilization at Colgate-Palmolive's Morristown facility (no longer thought of by anyone as the Mennen plant) was up 48 percent. Production volume increased by 67 percent, and the number of cases produced per person increased by a dramatic 64 percent. The cost per case of product decreased by 42 percent, and the cases held decreased by 82 percent. Surprisingly, all of these results were achieved with many of the same employees who had worked at the facility before Frazier's arrival.

Let's recap how Frazier achieved such dramatic results: First he met with all employees, eight to ten at a time, to understand the issues. Then he started writing the newsletter himself to explain who "Rob Frazier" was and "Where the plant needed to go." He held plantwide meetings clearly telling people "Where they were" and "Where they needed to go." He continually repeated the key messages: "Where we are," and "Where we need to go" to his employees.

As for the form of communication, Frazier had only a few rules. He wanted everyone to use the white boards so the communication would manifest itself visually. He told supervisors that the boards had to be changed and updated daily, that facts had to be presented, and that communication had to focus on business needs and goals. Other than that, they were on their own.

Frazier's Contribution to Our Understanding of Employee Care

What has Rob Frazier shown us about employee care? One important lesson we can take away is the importance of leadership in the employee-care value chain. When we asked Frazier about the placement of communication in his organization—in other words, who is in charge of employee communication here?—he seemed puzzled. "I am in charge of communications here. What priority could be more important than communicating and leading the people under my direction? I can't delegate that to someone else! But really, everybody 'does' communications here." It's hard to imagine anything more essential to a company's successful implementation of strategy than a strong leader who believes in the power of communication.

Frazier also demonstrates that a specific marketplace orientation is crucial to the success of an effective employee communication program. Employees need to have a common understanding of what the business is striving for in the marketplace; education is key to achieving this. As consultant Roger D'Aprix has written:

> It is not enough to talk about survival, it is not enough to threaten people's livelihoods, and it is not enough—especially today—to appeal to their loyalty. *The only argument powerful enough to encourage people to embrace change is one that is rooted in the marketplace.* If the customer insists on change, we have no alternative.[9]

We also can see that an organization does not need an expensive and sophisticated communication channel to be successful. Note that one of the keys to Frazier's success was the face-to-face meetings he conducted with his employees. Besides being one of the oldest forms of human communication, face-to-face communication is also one of the most effective. In particular, the small size of the groups made his employees feel he was listening to what they had to say. The ability to listen well is part of all relationships, and managers often forget that listening is important in business relationships as well. The other inexpensive, yet effective communication channel Frazier used was white boards. The collective power that is produced by all the white boards, banners, posters, signs, and information boards scattered throughout the plant creates tangible excitement at Colgate's Morristown facility. Finally, Frazier emphasizes the importance of current information. Boards change daily not monthly, and improvements occur constantly.

Let's leave Rob Frazier and Colgate's Morristown facility and travel to Princeton, New Jersey to see what David McCourt at RCN has to tell us about the power of communication.

BUILDING EMPLOYEE CARE FROM THE GROUND UP

One of the most compelling phenomena in American business late in the twentieth century was the rise of entrepreneurial high-tech ventures. Internet stocks soared throughout the late 1990s, and companies without profits had market values that made the *Fortune* 500 envious. It was in this environment that David C. McCourt, founder, chairman, and CEO of RCN found himself in late 1999. (The firm was originally called Residential Communications Network, emphasizing the company's focus on residential services as opposed to business services.)

McCourt built his company for the long term, basing many of his theories for managing the company on Porras and Collins' book *Built to Last*. McCourt spent the period from 1997 to 2000 convincing Wall Street investors as well as mogul Paul Allen to invest over $4 billion in McCourt's vision of the telecommunications industry for the twenty-first century.

Building Employee Care along with RCN

Communication strategy has been at the heart of this company from the day that it went public in October 1997.

> We focused our initial attention on Wall Street analysts to raise money. If we didn't have the money, there's no way we could make this idea of bundled telecommunications services work. But now we have the money, and the hard work of making an

entrepreneurial venture into a billion-dollar-a-year business inevitably has us focused on employee service, a concept that equates employees and customers as coequals in terms of corporate importance.[10]

By the way, you know it was my ten-year-old son, David Tyler who thought of that term, "employee care." One day we were riding along in the car and he heard me talking on the phone about our customer service program. And he said, "Dad, why don't you have something for your employees as well?" I didn't listen to him at first, but then I realized he was on to something. "Yeah, Dad, you can call it 'employee care' just like you do for customers!" David Tyler also came up with another idea that I used almost immediately. "Hey, you ought to send your employees to camp for the summer. You can call it Cable Camp!"

At first McCourt didn't realize just what a great idea that was. Six months later RCN's turnover rate among those employees who had attended Cable Camp had dropped by 75 percent.

Cable Camp is a program designed to promote RCN's values. Employees appreciate the strength and conviction behind these corporate guidelines and begin to use them in their own daily practices. Attendees are also exposed to and educated about the business workings of their company. As a final symbol of the significance of corporate unity, a rock engraved with corporate values is distributed to every employee, a tangible symbol of the importance these ideals hold. The values are:

- Understand the customer
- Seek innovation and efficiency everywhere
- Develop awareness
- Be a builder, not an employee
- Reward the best
- Be driven by enthusiasm

In addition to Cable Camp, RCN's annual meeting has been a huge success. The annual meeting has become one of the events that McCourt most looks forward to every year. That is where RCN can put its values on display for everyone in the company to see.

The meeting is part rally, part education, and part spiritual retreat. A definite mixture of hard work (the employees meet for 6 to 7 hours a day for 2 days) and hard partying. Banners proudly announce RCN's values. Gene Krantz, the flight commander of *Apollo 13*, speaks passionately about what it takes to be a leader.

His emotional story about the rescue of the space capsule grabs the attention of everyone. The job of the *Apollo 13* ground crew was to bring three men back from the moon with virtually no power, no heat, no navigational system, and, for assistance, only a bunch of unrelated items scattered around the ship.

McCourt tells us that the task he and his team have set for RCN's employees is equally daunting: Their goal is to become the dominant provider of telecommunications services, including local and long-distance phone, cable, and Internet, from Boston to Washington and San Francisco to San Diego.

Will RCN be able to prove itself in the economic realities of a post.com world? While the future may be uncertain, David McCourt knows who he has on the front lines, and that is more than many of the former CEOs of failed dot.coms can say.

McCourt believes that companies like RCN are the ones that succeed when the rules of the game are changing. Trying to keep the morale of employees up in an environment filled with change, opportunity, and fear, however, often seems next to impossible. At RCN, company leaders do everything they can to bring the right people in the door, and then they do everything humanly possible to keep them working for the company. Although the economy may be tougher today than it was in 1999, RCN is being repaid for the investment it made in employee relationships when the economy was at its peak; it can now count on increased employee retention and morale when times are bad.

At RCN's annual meeting, McCourt stands at the podium. His inspiring rhetoric has the employees literally on their feet as he talks to them about what it will take to be successful in the coming year:

> And I want each and every one of you to know that we realize how hard you are all working to make this company a success. To recognize that effort, my fellow employees, the board has approved a plan to give each and every one of you stock options. As of today, you are not just my fellow employees, but fellow owners of this company. With ownership comes responsibility. A responsibility that all of us will do the best we can for our customers, the best we can for our investors, the best we can for the communities we work in, the best we can for each other. And, we also have to do what's best for our families. You all need to keep your families securely at the center of all that you do. I know that's hard, but I try to do the same thing each and every day.

A video with the song "Taking Care of Business" plays in the background. We see RCN on the move in the investment community, building the infrastructure to support its services, installing the bundled services in customers' homes and on their streets. We also see McCourt on 10 to 15 broadcasts selling the company story. The pulsating music reinforces the company's value system, as RCN appears to move at rocket speed.

Soon a group of employees appears on stage to present a skit, the message of which is clear: "This is what it takes to serve customers well." The skit shows how difficult customers can be in a variety of situations. Despite the setbacks, RCN installers and customer-care personnel never lose their cool. RCN, like Navistar and Colgate-Palmolive, believes in connecting the marketplace to employee care.

Energy and a feeling of esprit de corps permeate the annual meeting. No one leaves the room for almost two hours as a variety of employees in skits, speeches, and self-made videos communicate about what the employees do, who they are, and what they believe in. Employees will remember this feeling of belonging to something greater than themselves when the economy and industry are stacked against RCN and McCourt has to ask for sacrifices from all those who are working to make the company a success.

During the meeting, we join McCourt aboard a boat that moves the 250 meeting attendees up the Potomac. In the world of RCN, senior officers mingle with the sales force, installers, and operators. Ten at a time line up to chat with the CEO, who obviously loves being close to the employees in his company.

The next morning, employees are treated to a video playback of the previous day's events, complete with fireworks at the end. This entire show will later be taken on the road by McCourt and others who spoke at the meeting, to give the employees who could not attend a sense of what went on.

"Next year my goal is to do the same kind of road shows that we do for Wall Street for employees instead. We need to get these people motivated to do battle over the next several months. This is such a competitive business. I need to be in touch with them in the same way we have been in touch with analysts who are following our stock," says McCourt.

McCourt's Contribution to Our Understanding of Employee Care

How was RCN able to achieve such a unified movement and to secure tremendous employee loyalty and support under such trying market conditions? What can we learn from the RCN experience?

First, RCN, like some of the other companies that are excelling in employee care, had a clear vision and goal that everyone can see, touch, feel, and measure against. Either the company's employees were making progress in their quest to wire the area from Boston to Washington and San Francisco to San Diego, or they were not. Although the dot.com crash has made the challenge facing RCN much greater, with employees who care about the company and understand what it seeks to achieve, success is still possible.

Second, the CEO is passionate about moving this company in the right direction. Every one of his speeches, his employee meetings, the endless details he oversees to make sure the jobs are getting done, convinces employees that David McCourt cares about his company. He is not satisfied to sit in the rarefied world of corporate headquarters; he has made a commitment to reach out and meet with his employees on a level where they can truly connect with him and his mission.

Third, the employee meeting, often a boring display of corporate bureaucracy, seems at RCN to be a truly exciting event that defines for employees who they are as a company. Speeches, skits, videos, and parties all provide employees with an awareness of the corporate culture. When they leave, RCN employees know what the company is all about, are inspired by it, and feel ready to do battle in the marketplace.

Fourth, tapping into people's excitement about something that is truly new (such as RCN's bundled services) helped RCN compete against the established telecom companies. RCN's new approach to telecommunications contributed to the company's appeal to employees. They were part of a revolution. The song "Revolution," played endlessly at company meetings, is genuinely the theme song for the company. The people at RCN are fighting against established companies like AT&T and Verizon. Similar to Apple Computer's fight against IBM in the mid-1980s, RCN's battle seems almost heroic. The company's initial ad campaign was focused on crushing the evil empire in its track. Lenin appeared in RCN ads with a noose around his neck. The tag line read: "No empire lasts forever; especially one that keeps you waiting for a repairman for five hours!"

And, finally, Cable Camp—that mixture of training, development, and indoctrination—is the company's way of teaching everyone what it means to be an RCN employee and what the task ahead is all about. In an atmosphere similar to what we saw at the employee meeting, but much more focused on a smaller set of employees, this program contributes substantially to the company's success in reducing employee turnover. Reducing turnover is never more important than in times when the economic focus is on the bottom line and profit making.

LESSONS ABOUT EMPLOYEE CARE
PROVIDED BY THE THREE COMPANIES

Taken as a whole, the three companies we have studied offer several important lessons about employee care that you may be able to apply to your own organization.

1. *Choose the right champion.* Each company picked the right champion to formulate and convey its key messages about employee care. As Navistar's new CEO, Horne placed employee interests at the heart of his vision which, in turn, he conveyed to all levels of the company—from plant workers to senior management. At Colgate-Palmolive, it was someone besides the CEO who acted as the driving force behind the change and focus on employees. The RCN example showed us, however, that a CEO has the potential to be the most valuable asset in employee relations; she or he can serve as an inspiration.

2. *Create the right settings for getting across the message about employee care.* Like the directors of a theatrical production, the champions of employee care at each company knew how to create and use the right settings for establishing an environment of employee care. Horne broke down old internal communication barriers by forcing managers and employees to meet face to face. Frazier discarded the old plant manager's office, isolated from the production line, and shaped a whole new setting for communication: a stand-up forum, complete with white boards, to promote timely exchange of ideas and information, to reinforce company goals and values, and to inspire employees to increased performance. With a director's sense of timing and scene setting, McCourt orchestrated an annual meeting full of skits, videos, and inspirational speeches to move his employees to greater achievements

3. *Repeat, repeat, repeat.* Employee communications is an iterative process, not a single communication, which, like an edict from the higher-ups, is sent out just once. Gone are the days of "command-and-control" when senior management could coerce workers to follow orders. Each of the companies we studied developed a "voice" that listened as well as spoke, taking into account employees' points of view and repeatedly engaging in a give-and-take with this most important constituency. Moreover, the messages each company sent out were distributed across multiple communication channels, such as newsletters, the Intranet, informal forums, formal meetings, posters, banners, videos, and written guidelines.

4. *Recognize that employee care means good company care.* As diverse as their businesses are, all three companies know that successful internal communications allow them to implement important organizational goals. Unlike many other organizations that shove employee communication into a closet, these companies place communication at the center of major organizational change. At Navistar, the new focus on employee communications paved the way for a remarkable turnaround in the company's reputation and financial status. At Colgate-Palmolive's Mennen plant, employee care yielded increased morale and productivity. At RCN, it galvanized support for the company's expansion. In all three companies, employee care contributes to the bottom line.

CONCLUSION

Companies in different developmental stages and different industries can institute programs that nurture and promote the pursuit of excellence in internal communication. Navistar had contended with years of union strife and negative press; The Morristown plant of Colgate-Palmolive was once part of a private company that no longer exists; and RCN is just a few years old. Employee communication at these diverse companies has a common focus—providing care to employees as a way to support the growth of business in the ever-changing economy.

What seems to be at the heart of these companies is the notion that employee care really means good company care. John Horne, Robert Frazier, and David McCourt understand that the marketplace is the place for business, but employees give us key access to that marketplace every day in their ability to deliver quality service.

Enlightened managers know that the more relevant and timely the information they provide to employees, the more likely the employees are to be highly motivated to do a better job, to advance in their positions, and to further the goals of the organization itself.

Such enlightened thinking leads to an atmosphere of respect for all employees within the organization. This goal can be accomplished in many ways, but the best way to create this atmosphere is through the communication that managers have with employees, most of which should, ideally, come directly from supervisor to employee.

In the twenty-first century and in the wake of the dot.com decline, the qualities we see on display in the companies we have visited will become more important than ever. Leaders will always have to find ways to make work exciting. Companies will have to give employees a reason to believe that coming to work is associated with something far grander than maximizing shareholder value. It should come to mean, for instance, participating in building a business, doing things better, and taking on productive roles in pursuit of a common goal. Leaders who are aware of the need for employee care will realize that managing internal communications well requires the same dedication they have typically given to other aspects of running a business.

C H A P T E R

INVESTOR RELATIONS: ENHANCING YOUR COMPANY'S HEALTH AND WEALTH

On weekdays, 28,000 to 30,000 people faithfully flocked to Wrigley Field in the 2001 baseball season to root the Chicago Cubs to victory. In contrast, more than 34,000 people tuned into the Webcast of Cisco Systems Inc.'s quarterly earning announcement, a 120-minute presentation about earnings and sales by executives and accountants. Perhaps Americans are developing a new favorite pastime.

Only a few years ago the majority of companies prohibited individuals access to their briefings with analysts. Today companies encourage close contact with individual investors—one in five entice individual investors to call by withholding long-term predictions from their news releases.[1] Personalized investor relations (IR) efforts—including the increasing number of annual meetings that your company Webcasts—can help your company construct and promote its reputation. R. R. Donnelly Sons & Co. Director of IR, Chris Curtis, agrees: "We're very much in a world in which communications with investors are sterile. Annual meetings are a human experience, and shareholders deserve that interaction."[2] Just as companies need close interaction with employees, customers, and members of the media, they also need to move investor relations away from a purely financial function to both a financial and a communication-oriented operation.

Most experts agree that investors deserve personal interactions with the companies they own, but perhaps more important, investors have come to expect nothing less. With the democratization of the stock market, investing in the late 1990s became as common a pastime as baseball. But this does not mean that all companies competing in a particular market have the same ability to communicate with investors. Unlike large, well-known companies, such as those in the *Fortune* 500, smaller companies need to communicate aggressively to get the right information about their company to the investment community. A strong investor-relations function directly influences the success of companies in communicating with this key constituency.

What makes investors stop and listen? Why do investors value one stock over another? When you consider that, entering the year 2000, 76 percent of the average U.S. company shares listed on the New York Stock Exchange had turned over in the previous year, investors seem to be restless, focused on the short term, and largely difficult to please. As discussed in Chapter 4, on corporate reputation, the dominant factor attracting investors to companies has been vision, not an exclusive focus on the bottom line. As James Collins and Jerry Porras note in *Built to Last*, "Visionary companies pursue a cluster of objectives, of which making money is only one—and not necessarily the primary one. Yes, they seek profits, but they're equally guided by a core ideology....Yet, paradoxically, the visionary companies make more money than the more purely profit-driven comparison companies."[3]

Given the importance of having vision as well as making profits in the investment community, this chapter will help you understand the importance of investor relations as well as how to communicate with this important constituency. First we provide an overview of the investor relations area, by tracing the evolution of investor relations from minimal communications 50 years ago to its present standing as a sophisticated communication function. Next we'll discuss why IR matters to you. Finally, we'll outline how your company can diligently develop its IR function to maximize shareholder value.

As you read this chapter, keep the following questions in mind:

- How is your company valued on Wall Street? If it is undervalued, why? Could it be that investors simply don't know enough about your company? How does your company currently communicate with its shareholders, financial analysts, and the media?
- Where is the IR function on your organizational chart?

INVESTOR RELATIONS: AN EVOLVING CONCEPT

First, what is investor relations, and how did it evolve? Investor relations is a strategic function of corporate management, combining the disciplines of marketing, finance, and communication to provide current and potential investors with an accurate portrayal of the company's performance and prospects. This function serves as the voice of the company to both the financial community and the capital markets.

Investor-relations teams at even the largest companies usually include only one or two people. In the United States, two-thirds of these professionals report to the chief financial officer (CFO). In smaller companies, the CFO often handles IR him- or herself, with the help of an agency that performs tasks such as writing analyst reports. Even in companies where IR reports to the CFO, however, the function is often tied in some way to the corporate communication function.

Let's look at the roots of investor relations. Investor relations first became a separate business function at General Electric over 50 years ago. The objective then, as it still is today, was to ensure that the investment community fully and accurately understood the investment potential of the company. This work goes beyond the regular practices of producing and distributing annual and quarterly reports, answering shareholder questions, and sending information to securities analysts. Although your company certainly must remember these mandatory, traditional activities, today it must also think in broader, more creative terms. Investor relations can have a profound effect on your company's reputation and positioning with customers, employees, and creditors.

To truly understand the history of investor relations, we need to begin with the 1950s and examine how the function unfolded over the past half-century. Despite the enactment of federal securities law in the 1930s requiring the continuous disclosure of financial information by public companies, IR didn't begin to move toward the function we know today until the 1950s. A decade later, the National Investor Relations Institute (NIRI) officially recognized the IR function. NIRI was established as a professional association of corporate officers and investor relations consultants who were responsible for communicating with corporate management, the investing public, and the financial community. By 2001, NIRI had over 5000 members in 33 chapters around the United States. Its official mission is to set the highest standards in education designed to advance the practice of investor relations and meet the growing professional development needs of those people who are engaged in the field. NIRI's membership spans the majority of the largest publicly held corporations in the United States and an increasing number of small and midsized companies, demonstrating the need for all companies to build a strong and robust investor-relations program.

By the 1970s the Financial Relations Board (FRB) had pioneered the distribution of investment profiles that laid out a company's long-term aspirations and strategies. Prior to this innovation, getting information to potential investors was done through local stockbroker clubs or analysts' societies. FRB also helped Sprint host the first conference calls involving hundreds of investors in the 1980s, making huge leaps in corporate credibility by putting a voice and personality to what had been previously seen as lofty and inaccessible upper management. Soon thereafter, quarterly conference calls became the norm at many companies.

The most radical innovations in IR started in the 1990s with the Internet boom. Companies altered the way they communicated with their constituencies, including the investment community, by posting information, including annual reports, on their Web pages. By December 1999, companies were regularly Webcasting annual meetings so investors who were physically unable to be present could gather information in real time. FRB reported in 1999 that of their 85 hour-long Webcasts, each earned approximately 200,000 hits. Investor interest was clearly sparked; the feedback was so positive, in fact, that the respective stock prices of each company rose as much as 10 percent following the on-line presentations. Investors worldwide were thrilled that they were suddenly able to share viewpoints and commentary with fellow investors near and far, and that they could get all their questions fielded directly by CEOs and CFOs.[4]

These changes have transformed the modern investment world into one that is radically different from its early beginnings. Over the decades, major external forces have prompted these changes, propelling IR from an idea into an active, much-needed function. As we mentioned previously, the democratization of the stock market caused many individual shareholders to invest in publicly held companies. The proliferation of these individual investors created a vital need for companies to attract investor interest in an unprecedented competitive investing environment.

Institutional investors have also invested their reserves of excess cash in the stock market, dramatically increasing their share of total equity holdings. Since this increase, the role of institutional investors— pension funds, mutual funds, insurance companies, and banks—has continued to expand, and today these investors exert more influence than ever on corporate management. The institutional constituency is an important one for your company to consider because their block trading activities can have a huge short-term effect on your company's stock price performance. And since, as you will see, investors have traditionally set their sights on relatively short-term goals, institutions' approval or disapproval influences individual preferences. As Darrell K. Rigby, Bain & Company director, has commented: "I've seen so many senior executives saying and doing things to deliver short-term news lately that it's a little frightening.... Their time horizons are shortening. They're thinking more about retiring rich at 45 or 50 and less about the institution they will leave behind."[5]

Beyond the Bottom Line

Although the time an individual investor holds your company's stock is shortening, investors are more closely examining all aspects of your company. Today, investors must understand more than your company's financial information; they must fully understand the vision driving your company. Beyond the strictly financial terms, investors will consider how you are faring in everything from employee relations to your company's reputation in its local community.

Considering this, you should hardly find it surprising to learn that in August 2001, three-quarters of Americans stated that they considered social responsibility when making investment decisions. Twelve percent of these investors would go so far as to buy the stock of a socially commendable company even if that meant settling for lower returns on their investment, as our discussion of corporate philanthropy in Chapter 8 corroborates.[6]

Consequently, Arthur Thompson, CEO of Phezulu Financial Services in South Africa, defines investor relations as more than merely the communication between companies and investors; it is also a function whose "purpose is to give a clear picture of what the company stands for and its goals."[7] Nonfinancial considerations—ethics, vision, and ideology, as well as social responsibility—can positively influence your company's bottom line. But your organization's nonfinancial commitments must be heartfelt to be credible to the public. For external constituencies to believe in your company's dedication, the company must be actively involved in fund-raising and volunteering.

The Current State of Affairs

Before delving specifically into how you can successfully build and manage your own investor relations program, let's get a better idea of what the IR function means today. The term "investor relations" encompasses both relations with individuals—shareholders of record—and institutional investors—pension funds, mutual funds, insurance companies, and banks. Insiders—the managers and employees within your company—represent the final type of investors in your company, such as Starbucks employees buying into Bean Stock. Typically, companies target the financial community via "buy-side" and "sell-side" analysts. The buy side represents institutional analysts, fund/portfolio managers, and individuals. On the other hand, the sell side represents research analysts at investment banks, institutional brokers, and individual brokers.

Your company can reach these investors through various channels. Your company's IR managers can reach investment institutions through phone contact and one-on-one meetings daily with buy- or sell-side analysts, sometimes involving your company's CEO or CFO. More formally, your organization can contact institutions by holding meetings in which your CEO addresses the analysts of brokerage societies or industry conferences. Another option is hosting your own meetings in major financial centers such as New York or Boston and inviting institutional investors who either own or may be interested in owning your company's stock.

While these options can give you access to institutions, reaching individual investors can prove to be much more difficult. Think about your existing IR program. How does your company communicate with individual investors? Sending direct mail to affinity groups such as shareholders, employees, customers, and suppliers may be an option to consider. In addition, your company can use the brokerage community or attempt to generate positive visibility in the media to attract the attention of individuals. And, as we discussed in our chapter on corporate advertising, targeted image advertising is another potentially effective way to speak to a broad range of individual investors.

Simultaneously communicating with both institutional and individual investors is quite efficient. Companies do so through financial reports including the annual report/10K, quarterly report/10Q, proxy statements, and earnings/news releases. Annual meetings also are an opportunity for your company to review its fiscal year as well as provide a useful forum for investors' questions.

A WHOLE NEW BALLGAME: WHY INVESTOR RELATIONS MATTERS TO YOUR COMPANY

Why should you and your company work conscientiously to build close and positive relations with the investment community? Perhaps because the average American is doing more these days than just watching baseball. As Gary Mednick, president of On-Site Trading Inc., a Great Neck,

New York, company (that recently set up a day-trading office in Bethesda, Maryland) explains: "The public is more aware of what's happening in the stock market than ever.... People sit around and talk about what's going on in the stock market like they used to talk about sports."[8] As discussed in Chapter 4, business news has a wider audience than ever before, since on average Americans have 40 percent of their financial assets in the stock market.[9]

With public attention focused on your company, it must be even more diligent about building strong relationships with investors, in both good times and bad. Arthur Thompson cites this relationship building as the chief contributor to a better assessment of a share's value by Wall Street. The frequency and type of communications companies direct toward investors directly affect whether the investor wishes to be associated with the company, as well as the potential for returns. Penelope Gracie of Penelope Gracie Investor Relations agrees with Thompson, stating that, "Conducted effectively, IR can have a positive effect on a company's total value relative to that of the overall market and the company's cost of capital."[10]

The upper management of *Fortune* 500 companies undoubtedly acknowledge the importance of building a successful IR program. One *Fortune* 500 CEO recently told us that he spends approximately 35 percent of his time talking to analysts and major shareholders and generally thinking about the prevalent issues on Wall Street. He explained that there is always the stock price to think about, especially considering how the compensation of many CEOs is connected to share price.

When you consider how crucial a strong investor relations program is for your company's success, why is it that so many companies underestimate the importance of IR? For example, by February 2001, 11,000 publicly held companies in the United States had substantial market capitalization, but one-third had no professional investor-relations guidance. Instead, finance, general public relations, or advertising executives handled investor relations for these companies.[11]

What are the risks of having public-relations professionals spearheading your company's IR programs? Given the hybrid nature of IR, the field of investor relations qualifies as both a financial discipline and a corporate communication function. Over the past 15 years the way corporations decide how, to whom, and to what extent they convey financial and operating information has evolved tremendously. Now, an expanded range of activities fall under the investor-relations heading, and therefore your company's IR executives must have a broader range of skills. Most important, these executives must have both excellent communication abilities (to market your company's stock) as well as a sophisticated financial background. Increasingly, they also need to be Web savvy to understand the needs of analysts and investors.

THE MODERN INVESTOR—A DIFFERENT KIND OF ANIMAL

The increased traffic to CNNfn.com and CNBC.com over the past decade indicates that consumers are turning to the Internet to learn about the current state of their stocks. For example, General Electric Co. has approximately two million investors and receives an average of 7000 hits per day on its investor relations Web site alone. Investor relations pages, which ideally highlight stock quotes, news releases, and stock charts, are increasingly popular. Investors find this kind of instantaneous access to information comforting and stabilizing during tumultuous stock market periods, as such access implies that companies are being open and honest. Also remember that investors are frequently looking to the Web to compare your company's stock strengths to your competitors', as well as keeping an eye on immediate updates on any breaking company financial news.

Given this surge in on-line activity, delivering your company's annual report on CD-ROM and having your CEO appear live on the Web in real time to talk about the company's future will become standard in the next couple of years. Yet Web-reliant communication is not without its dangers, as we discuss in Chapter 9, on generating a powerful media-relations strategy in today's news-hungry world. The Internet has essentially handed the average person a megaphone with which he or she can spread rumors and falsehoods about your company. Ted Pincus, founder of the Financial Relations Board, the first investor-relations firm, insists that such troublemakers have always been around: "They used to show up at annual meetings; now they just hop online."[12]

From the company's perspective, operating on-line is a useful cost-saving tactic. Although federal laws require that all shareholders receive paper copies of annual reports by mail, potential investors may appreciate your company's making its annual report available on-line. Paper reports cost several dollars per copy to print and stamp, while electronic versions are essentially free. Clearly, the cost incentives alone—and the speed at which you can reach thousands of investors—are reason enough to supplement your company's existing investor-relations program with a strong on-line presence. Boeing diligently posts up-to-the-day information on airplane orders and deliveries on its Web site, enabling investment houses and analysts to track this information easily.

Displaying such information on the Internet saves the weeks it would otherwise take to print and mail the same information; by the time the printed information arrives, it is less relevant because it will be slightly dated. Similarly, investors purchasing shares from General Electric can save days over the usual time it takes to make a transaction, because they have the option to view a prospectus on-line and apply by e-mail, without using a broker.

What the Modern Investor Values

Adding to the already chaotic world of investor relations is the daily, incessant change in the stock market itself. As investors watch stocks oscillate daily, one wonders what drives companies' stocks up and down—besides the market's inherently fickle nature? First and foremost, the confidence investors have in your organization drives stock price, and that confidence is founded on management's ability to make and keep important promises.

Your company can generate confidence effectively by offering investors stability and predictability. A major overhaul in operations or spin-offs of part of the company can create a sense of volatility. Any sort of transition, in fact, particularly in management, serves as a red flag for investors. Charles C. Conaway, president of CVS Corporation, the $17 billion U.S. drugstore chain, explains: "Where there is a change in the strategic direction of the company, you've got monster turnover in shareholders."[13] Conway endured this high level of turnover in 1995 when CVS underwent a major restructuring, prompting almost a complete investor turnover in a single year. After this incredible transition, CVS actively recruited longer-term institutional investors more suited to CVS's new growth profile, meeting with almost 40 potential shareholders. Through focused, strategic communications, the company was able to enhance shareholder value.[14]

The promises your company makes to its shareholders are directly determined by what kind of planning it has done. Planning can be defined as knowing where you are today, deciding where you want to go, determining how to get there, and monitoring your progress along the way. Essentially, planning is the series of steps your company needs to take to ensure that its vision is realized. However, shareholder value should not be your company's only agenda. Instead of basing your company's vision on what analysts and individual investors want to hear, determine your own hopes and expectations and the steps you will need to take to achieve them. This proactive approach will ensure that your company is secure in its identity. As Harlan Teller, Hill & Knowlton director of worldwide corporate practice, has pointed out: "Companies continually misread the desire by people to invest in companies they feel have their own principles. Companies never seem to get it, but the public sure does."[15]

And when things don't go according to your plans, as in a crisis, directness and forthrightness are what investors prize most. There are three questions investors want answered during turbulent times, such as Johnson and Johnson's Tylenol crisis or Coca Cola's recall in Belgium: Why did the incident happen? What is the implication for future earnings? What is your company going to do about it to counter the negative effects? The swiftness, directness, and thoroughness with which your company answers these questions will have an enormous influence on investors' confidence in your company.

Thoroughly mapping your company's IR plan includes stating in detail the assumptions the plan is based on. With a plan that includes such detail, if your company experiences an earnings shortfall somewhere along the way, it will be able to pinpoint precisely what caused the divergence. Having this information at your company's fingertips will enable your company to deliver swift and accurate responses to information-hungry investors, which will assure them that your company is in control of the situation. Accounting for mistakes makes the investment community more understanding of them. As Lawrence Serven, founder of the research and consulting firm Buttonwood Group, stated, "If your company misses one quarterly forecast and makes it up later, Wall Street can be forgiving. But if you miss the annual earnings number, your stock can be decimated because it indicates precarious and imprudent planning—the real investor confidence crushers."[16]

Building from the Ashes

What happens if your company establishes a strong reputation among investors but a crisis shatters that reputation? How can your company pick up the pieces? And how does it build back the fragile trust it has worked so hard to gain?

Let's take a look at an example of investor relations gone wrong. Cendant was a company born of the merger of Walter Forbes's CUC International and Henry Silverman's franchising giant HFS (franchiser of brand names such as Ramada, Avis, and Century 21)—two of the most reputable names in the investing world. The merger revealed that CUC had concocted $500 million in phony operating income. When the news hit Wall Street in April 1998, a one-day, $14 billion stock meltdown occurred, and shareholders filed class-action lawsuits. Four months after the scandal of CUC's overstated operating income broke, Cendant had lost almost half its market value. The incident became one of the largest financial frauds ever brought before the Securities and Exchange Commission.[17]

HFS CEO Henry Silverman appeared on television with self-assurance immediately following the blowup, vowing that HFS was not involved with the fraud and that his primary mission was to "make things right again." Instantly he channeled his energies toward building back the investment world's confidence in his company. He began to "make things right" by announcing that Cendant had reached a preliminary $2.38 billion agreement to settle the class-action lawsuit filed by shareholders. AT&T's Liberty Media invested $400 million and received 18 million Cendant shares in return; Liberty Media's John Malone also agreed, along with Cendant's board, to personally purchase 1 million Cendant shares—all of these actions boosting the investment world's faith and confidence in the company. A huge delivery on Silverman's promise also happened in December: CUC's auditors, Ernst & Young, agreed to pay Cendant shareholders $335 million.[18]

What did all of this mean for Cendant's stocks? The stock, once standing at $7.50 in October 1998, reached $25 by January 2000. Silverman's unflinching confidence and his willingness to face the music at the outbreak of the scandal paid off by smoothing the ruffled feathers of investors and rebuilding confidence levels.

Now that we've considered what modern investors, both individual and institutional, value in companies, let's take a different tack to explore how you can ensure that your company is thoroughly fulfilling its need to communicate with these important constituencies. More specifically, let's consider how your organization can initiate and execute the successful development of a strong IR program to boost your company's share value.

DEVELOPING A SUCCESSFUL INVESTOR-RELATIONS PROGRAM FOR YOUR COMPANY

To begin developing the crucial tenets of an IR program, your company should first consider where the function will fit within your organizational blueprint. Although the investment community is external to your company, it is not the same as other external constituencies handled by the corporate communication function. Graeme Lillie, managing director of FCB Investor Connexion, makes a distinction between traditional PR and the new realm of investor relations: "True IR can and does play a more strategic and financial role in a company, and there needs to be a distinction between professional IR consultants and press release factories."[19]

IR professionals require a separate skill set from that which is necessary for traditional communication activities. In addition to outstanding communication skills and the ability to craft an appropriate message, an IR professional must have a firm grasp of the workings and fluctuations of the investment world, as well as a strategic understanding of how your company fits into that equation. This person must also have a finger on the pulse of your industry as well as knowledge of the existing investor perceptions and requirements, and a handle on managing the rapidly evolving relationships between the company and its individual and institutional investors.

But besides hiring the right IR professional to lead the function within your company, how do you ensure that the IR program your company develops will be a successful one? Here are some key ideas to consider when dealing with the often-erratic realm of investors.

A Little Help from the Web

Given the Web-savvy nature of today's investors, you must ensure that the Internet helps, not hinders, your IR efforts. As we are well aware, the Internet travels at such speed that it effectively transfers news across the globe before those involved in the story figure out what is actually going on. Fleishman-Hillard Inc.'s survey on investor relations and the Internet found that one out of eight executive respondents admitted that, at some point, they had seen material news break on-line before they had a chance to officially disseminate anything.

Businesses that ignore or underestimate the Internet and the IR function today do so at their peril. Eighty-four percent of businesses surveyed by Fleishman-Hillard agreed that the Internet is the most influential source of information for investors. The majority of businesses have implemented Internet crisis policies, in case Web communication comes back to haunt them. Such a crisis policy becomes crucial when you consider that almost three-quarters of the companies that responded to the survey admitted to being worried when they heard themselves being discussed in on-line message boards or in chatrooms. If your company has an official written crisis communication strategy, does it address the possibility of a crisis originating on-line?[20]

Don't be fooled—the possibility of an on-line crisis certainly exists. The experience of Sun Microsystem Inc. serves as a good example of how valuable an effective Web crisis policy can be when the unthinkable does happen. On October 18, 2000, the company was scheduled to send out a news release around noon, but the headline was accidentally released to the company's external Web site at 4 A.M. that morning. Luckily, Sun's IR director, Mark Paisley, was aware of the situation; by 7 A.M. he had called the legal department and asked the Nasdaq to stop trading, and by 10 A.M., Sun had sent out a press release calling for a 1:30 P.M. conference call with investors and the media. The headline had leaked to the outside press because Sun's Intranet typically "pushed" confidential documents onto the external server unless they were manually tagged. In the wake of the incident, the IR department now has its own secure server, minus the "auto-push" function. Paisley, in retrospect, offers sound advice to other IR departments: "To plan for success, you have to anticipate the worst."

Monitoring on-line rumors and initiating confident, swift responses to them is one way to follow Paisley's advice. Fleishman-Hillard senior VP and partner Anne LaChance explains, "While I would maintain that companies should never respond to rumors, what we're suggesting is a strong monitoring system that allows companies to anticipate the types of information investors are looking for instead of having them speculate in chatrooms." Having an extensive and detailed Frequently Asked Questions (FAQ) segment on your company Web site is a simple way to combat misperceptions about your company before they have a chance to spread.[21]

Earnings Webcasts, such as those offered by Cisco, also afford investors the opportunity to witness first-hand how companies' top executives handle themselves, and the general tone of their presentation and core messages—bringing an otherwise two-dimensional upper management vividly to life.

Initially, many of the first Webcasts were closed to individual investors, since companies worried that they would otherwise be opening up the floodgates for questions and demands to companies' investor relations departments. In reality, the reverse happened: More individual investors received the information they were seeking through the Webcast, resulting in fewer calls from investors.

Plus a Little Help from Some Friends

Getting your company's voice heard by the investor community requires help from traditional media, in addition to the Internet. In light of this, your organization must conscientiously build strong, personal relationships with reporters for financial media such as CNBC and *The Financial Times*.

Yahoo! Inc.'s annual meeting tactics are an example of how a company can fail to develop relationships, generating a lot of hostility between members of the media and the company. For the past five years, Yahoo! has barred reporters from its annual meeting, claiming that it does not want the media to take up the valuable space interested share-holders have prior claim to. The crucial point Yahoo! seemed to miss is that today's constituencies overlap more then ever, as evidenced in our discussion in Chapter 4 about the challenges of managing a reputation. Although not every reporter may be an investor, most will be more than willing to pose as one to get the inside scoop on a company at an annual meeting. If not, they can easily hop on-line to catch Webcast meetings. Whether the audience member is an investor or a reporter, the fact remains that turning interested spectators away from your company's meetings generates negative publicity. Former Council of Public Relations Firm's president Jack Bergen explains that turning anyone away from your company's public meetings—even disgruntled anti-management advocates—indicates to the public that your company's management is unwilling to have a civil dialogue about the issues at hand. The only conclusion most people will draw is that, ultimately, your company has something to hide.[22]

Even if your illogical hope is to avoid media presence entirely, this is no more than a dream. Financial Relations Board President Ted Pincus explains: "Some reporters have bought one share in a company just to gain admittance, but I don't see why they should have to go to that extent. From an IR perspective, it's poor policy."[23] Instead, Martha Stephens, the director of business development at the National Association of Investors Corp., suggests that a better strategy for Yahoo! would have been to invite press members but to closely monitor who turned up and whether any press member caused a disturbance.[24]

A persistent problem with members of the press attending a Yahoo! annual meeting could have been addressed by providing the press with real data to back up the company's response. The company missed the opportunity to put a positive spin on the episode by hosting a press con-ference for members of the press only, following the meeting, to answer any questions that still might be lingering in their minds.[25]

The media is not the only external body that you can draw on as a useful resource for investor relations. Shareholder turnover has been so high recently that the equivalent of an investment dating service has been created to help potential investors in your company with making a com-mitment to investing in your company. For example, Thompson Financial Services continually analyzes daily investor turnover, looking at over 1700 institutional shareholders and their portfolios. Thompson arranges matches and can help your company increase its appeal among investors. Such third-party credibility can often be a valuable help when you are try-ing to persuade prospective long-term shareholders to buy your stock.[26]

Communicating What Counts

Whether dealing with the media or customers, we all know that things out of sight are also often out of mind. This certainly holds true in the investment community as well: Companies who are out of transmission range when it comes to communicating with investors do not earn the respectful attention of investors. Using the right communication channel and frequency is pivotal when a company is building a successful investor-relations program. Too often companies tend to undercommunicate to the investment world. As Harvard Business School Professor John Kotter has commented, one of the biggest challenges faced by organizations is that "their messages are typically undercommunicated by a factor of 10."[27]

Part of the reason for this "undercommunication" is that your company cannot communicate its worth to the investment world on its own. Having people—namely key analysts—on Wall Street promote your company and stock is crucial. For example, Salomon Smith Barney telecommunications analyst Jack Grubman has been dubbed far and wide as a "guru" whose comments have immediate influence, both positive and negative, on stock prices. As one CEO phrased it to *Business Week* in May 2000, "[the man] is almost a demi-god." Similarly, claims have been made that Merrill Lynch's entertainment analyst Jessica Reif Cohen can, in her own words, "instantly add—or subtract—billions in market value."[28] And, at the height of the dot.com boom, Morgan Stanley's Mary Meeker was even profiled in the *New Yorker*, placing the world of analysts right before the eyes of America's intelligentsia.

Taming the Hype

Remember, however, that having too much analyst hype generated about your company can easily leave thousands of investors disgruntled if the analysts' predictions fall short of the mark, as they often do. Witness the *Wall Street Journal*'s contest between analysts' predictions and dart throwing as a way to pick stocks. The dart-throwing method often wins the contest. When the bull market emerged at the outset of the 1990s, thousands of people eagerly leapt onto the investing bandwagon. Enthusiasm was high, but patience was frighteningly low: Short-term performance was the primary concern of investors everywhere. Investing seemed to be a breeze, CNBC surpassed most sporting events in drawing television audiences, IPOs sold like proverbial hot cakes, and research analysts like Grubman and Meeker were trusted as the guides that would usher in prosperity for all.

When the gurus' predictions started to go sour, however, the stars in the financial analyst world began to crash and burn. Mary Meeker, the darling of the group, found herself vilified in a *Fortune* cover story with the title "Can We Ever Trust Wall St. Again?"[29]

And, as a Web posting about Salomon Smith Barney analyst Jack Grubman read: "The only way to view Grubman is that he makes price predictions based on INCOME ...HIS and not yours." Winstar Communications—offering local phone and Internet services to businesses—was one of the most conspicuous of Grubman's failed predictions. He staunchly supported them, helping them sell $1.2 billion in junk bonds, right up until April 18, 2001, when the company filed for Chapter 11 bankruptcy protection.[30]

With such accusations of analyst corruption flying about Wall Street, your company's upper management must ensure that they are presenting themselves to the investment community as honestly as possible. All too often, CEOs regard skewing reported earnings as par for the course. An anonymous but prominent *Fortune* 500 company employee tells the story of the wrath his CEO unleashed at the financial managers and lawyers when they informed him that the quarterly earnings he was about to announce were hardly accurate. The CEO screamed: "Stop fooling around with my numbers! The No. 1 job of management is to smooth out earnings."[31]

Show Me More than Just the Money

The motivation to make a profit drives investors just as it drives businesses themselves. But today you should be well aware that earnings and profit are only two of many motivational factors propelling people to invest in your company. In fact, an August 2001 Hill & Knowlton survey reveals that almost three-quarters of Americans consider social responsibility when making decisions about their investments.[32] *Fortune* cites social responsibility as one of the main criteria for its coveted Most Admired Company list.[33] Given this growing emphasis on ethics, it's surprising to find that most businesses aren't jumping at the chance to impress and win over investors. In fact, 53 percent of Americans still believe that U.S. companies are not performing adequately in the area of social responsibility. And 85 percent say that business does a poor job of balancing profit and public interest.[34]

The majority of investors are looking for signs that your company is visibly committed to a cause, both internally with its own vision and externally through involvement in philanthropic programs and the adoption of conscientious environmental practices, to name a few. Donations of money alone are not particularly compelling. Instead, your company should encourage employees to participate actively in local programs that will commit your company's time and energy in addition to whatever funds it donates. This commitment from your company and its people reinforces its vision as well as its credibility. Hill & Knowlton's director of worldwide corporate practice Harlan Teller reiterates that you must convincingly show, not just tell: "Companies need to show the results of their programs so the public can see it's more than just an act. Companies that get real results that impact the welfare of the community will lower [consumer and investor] skepticism."[35] Gaining a reputation as a socially and environmentally conscious company gives your company political leverage in times of need and thus grants it more leeway with investors when it does make inevitable blunders.[36]

These nonfinancial factors make all the difference in gaining the admiration of the investment world. Elizabeth Laurienzo, director of communications at Calvert Funds, explains the tie-breaking quality that socially responsible programs can have: "Given two identically appropriate companies, a philanthropic program would weigh more positively in a company's favor. Social investors call this positive screening—it always helps to have something in addition to just meeting the standards."[37]

Socially responsible programs can start a positive chain reaction that leads directly to increased shareholder value; the programs can be used as a recruitment tool for attracting bright and talented employees who, in turn, are likely to contribute enthusiastically to consumer satisfaction, driving profits and stock value upward.

Bringing Your Troops Onboard

Employee motivation can have an impact on much more than just the success of your social program. As we've discussed throughout the book, to be successful in communicating externally, your company must start by communicating well internally. Your employees must be familiar with, comfortable with, and vested in *all* of the messages your company is delivering to its other constituencies. If they are loyal to your company's vision, employees can assume the crucial role as the apostles of all your company stands for, and all you want to convey to the investment world. The public is more likely to believe messages delivered to them individually, by a personable individual, rather than the faceless proclamations of your entire organization.

Peter Kinder, president of the corporate social responsibility research firm Kinder, Lydenberg & Domini explains the value of involving employees in strong IR messaging: "Companies really need to use employees in a high-impact way—it's a lot easier to trust people than it is to trust big institutions. Most Americans are distrustful of big businesses. The more a company can humanize its...programs, the more the community will identify with the company."[38] Your company's upper management must consciously try to reinforce your organization's purpose, goals, and vision to ensure that these core messages are internalized before investors even begin to try to grasp them.

Getting Your House in Order First

Despite the increasing attention investors are paying to nontraditional areas such as corporate social responsibility, ultimately they still want your company to be a well-managed, well-oiled machine. Corporate philosophy is just one of the many criteria investors heed, along with your business model, employment standards, vision, and environmental practices. Investor Responsibility Research Center Social Issues Service Director Meg Voorhes said that "corporate philanthropy is one small part of the screening mix."[39] Once basic standards are met, however, nonfinancial entities can serve as a tiebreaker of sorts for investors trying to choose between various investment options. In the competitive investment environment of today, any edge your company can gain on its rivals should be maximized.[40]

Here Comes the Pitch

Contacting journalists to build relationships can give your company the edge necessary for garnering positive press and a strong reputation in the investment community. *PR Newswire* conducted research at the outset of 2000 analyzing the preferences and personalities of business news journalists, and offered the following tips for interacting with them:

- Establish contacts with reporters when you are not pitching a story, just to provide them with industry and/or trend infomation they might find valuable. This enables you to establish the journalist's beat and figure out upcoming stories that she will be covering. Most important, it establishes your credibility with the journalist and contributes to relationship building for the future time when you *will* phone with a story to pitch.
- Post a version of your press kits on a user-friendly Web site with all of the latest-breaking company literature.
- When pitching a story, have other sources readily available to help the reporter fill out the story.
- Keep press materials and the pitch itself short and crisp. Also be sure to keep your diction and phrasing clear—business editors and writers often attribute unclear writing to some kind of corporate cover-up.[41]

Why is a good media pitching strategy so crucial? Because in the investment world, media coverage is the most valuable form of currency. Generating good press as well as positive analyst reports about your company will enable it to attract more customers, capital, suppliers, as well as future acquirers. Zacks Investment Research unveiled statistics that drive this point home; between 1985 and 2000, stocks that attracted coverage by three or more analysts fared 37 percent better over the ensuing six months than did those stocks that were overlooked. Be sure not to forget that publicity is only publicity because it is selective and is won by only a few companies at a time. As C. Anthony Rider, chief financial officer of Astronics, a $50 million electronics and paper-packaging maker, explains: "You're competing for the investment dollar."[42] Your company's story must appeal to the investment world more than the next guy's, or you can't expect to win the coveted shelf space for which everyone is fighting.[43]

Track Your Success

Once you begin to implement new communication strategies with investors, be sure to keep track of what parts of your IR program are working and which are falling flat. Ways to track success include comparing your company to its competitor using an index of some sort (the *WSJ* publishes annual rankings). Nonfinancial measurement tools can also be telling, including employee turnover, customer satisfaction, and process improvement.[44] Happy customers demonstrate loyalty for a company, rave about it openly, and, consequently, drive profits upward, translating into high stock prices and greater shareholder value. A 2001 American Customer Satisfaction Index survey of companies across most industries revealed that those scoring in the top 50 percent in overall customer satisfaction created over $24 billion in shareholder value, while the bottom 50 percent created only $14 billion, almost half. Employees play a pivotal role in customer satisfaction: Pay attention to this direct correlation between loyal employees and shareholder value. Tracking your progress before and after key interactions with investors determines what exactly you are doing right and wrong, thus helping to streamline your IR strategy and pushing your company along the path to success.[45]

CONCLUSION

Keeping these guidelines in mind, remember that no two IR programs will be identical, as they are contingent on a company's type, industry, and size. While investors as a constituency demonstrate some distinct characteristics, such as short-term goals, they have a lot in common with the other constituencies we have discussed throughout the book—from consumers to employees. Thus the way your company approaches investor relations should be similar to the way your company communicates with other constituencies. As with any group, communicating with institutional and individual investors should rest on a clear explanation of your company's vision and mission, a thorough grasp of the external environment in which your company is situated, the development of the appropriate message to target the constituency at hand, and the recording of all successful efforts and feedback from interactions for future reference. And, in today's world, this means the successful integration of the Internet as a key communication channel.

Although Woody Allen claimed that 90 percent of life is just showing up, your company needs not only to show up but also to become an identifiable, confident face that the investment world can look to and—above all—trust. That trust is born of the stability your company can generate by holding fast to its core vision in both good times and bad. As Jim Collins and Jerry Porras insist, "visionary companies display a remarkable resiliency, an ability to bounce back from adversity."[46] This resiliency can easily become the very lifeboat many investors are searching for in the turbulent sea of twenty-first-century investing.

CHAPTER

MANAGING OUTREACH TO THE COMMUNITY: GOVERNMENT RELATIONS AND CORPORATE PHILANTHROPY

A T THE BEGINNING OF THE NEW MILLENNIUM, we are far removed from the laissez-faire environment that marked the height of the robber barons' power more than a century ago. Today, no matter what business you're in, you are subject to government regulations, be they federal, state, or local. You need to comply with zoning laws, with employment regulations for maintaining a safe work environment, and with tax laws specific to your business. Even a small business such as a local restaurant needs to comply with legal requirements—about sufficient parking, liquor licenses, sanitary regulations, among other things. At the other end of the spectrum, huge multinational corporations such as the pharmaceutical, tobacco, and oil and gas industries routinely grapple with complex government regulations that are specific to each industry as well as those that cut across all businesses. All of these businesses must pay attention to how they communicate with the government.

Historically, as U.S. presidents have succeeded one another, there has been a shift in the amount and kind of regulation imposed on business. During the Clinton years, the North American Free Trade Agreement (NAFTA) was signed, and tariffs were all but eliminated between the United States, Canada, and Mexico. As a result, trade expanded, and companies engaged in North American import-export businesses got a boost. On the other hand, pollution-producing companies, such as heavy manufacturing and oil and gas, were subjected to increased regulation, including a number of regulations that President Clinton signed on his last day in office.

With the election of George W. Bush, it became immediately evident that pollution-producing companies were going to get a break, and big business, more generally, would be favored: In less than two months in office, President Bush reneged on a campaign promise to regulate carbon dioxide emissions, a move that favored coal and utility companies; voted to release more public land to mining and drilling, pleasing the oil and natural gas industry; and signed a repeal of a workplace safety rule that could have cost companies millions of dollars.[1] During his first five months in office, President Bush suspended environmental investigations of eleven utilities and four refineries for suspected violation of the Clean Air Act.[2]

Regardless of the party that holds the White House, however, regulation is a fact of business life. Moreover, antibusiness elements—whether congressional representatives, the White House, or special interest groups—are permanent forces in political debates about regulating business.

Government and business have traditionally been adversaries in the United States as business tries to keep government off its back, and government tries to manage the needs of all citizens to provide the greatest good for the greatest number. Some contend that Americans have used government to control business ever since the first pilgrims landed on Plymouth Rock in the seventeenth century. This is not to say that the relationship between government and business is always adversarial; increasingly, business is attempting to develop cooperative alliances with government agencies, but on balance, the struggles between government and business have been fierce, and the costs to business, some would argue, are greater in the United States than in most Western nations. In fact, the U.S. government has created more regulations stipulating what constitutes white-collar criminal behavior on the part of businesspeople than any other industrial democracy.[3] Today, corporations have more interest than ever before in finding ways to manage relations with government at the federal, state, and local level.

This chapter begins with a discussion of the government's long history of regulating business, giving special attention to the highly regulated tobacco industry. We then make a 180-degree turn and look at corporations' attempts to manage their relationships with government through alliances, lobbying, and PACs (political action committees), and consider the efforts of government affairs departments to influence government on behalf of companies. Finally, we look at business's attempts to shape the decisions of local governments, and the ways in which companies manage their relationships to local and global citizenry, especially through corporate philanthropy. We move, then, in this chapter from government to community relations, recognizing the need for companies to become good corporate citizens who give back to the communities in which they operate and to the individual citizens who can affect governmental decisions.

Before considering these issues, however, we'd like you to answer the following questions about your organization and its relationship to government:

- In what ways is government involved in your business? What are the most important links?
- How does your company manage government relations? For instance, do you have a government affairs department? If so, what does it do?
- Are the company's efforts successful? If so, how? If not, why not?
- In what ways does your company reach out to the larger society as a good corporate citizen? How effective are these efforts in serving the company's goals while helping communities?

The most powerful way that government can influence activities in business is through regulation. Government regulation was first applied to industries where the cost of entry was so great that some sort of monopoly seemed inevitable. In these cases, regulation was meant to replace Adam Smith's "invisible hand" in protecting consumers from high prices, bad service, and discrimination. Let's look now at how government uses regulation to influence, if not altogether control, more and more of the basic business functions ranging from setting prices to extending market share.

GOVERNMENT REGULATION OF BUSINESS

Today, government is involved throughout the life of a business. For instance, many enterprises cannot begin operations until they receive a license that is obtained by going through regulatory agencies such as the Federal Communications Commission (FCC) or the Food and Drug Administration (FDA). Once an enterprise has been approved, the products the company makes must be inspected and approved by the government as well. Clothes, for example, must meet the Wool Labeling Act standards, and drugs must be approved by the FDA. The Consumer Product Safety Commission is involved in setting up safety standards for consumer products, and most products must pass this "test" or never be allowed out in the market.[4] More recently, the U.S. Patents and Trademark Office as well as Congress and the President are considering the need for regulation of cloning technology and embryonic stem cell research.

Although government has an impact on nearly every area of the private sector, government's influence and control vary across industries and evolve as society's values change. Transportation, pharmaceuticals, tobacco, communications, and utility companies are heavily influenced by the government. Strict regulation of these and other businesses may be the result of fear of monopolies and trusts, which has been a pervasive attitude in America for over 100 years, and is dramatically evident today in the government's case against Microsoft for monopolistic practices.

The Development of a Regulatory Environment

In 1877, the Supreme Court handed down decisions on what became collectively known as the Granger Cases. These cases involved legislation by Midwest states to control the railroads. One of the main cases, *Munn v. Illinois*, dealt with the refusal of a warehouse firm, Munn and Scott, to apply for a state license and to be controlled. The Court said that Munn and Scott had to comply with the ruling to stay in that business. The company conceded, thereby becoming one of the first private businesses to be regulated by the state. In addition, Munn and Scott came to symbolize the growing American businesses that had begun to overstep their bounds and were in need of governmental regulation.[5]

The largest of such business giants were the railroads. The railroads opened new opportunities for people all over the United States as never before. They triumphed over all rival forms of land transportation and, within half a century, the rail system became the lifeline of a growing industrial society in the United States. However, the railroads also presented the country with enormous problems. Competition, which according to laissez-faire, was meant to regulate business, failed to regulate the railroads. As a result, corrupt practices began to characterize the industry.

For instance, many communities were served by two or more railroads competing for traffic, and competition led to rate cutting and widespread use of rebates. Discrimination occurred when freight rates and passenger fares were cut by rival railroads, while the rates and fares between, to, or from noncompetitive points served by only one railroad were not reduced. Further, rates were reduced for certain preferred shippers but not for the average farmer or merchant. In other cases, lower rates would be given on certain types of traffic moving in large quantities with regularity, while rates on traffic moving in smaller quantities and with less regularity were never reduced. These conditions resulted in numerous public complaints. At the height of their success, the railroads failed to solve their own problems and thus government was forced to intervene.

Finally, in 1886 in *Wabash, St. Louis & Pacific Railway v. Illinois*, the railroads were charged with the "tapering principle," charging higher rates for short hauls than long hauls. The Supreme Court, however, decreed that Illinois could not interfere with commerce between states (as mentioned in the Constitution) and thus the case became an issue in the federal courts.[6]

In the following year, Congress's passage of the Act to Regulate Commerce, which established the Interstate Commerce Commission (ICC), began the federal government's regulation of business. Three years later came another crucial regulatory bill, the Sherman Antitrust Act (1890).[7] From antitrust laws to the huge number of environmental bills passed every day, the federal government has continued to establish new agencies and laws to address problems that arise in society that are attributed to business.

Regulatory agencies have evolved into sophisticated organizations through the years. During the two world wars and the Great Depression of the 1930s, federal powers fluctuated enormously as the economic needs of the nation changed. For instance, Franklin Roosevelt's New Deal gave government huge amounts of power to regulate. The Securities and Exchange Commission (SEC) was created to stabilize financial markets and the National Labor Relations Board (NLRB) was given the power to remedy labor problems and issues. Radio, television, and telephones were regulated by the Federal Communications Commission (FCC), and the airlines were controlled by the Civil Aeronautics Board (CAB). Despite the growth of regulation in the first half of the twentieth century, most businesses were affected by relatively few federal regulations until the mid-1960s; in the latter half of the twentieth century, government regulation expanded in the areas of environmental protection, taxation, energy, health, safety, and technology policy.[8]

In recent years, technology policy has been on the government's radar screen, especially because of the privacy issues raised by Internet usage. According to a recent report on the global impact of the Internet by the UCLA Center for Communication Policy,[9] the privacy of individuals tops the list of concerns that respondents have about the use of the Internet. A second survey confirms and extends this finding: People express the most fear about open access to bank information, credit card numbers, and information requests about their children, political affiliation, medical history, income, and salary. Moreover, many believe that business alone cannot solve this problem; government needs to intervene.[10] Use of the Internet shows no sign of decreasing, and, as public demand grows for government protection of individual privacy, we are likely to see new federal policy in this area.

As we'd expect, American industry has complained that the mounting regulations hurt American business, especially with overseas competitors, who, according to American companies, are not subjected to these regulatory bills. Thus, American products are often more expensive than foreign goods, and the American economy has suffered as a result. Further, the bureaucracy and paperwork needed to get through regulatory agencies delay release of new products. This is particularly detrimental to American pharmaceutical companies.

Government regulation has created a lag in the release of new drugs, especially in the cardiovascular, diuretic, respiratory, antibacterial, and gastrointestinal areas. Moreover, the process of getting approval for new drugs from the FDA is so arduous and costly that it presents a significant—and sometimes insuperable—barrier to the business prospects for start-up companies in the pharmaceutical industry. As one venture capitalist has told us, "As soon as we see that the firm needs FDA approval, we're likely to cut off discussion for funds."

The pharmaceutical industry as a whole has been hard hit in recent decades, but the most publicized government battle against industry since the 1990s is the Microsoft case. Accused of monopolistic practices by the federal government and many state governments, the company was first subjected to investigations by the Federal Trade Commission (FTC) and the Justice Department's Antitrust Division, and to a series of trials that began in the mid-1990s.[11] The trials ended in contested decisions that created lots of negative media attention for the company and led to new motions, new appeals, and more bad press. Fueled by a group of rival companies, government attacks on Microsoft focused on the company's alleged attempts to cut off the competition and stifle product innovation. Even with the shifts from a Republican (George H. Bush) to a Democratic (Bill Clinton) and back again to a Republican (George W. Bush) administration, the company remains on the government radar screen. In all likelihood, there will be curbs placed on its contractual agreements and uses of its industry-standard Windows operating system. Through it all, the company's corporate communication department has been hard pressed to get constituencies to see Microsoft as a corporate do-gooder in the community and as a customer-friendly organization that sells high-quality products at a fair price.

As we saw in Chapter 2, the tobacco industry was one of the first to use communications systematically to market its products in the first half of the twentieth century. For example, the industry used Bernays's ability to tap into the social values of the time—the upsurge in women's independence in the 1920s—to expand its customer base to include women. Ironically, this industry, which earlier pioneered the use of public relations to market its products, has failed to fully analyze the implications of the public's growing concern about tobacco's health hazards and to reach out to the government and the public in ways that would acknowledge the evidence but market the product. On the other hand, this may be a case where the damage caused by the product makes an effective corporate communication campaign either impossible or deceptive.

Even though the pharmaceutical industry and the high-tech giant Microsoft claim that regulation has hurt business and even stymied the creation of new initiatives, no industry has been hit harder than tobacco.

Regulations Affect the Tobacco Industry

All three branches of government—Congress, regulatory agencies, and the courts—have had a role in the government's attempts to regulate the tobacco industry. Although tobacco has had some significant successes over the years, on balance government restriction is the bigger winner, especially since the health dangers of cigarette smoking are widely acknowledged, and society increasingly values the role of government in protecting public health.

In the early 1960s, the American Cancer Society and a number of private health organizations began urging the government to take notice of the relationship between smoking and disease, and to take action. In 1962, a panel of 10 scientists was formed and concluded in January of 1964 that smoking was related to lung cancer, chronic bronchitis, emphysema, heart disease, and cancer of the larynx. The FTC announced that it would hold hearings to establish new regulations for labeling and advertising of cigarettes and in June of that year they issued regulations requiring all cigarette packages and advertisements to add warning labels about the health hazards of smoking.

The tobacco industry reacted first by agreeing to the regulation of package labeling if the industry would be protected against further advertising requirements and state regulation. At the same time, the industry decided to challenge the FTC's ruling by appealing to Congress rather than to the courts. To accomplish this end, a committee of tobacco advocates was formed consisting of six prominent lawyers, one of whom, Abe Fortas, was a close personal friend of President Johnson's (and later a Supreme Court nominee). The committee represented the tobacco industry at the FTC and congressional hearings.

The tobacco industry had some advantages in Congress. The industry was important in the South and thus the committee could count on southern sympathies. Also, since the issue involved further governmental regulation of business, most Republicans would be opposed to it. Broadcasting companies also did not like the regulation because they feared that it would cause a decrease in revenues since tobacco advertising would be lost. With all of these advantages, it is not surprising that the tobacco industry was successful in its efforts. As one member of Congress stated, "Let's face it...When you combine the money and power of the tobacco and liqueur interests with advertising agencies, newspapers, radio and television...it is too much political muscle involved to expect much accomplishment."[12]

The congressional hearings were a success for the tobacco industry. Although a bill requiring warning labels was approved, all that it required was that the warning "appear in conspicuous and legible type."[13] More importantly, restrictions on advertising were suspended for five years. In addition, Congress prohibited both state and local governments from enacting legislation that would affect the labeling and advertising of cigarettes.

Despite the series of decisions about tobacco, the debate was far from over. The public's concern about the health hazards created by the industry and the public's push for more government intervention in the industry's practices had just begun. Five years after the initial ruling by Congress to keep tobacco ads on the air, Congress completely banned tobacco advertisements from both radio and television.

Although in 1965 Congress prohibited the requirement of health warnings in cigarette ads, in 1970, they ruled that the tobacco industry could not advertise at all. The FTC had issued a report to the government recommending this action be taken, and this time, Congress agreed. Another factor that went against the tobacco industry was that the FCC had gotten involved. The FCC decided to apply what they term the "fairness doctrine" to cigarette commercials. This required television and radio stations to provide airtime for antismoking advertisements. The National Association of Broadcasters (NAB) was appalled, describing this action as a dangerous intrusion by government into business, and the tobacco industry appealed the decision in the U.S. Court of Appeals for the District of Columbia. Unfortunately for the tobacco industry, the courts ruled in favor of the commission and shortly after the decision antismoking ads began to appear.

With public opinion influenced by the ads, as well as the increased influence of antismoking organizations, the tobacco industry lost the battle and the Cigarette Advertising Act of 1970 was passed. All tobacco ads were banned from television and radio as of January 2, 1971.

In the 1990s and the new millennium, tobacco has once again been in the spotlight, and the victory once again seesaws between government and industry. In 1996, attorneys general (AGs) from 40 states negotiated a settlement with the industry—subject to congressional approval—that included the following concessions:

- Annual payment by the tobacco industry of $10 billion initially and then rising to $15 billion to be divided among the AGs , public health groups, and a fund to pay for damage claims from sick smokers.
- $50 billion up front in return for a ban on future punitive damages awards against the tobacco companies.
- $2 billion per year for programs to help people stop smoking and to get medical treatment.
- Requirement that tobacco companies reduce smoking among youths by 67 percent within the next 10 years; otherwise up to $2 billion a year in penalties.
- A ban on advertising on billboards, the Internet, and sports promotions.
- A ban on cigarette vending machines.
- The need for tobacco products to be sold behind the counter.
- Tobacco companies required to pay for antitobacco ads.
- Tobacco ads limited to text only and in black and white, except in adult establishments.
- Elimination of all human images like the Marlboro Man and Joe Camel in tobacco ads.
- Larger and sterner warning labels on cigarettes like "Smoking Can Kill You" and "Smoking Causes Cancer."
- No smoking allowed in public places, workplaces, fast food restaurants.

- Need for cigarette producers to disclose ingredients and additives.
- Nicotine regulated by the FDA as a drug. This means that the FDA can reduce the amount of nicotine in cigarettes and completely ban it by 2009.[14,15]

Yet Congress had to approve this settlement, and conditions shifted in favor of tobacco in 1998 and 2000. Although the states and the tobacco companies did reach an independent settlement, in 1998, the Senate defeated a $500 billion tobacco bill that would have given the FDA authority to regulate cigarettes and to raise the price. The money collected would have helped pay for health research and antismoking advertising.[16] In March 2000, the Supreme Court declared that the FDA does not have the authority to regulate tobacco under current laws.[17]

In 2001, several bills were being discussed in Congress that would impose restrictions on tobacco, including the *Davis* bill and the *Ganske* bill. The *Davis* bill would grant the FDA authority to regulate tobacco, but not as a drug or medical device; allow the FDA to adopt standards for the ingredients in tobacco products, as long as these standards would make the product legal for adult consumption; prohibit the FDA from outlawing a class of tobacco products (for example, cigarettes and chewing tobacco) and from outlawing the use of nicotine in these products; require manufacturers to reveal the ingredients in tobacco products to the public; and restrict use of labels like "light" or "low tar." The *Ganske* bill is more restrictive. It would give the FDA authority to regulate tobacco as a drug, allow the FDA to adopt standards for ingredients—without limitations, allow the FDA to ban a class of tobacco products, and grant the FDA the authority to require ingredient disclosure with the latitude the agency exercises with other foods and drugs.[18]

The lineup supporting each bill cuts across the typical government-industry antagonism. The Philip Morris company has joined forces with congressional representatives from Missouri and Virginia to cosponsor the less restrictive Davis bill. In response to questions about the company's apparently strange alliance, Philip Morris's associate general counsel Mark Berlind said, "Essentially we have concluded that regulation will be good for our business and good for our company. When you have a product like we do that is addictive and that harms people…there ought to be appropriate regulation."[19] Public health advocates in favor of stricter regulation argue that Philip Morris supports the Davis bill because the bill has no real clout; other tobacco companies like RJ Reynolds and Brown & Williamson—which are against the Davis bill too—claim that Philip Morris favors the bill because it would strengthen the company's competitive position by limiting the introduction of new products.

In the new millennium, there have also been continued aggressive attempts to extend restrictions on smoking—banning smoking from outdoor venues frequented by the public and developing worldwide regulation of tobacco. Lobbied by a local antismoking advocacy group, the San Diego City Council has prohibited smoking near playgrounds, and the American Lung Association of San Diego and Imperial counties plans to lobby family tourist destinations like the San Diego Zoo and SeaWorld to ban smoking as well. The outdoor ban has also been approved by municipalities in Texas, Hawaii, Massachusetts, and New York.[20]

Attempts to restrict smoking have moved into the global arena as well. For the first time, the World Health Organization (WHO) has launched an effort to create an international treaty restricting smoking. Eighty percent of smokers live in developing countries, and 4 million people die each year from tobacco-related illnesses. As a result, the WHO would like to see government regulations like taxes on cigarettes and restrictions on advertising imposed worldwide.[21]

In light of the great impact of government on the business affairs of industries like pharmaceuticals and tobacco, business realized the need to have a say in activities on Capitol Hill and at lower levels of government. Let's look now at how companies try to influence government.

BUSINESS BEGINS TO MANAGE ITS RELATIONSHIP TO GOVERNMENT

In recent decades, as government intervention has continued to grow, so has the proliferation of organized efforts to present the views of business in Congress, the White House, regulatory agencies, and state and local governmental entities. Business employs several approaches to manage its relationship to government, including coalition building and CEO activism, lobbying and political action committees (PACs).

Coalition Building and CEO Activism

As government regulation of business intensified in the late 1960s and 1970s, business increased its efforts to exert political influence on decision makers through coalition building. Prior to this move, many businesses took a solo approach to advocacy. As a result, when a particular company was in trouble, it would have to fight alone to put forward its point of view even though it often was fighting a battle that affected many other corporations in the same industry or—for that matter—in all businesses.

As a result of these shared concerns, companies in the same industry began to band together in trade associations to represent industry issues—for commercial airlines, for pharmaceuticals, for tobacco—and to create a presence in government beyond what any individual company might be able to achieve. Businesses across the board began forming coalitions, particularly in the 1970s, because the form of governmental regulation changed. While in previous years regulations affected one or a small number of industries, new legislation concerning consumer safety and labor reform affected most, if not all, businesses. Businesses worked together to battle legislation through lobbying, which is a communication function. When one company would be affected by new regulations, it would find other firms that were in a similar situation and form ad hoc committees with these firms. Having formed such alliances, companies now had more support in congressional districts and states. Such coalition building was especially effective in combating the consumer protection agency, labor-law reform, and in arguing for rollbacks in the powers of the FTC.

In the early 1970s, companies also established the Business Roundtable, formed by a merger of three smaller ad hoc groups: the Construction Users Anti-Inflation Roundtable, the March Group (a group of CEOs who wanted to increase the political influence of business), and the Labor Law Study Committee. Because the members are the CEOs of 150 major corporations—and the group is restricted exclusively to CEOs—the Roundtable's visibility and clout are substantial. Enjoying a reputation based on the cumulative prestige of its membership, the Roundtable also manages to act quickly in times of crisis. One week after the September 11th attack on the United States, the group organized a conference call of the membership out of which came a letter sent to President Bush and signed by the group's Chairman, John T. Dillon (CEO of International Paper Company), urging the President to lead broad-based initiatives to stimulate the national economy.[22]

As members of the Business Roundtable, but also individually, CEOs are making their presence felt in government circles. This is especially important for heavily regulated industries such as many public utilities whose customers also elect the government officials who oversee the utilities' operations; however, the need for a strong CEO presence in the halls of government goes beyond companies in government-regulated monopolies.

CEOs in everything from start-ups to multinational corporations can find that their most memorable, high-impact presentations are the ones they make on Capitol Hill or in the courts. On July 20, 2000, Jeff Katz, the President and CEO of Orbitz—a small online flight reservation company—spoke with passion and clarity to a U.S. Senate committee investigating the company's practices, which were brought into question by the significantly larger, more established duopoly of Sabre/Travelocity and Microsoft/Expedia. Katz successfully portrayed the company as an underdog, a version of the "American Dream" that is so powerful in creating good reputations. He used this quintessential American story to enter the formidable competitive arena of online travel services, providing the traveling public with cheaper fares and access to more airlines than the larger competition. He also managed to explain the advanced technology his company possesses in terms that senators could relate to: Orbitz, he claimed, could help them find the most convenient and cheapest flight to get from City A to City B.

By contrast to Katz's polished performance, Bill Gates, one of the most famous CEOs to speak before Congress, performed very poorly during the hearings in the 1990s about Microsoft's business practices. Gates, who testified in the early 1990s, seemed to be self-absorbed and indirect, speaking down into his notes rather than to the audience and dressed too casually, even sloppily, for the occasion. Later in the decade, his videotaped deposition taken for the Justice Department's case against Microsoft for monopolistic activities showed him to be ill-informed about company activities—therefore lacking credibility—and arrogant or defensive in his responses when asked to comment on Microsoft's strong-arm tactics to squelch the competition.

By 2000, however, Gates's appearances before the public were very different. He seemed to be open, well groomed, able to engage conversationally. A more human Gates had been crafted. Even Microsoft—which, according to one critic, used to think the only Washington was a state in the Northwest—has learned the necessity of its leadership representing the company in the other Washington—D.C. As we will see later in this chapter, the Gates foundation, which became quite visible while the company was being attacked by some of its competitors and investigated by state and federal governments, may now be the former CEO's greatest activism—albeit less direct than appearing in Congress to defend his company—in seeking public and government support.

As powerful as coalition-building and CEO activism can be, often a firm decides to enlist lobbyists to represent the company's position and provide a mechanism for keeping track of shifts in trends on Capitol Hill.

Lobbying to Make a Difference

A company hires lobbyists to gain direct access to key political decision makers, and, once contact is established, to express its views, influence votes, and encourage modification of bills to either favor its business or reduce the impact of restrictive legislation. This last point is worth underscoring. Sometimes companies are not successful in changing a vote on a bill, but can influence the language of a bill such that its negative impact on a company is delayed or penalties for failing to comply with it are reduced. For instance, companies can be given more time to comply with environmental laws or with employee safety rules. Finally, in the case of some industries like defense or other government contractors, companies hire lobbyists to impress the customer who *is* the government. In these instances, there is a powerful overlap between the two constituencies.

Companies intensify their lobbying efforts during pivotal moments in government's decision-making cycles. To get a better sense of what this looks like, let's consider the role of lobbyists in a competition for a new generation of military planes in what may end up being the largest military contract in U.S. history.[23] The two contestants for the $200 billion contract were Lockheed Martin and Boeing—two giants in the defense industry where the government is, in fact, the customer. The loser, according to some analysts, would be forced out of the tactical fighter business.

The early fall of 2001 was peak season for lobbyists' involvement in both companies: The Pentagon was getting ready to award contracts; Congress was preparing to decide on the size of the Pentagon budget; and Secretary of Defense Donald H. Rumsfeld was completing his budget proposal, which included his recommendations for a number of billion-dollar programs. Both Lockheed Martin and Boeing hired top-name lobbyists. Haley Barbour, former chairman of the Republican National Committee, represented Lockheed Martin, and Rudy de Leon, Deputy Secretary of Defense during the Clinton administration, championed Boeing's cause. Not surprisingly, these lobbyists were former government insiders, a role that gave them greater credibility and access to Congress. In addition, lobbying reports indicated that Lockheed and Boeing would spend more than $10 million on lobbying in 2001, one-sixth of the lobbying budget for the entire defense industry. On October 26, 2001, the government announced that Lockheed Martin was the winner.

Of course, the companies' lobbying efforts—like any other effort to influence government—come into play in a larger corporate communication campaign that includes promotional videos of successful experimental plane flights sent to lawmakers and on-site demonstrations for them; corporate advertising, especially in the *Washington Post*, the "hometown" paper for Congress; contact with CNN to get the station to show their videos; and efforts on the part of trade associations and company employees to influence congressional representatives in the districts where production of the planes or parts is likely to occur.

Companies engage in lobbying not only on the federal level but also on the state and local level. Many companies have found that grassroots lobbying is particularly powerful because it can mobilize opinion out in the districts. Congressional representatives often comment on how effective it is to understand the opinions of those they represent. Grassroots lobbyists can help shape those opinions.

Some of the most effective and sophisticated grassroots lobbying has been conducted by the Chamber of Commerce. With many state and local chapters of the Chamber of Commerce across the country, and with many corporations being members, the Chamber of Commerce had a wide base to work from. By 1980, it had also created 2700 "Congressional Action Committees," which consisted of executives who were personally acquainted with their senators and representatives. These executives were kept informed about events in Washington through bulletins from the Washington office and were responsible for keeping in touch with their representatives and contacting them when called upon. This method of lobbying has been very effective: The Chamber of Commerce can do research quickly on the likely impact of a bill and then mobilize a grassroots campaign in time to affect the outcome of the vote.[24]

Political Action Committees (PACs)

Campaign finance reform, which legalized the formation of political action committees (PACs) in the 1970s, created a new opportunity for business participation in government through financial support of members of Congress. PACs are created to raise and spend money to support the election of candidates that a company favors because these candidates tend to share the company's concerns and interests. The PACs themselves can give only $5000 annually to a candidate's committee for a given election, but can raise and disseminate up to $5000 from each employee who contributes to the fund.

Besides supporting specific candidates, PACs offer many other benefits to a company. They can increase employees' political awareness, educate them about issues that affect their employer's well being and future, and encourage them to get involved directly in politics. For example, in an internally distributed pamphlet on PACs issued by the government affairs department of TRW (a large, diversified corporation with businesses in automotive parts, defense, aerospace, and advanced computing systems), employees are told how a PAC contribution will dramatically increase their influence on candidates, give them an opportunity to exert influence beyond the local or state level, and provide them with timely information about political developments that may affect TRW's future. Employees are even told that they may be invited to attend a political function when their legislator is present. Used especially by the larger *Fortune* 500 companies, which are the prime target of government regulation,[25] PACS are intended to give companies access to candidates, and companies tend to contribute to both incumbents and challengers to make sure that this will happen.

PACs, as well as other forms of political involvement of business, encourage corporations to coordinate their political activities and often to cooperate with other firms. In addition to establishing PACs, hiring lobbyists, forming coalitions with like-minded companies, and getting the CEO involved in influencing government, since the 1970s companies have been opening Washington offices and working to develop a sophisticated government affairs function. We look at that function in the next section.

The Modern Government Affairs Office

What constitutes an effective government affairs office today? To answer this question, let's look at one of the best: Sears Roebuck and Co.'s department, run by Penny Cate, vice president of government affairs.[26] As we follow her story, keep several things in mind:

- Her planning process, especially the establishment of a set of priority issues and the steps taken to address them
- Her management of relations to both external and internal constituencies
- Any approaches she uses that would work well in your own organization

Notice how Cate transformed the government affairs function from being a low-visibility and ad hoc function to a highly visible one engaged in purposive communication. In sum, her approach to government relations is strategic.

When Cate took over as vice president of government affairs, the department, as she described it, had no direction, inadequate resources, and no overall strategy. As a result, she began by doing a SWOT (strengths, weaknesses, opportunities, threats) analysis of Sears with a focus on the communication strategy needed for managing the influence of government on the company's business goals and practices. As you may be aware, a SWOT analysis is routinely used to develop a company's overall strategy by assessing a company's strengths (S) and weaknesses (W) against the opportunities (0) and threats (T) it finds in the competitive environment. Here, Cate applied this type of analysis to the company's *communication* strategy with the focus on public affairs. Her work resulted in a communication plan for influencing legislation at all levels of government, with primary emphasis on the federal and state level but with some attention to Chicago, where Sears has its headquarters. The plan identifies the issues Sears needs to address in descending order of importance.

On the first tier are issues that Sears needs to influence actively and for which the company needs to take a leadership role in industry efforts that champion the company's position. On Sears's top priority list are issues under federal or state jurisdiction that pose the greatest threats and opportunities: collection of taxes on Internet sales (federal and/or state), redefinition of maintenance agreements (state), changes in OSHA regulations (federal), and flexible use of customer information (federal and/or state).

Sears would like the government to collect taxes on Internet sales. The company's competitors who engage in online sales have the advantage of their customers not having to pay state taxes; by contrast, Sears's in-store customers who buy the same product have to pay state taxes. As a result, Sears favors imposing sales taxes regardless of location to remove the current competitive advantage for remote sellers.

Another top-priority issue concerns maintenance agreements. Some states define maintenance agreements for things like appliances as a type of insurance policy. Once categorized in this way, the seller of such a policy must be a licensed insurance agent, a position that requires special training. Sears believes that the intention of the law is not that product maintenance should have to be sold by a licensed insurance agent. The company wants the law changed to allow Sears sales reps to sell maintenance policies without being insurance agents. Also of top priority is the company's interest in the repeal or amendment of a recent expansion of OSHA regulations that mandate ergonomic training for virtually the entire Sears workforce and require the company to provide paid leave for up to three months for certain vaguely defined conditions. Yet another important issue concerns the privacy of consumer information. The company wants to obtain and use customer information for marketing and other business needs.

On the second tier—issues for which the company participates in industry coalition efforts—we find a local issue: opposing municipal minimum wage ordinances that the company feels artificially inflate wages within small geographic areas and make doing business there too costly. For example, Santa Monica, California, is considering a living wage that will cost one Sears store $650,000 a year in increased wages. On the second tier, we also saw support for President George W. Bush's broad-based individual tax reform package in 2001, which provided a tax rebate for families at all income levels. The rebate, Cate believes, may help generate increased disposable income and additional retail sales. On the third tier—issues the company monitors for opportunities—we find, among other things, support for legislation that strengthens shoplifting and employee theft laws and raises the allowable fees that can be collected for bad checks.

The department's primary focus is on the top 10 issues on the Sears priority list. For these, Cate asks, "Are the issues moving or dead?" To answer this question, she relies on a network of relationships that the company has built with members of Congress and their staff, lobbyists, and trade associations to which Sears belongs. Cate's department determines which members of Congress are concerned with the top-priority issues that affect Sears, who has leadership of key committees, and who has lots of Sears people in their district. Of the 50 or so members of Congress who match these criteria, Sears tries to influence them directly by giving political contributions, initiating meetings to explain the company's top-priority issues, and offering facility tours and opportunities to meet with the CEO. This approach is taken at the state level as well.

Sears wants a direct relationship with key members of Congress rather than relying primarily on lobbyists or trade associations. "It's fine to use lobbyists," says Cate, "but Sears needs a personal face. I need to go to political fundraisers, to be there myself to present the check to the Congress person. Just giving a contribution is not enough. When you depend too much on lobbyists, *they* have the relationship with Congress, *not the company.* What if you want to change lobbyists?" Cate emphasizes the importance of companies having their own strategic network in Congress independent of the lobbyists they hire: "I tell the candidate who the company is and why we are supporting him, for instance, because of his position on bankruptcy legislation," says Cate. "Sears has a credit card division. If it's easy for people to declare bankruptcy, the company is left holding the bag, including paying state tax on products the individual has purchased with the Sears credit card but never pays for."

Besides cultivating relationships with Congress, Sears uses lobbyists and trade associations at the federal and state level, the National Retail Federation at the federal level, and state retail associations in each of the

46 states where Sears has a presence. Since Sears has its headquarters in Chicago, the company is quite active in the Illinois Retail Association.

Relationship-building has an internal component as well. Cate informs senior management about the importance of top-priority issues, showing their relevance to the company's bottom line. In fact, for some of the communication specialists on staff in the government affairs department, "internal lobbying" is their main task. They explain the company's key issues to employees at all levels of the organization, request individual contributions to the company's PAC, and urge employees to write to local and national politicians on behalf of the company.

Although government affairs (also called public affairs) is a set of activities that is more important in some industries than others, virtually every company can benefit by having ties to legislators on both a local and national level. Whether a separate function or part of the corporate communication function, government affairs focuses on influencing one constituency—government—while keeping all the others in mind.

Grassroots Politics: Influencing Local Governments

Much of the discussion thus far has put the spotlight on business's relationship with the federal or state government. In fact, the most highly publicized encounters between business and government involve corporate giants facing off with the federal government, a giant in its own right. But many business/government issues have a local focus. For instance, an oil and gas company may want to build a plant in your community, or a cable company may need an operating license in your region. When the local community is the seat of decision making, company management successful at corporate communication uses a variety of techniques to influence local government bodies and voters: advertising in the local media, serving on school boards, and being active in the local Chamber of Commerce. Companies may also create and support community advisory panels (CAPs) that voice community concerns about the company's activities, such as the impact of a manufacturing facility on pollution, the drain on public services should a company expand, or the potential loss of jobs and tax revenue if a company moves production out of town. In many companies, this work is planned and coordinated by the community affairs group within the corporate communication department, and may be managed in the branch offices closest to the specific communities.

Increasingly, companies are finding that it is a useful communication strategy to enlist one constituency—company employees—to present the company's point of view to another constituency—local voters. Let's look at two examples.

Shell and MediaOne.   Shell needed to acquire permits to expand its factories in a Louisiana parish resistant to this kind of corporate growth. Top management decided that the best way to influence voters was to enlist the services of nonmanagement employees because, according to a company survey of 600 residents of the parish, the credibility of nonmanagerial plant workers was huge, nearly as big as that of doctors and the federal EPA.[27] As a result of this finding, the company initiated an internal communication program to keep employees well-informed about Shell's community service, a corporate effort that employees felt to be very important, and encouraged them to relay this information to members of the community.

Similarly, the cable company MediaOne turned to its employees to gain the public's consent to transfer operating licenses to AT&T, which wanted to buy MediaOne.[28] Communities in Massachusetts proved to be the most challenging because each community was required to hold a hearing to vote on the transfer. The legal and communication departments of MediaOne joined forces to gain employee support for, and direct action in, persuading key government officials in each community to vote for MediaOne's proposal. For each community, employees who lived in that community were enlisted for the effort. They were asked to send letters and attend regional hearings. The campaign was a huge success, resulting in a 98 percent unconditional approval in the 115 communities in Massachusetts that voted on this transfer. MediaOne spokesperson Carolyn Fischer explained: "These employees could present reasons why the merger would be good for customers and the community at large."[29]

What makes the use of employees as goodwill ambassadors so powerful is the overlap between the two constituencies: The employees that Shell and MediaOne enlisted were also residents in the communities where these companies needed voter approval. Thus, the same neighbors whom residents carpool with to soccer games and share potluck suppers with are also the people who are representing their companies. There is no substitute for the relationship that can be built between neighbors in face-to-face communication, the oldest and most trusted form of communication.

Just as companies need to focus attention on government at all levels, they also need to reach the public directly, who, after all, constitute the voters and sometimes the customers, employees, suppliers, and distributors with whom companies do business. The next section addresses one of the most powerful approaches to influencing the public, both globally and locally: corporate philanthropy.

CORPORATE PHILANTHROPY

In their glory days, the robber barons of the late nineteenth and early twentieth centuries could operate with blissful disregard for the concerns of the public, amassing huge fortunes and giving back nothing to the public unless they chose to. Fast forward to the beginning of the new millennium and we see a totally different picture. Not only are companies restrained in their actions by government regulation, but they are also expected to give back to the communities in which the company operates.

It's not enough for companies just to act with integrity, to be honest and fair. Today, the public expects even more: Companies need to be good corporate citizens. A recent worldwide survey reveals that people believe companies have a moral responsibility to improve society. Among Americans, "only 11 percent think they [companies] should focus only on making a profit, paying taxes, employing people and obeying the laws. Three times as many (35%) think they should also work to exceed lawful requirements, set higher ethical standards...."[30] The old rule of "Do no harm" has given way to a new, more stringent rule: "Do good beyond the narrow limits of making a profit."

Earlier in this book, we saw the old rule illustrated in, among other examples, the cautionary tale of the damage done to Hooker Chemical's reputation by its inadequate communication about, and denial of responsibility for, the pollutants spilled into Love Canal. Today, a company in similar straits would have to do more than clean up the mess and accept responsibility for it. The company would have to give the affected communities a say in its activities that have an impact on them, and invest in the communities by supporting a host of health, education, and cultural programs, among other things.

Companies give back to their communities, both global and local, through corporate philanthropy, showing with their dollars and with the commitment of their employees' time and talent that the company supports social goals. In this section, we explore the multiple benefits of corporate giving, the evolution of the activity, and the philanthropic work of two exemplary companies—Avon and Microsoft. But before we do, we'd like you to consider your company's philanthropic efforts:

- Is your business involved in philanthropic activities?
- Do the philanthropic activities help both the community and the firm? If so, how?
- Are the activities well suited to the company's vision, mission, and overall strategy?

The Case for Corporate Philanthropy:
Another Look at Building Reputation

In Chapter 4, we saw how products and services alone are not the only parts of your company that attract attention. Constituencies form perceptions of your company based on *all* the messages it sends out through names and logos, and through self-presentations—among which are included corporate philanthropic activities. These activities help build a company's reputation as a good corporate citizen, socially responsible to the communities in which the company operates, and in doing so, get the word out about what the company stands for. For example, TRW, a corporation with substantial involvement in aerospace and advanced computing systems, sends underprivileged children to Space Camp in Huntsville, Alabama; supports a computer center at the YMCA in Reston, Virginia, where a large number of TRW people work and live; and gave a large grant to the Smithsonian's Air and Space Museum for a new gallery on exploring the universe, which will include a TRW space telescope.[31] Not surprisingly, since TRW excels in state-of-the-art compuler systems and space exploration, much of its corporate giving reflects the company's identity.

When companies give to communities, they reap benefits from and beyond these constituencies. Giving to local communities in which your company has its headquarters, branch offices, or plants often means giving to your employees as well, many of whom live in the community. Corporate philanthropy at the local level can also improve relationships with local government, which is responsible for making and carrying out laws that can ease or restrain your business activity. Peter Davies, an expert in corporate giving, explains that philanthropy gives back to the corporate donor by enhancing the quality of life in the communities where the company operates: "Business performance is affected by the local level of literacy and numeracy, the crime rate, the opportunities for childcare and the available services for elderly relatives. Using CCI [corporate community investment] to provide social support and to develop the capacity of the local community enhances companies which are competing in a global market."[32]

When a company gives to causes that have a universal appeal, like public health or literacy, the company's reputation can improve across all constituencies. By giving to the global community, the company may see that customers feel greater loyalty, government may give the firm the benefit of the doubt when reviewing its practices, global markets may expand when giving extends across national borders, job seekers find the company more attractive, and employees enjoy a sense of pride through association with the firm's good deeds. Although some investors may feel that corporate giving puts a drag on profits, others are interested in investing in socially concerned companies and recognize that philanthropy can build a company's reputation, which spills over into the bottom line.

In addition to the local and global communities that benefit directly from corporate support, another constituency—employees—may feel the most impact from a company's philanthropic program. They too may be recipients in tangible ways if they live in the local community targeted for corporate grants or if their company has chosen to support social issues, like the environment or child care, that they themselves feel committed to. Moreover, employees can feel more closely attached to their organization if they are called on to get actively involved in corporate philanthropy. Many companies encourage employees to participate in corporate giving programs by, for instance, teaching basic reading and math skills in local schools, bringing meals and companionship to the elderly, or refurbishing youth centers and housing for the poor.

Employee activism builds especially strong bridges between companies and the communities that enjoy these services because the connections are established through personal, one-on-one relationships between employees and community members. In turn, these relationships build a company's reputation. Since 1993, the Points of Light Foundation, established to recognize outstanding employee volunteer programs, has sponsored a President's Service Award[33] that gives national visibility to the winners, including Bayer Corporation for its science learning program in the public schools and First Union Bank for its book donation and literacy drive.

Companies perceived as good corporate citizens benefit financially. A recent worldwide survey shows that "nearly half of U.S. respondents say their perception of a company led them to consider rewarding or punishing a company by purchasing its products or services—or by speaking up, either for or against an organization."[34] Moreover, as the products and services offered by companies become increasingly homogenized, a company's involvement or indifference to causes that benefit society becomes an important yardstick that consumers use to choose among similar products offered by competing firms. Corporate philanthropy is, then, a powerful way for your company to stand apart from the rest, amidst all the marketing static and proliferation of brands that tend to obscure your company's image with potential customers. Corporate giving can count at the cash register.

Corporate Philanthropy Comes of Age: From Supporting the CEO's Pet Project to Giving Strategically

The universe of causes a company can contribute to is nearly endless, and, before the last decade or so, many companies approached corporate philanthropy in a scatter-shot fashion. On one day the company gives to the CEO's favorite nonprofit organization, on another to a local charity drive, on yet another day to the favorite charity of the CEO's counterpart in the interests of building close ties between the companies. By contrast, in the new millennium, the landscape of corporate giving has clear definition. Today, corporate philanthropy, sometimes called "corporate social investment," represents well-placed giving, that is, giving linked to a company's mission and strategy. As Curt Weeden, former Johnson & Johnson vice president in charge of the corporation's philanthropy program, explains:

> Social investing *disciplines* a company's charity (or philanthropy) so that it is focused on the same general field of interest that the corporation has marked as its primary business territory, *strategically* applies funds paid to external nonprofit organizations…in a way that also helps the corporation, *leverages* whatever gifts or payments are made to nonprofits so that these allocations end up helping the company continue to be profitable.[35]

Companies try to align themselves with causes that are fundamentally linked to the products and services they sell. This approach not only keeps a company in the minds of constituencies as they learn about its good deeds but also lends greater credibility to the kind of charitable giving the company engages in than if it were to go off and give to causes it knows nothing about. Disney publicizes its support of children's causes; Weyerhauser helps the environment and publicizes these efforts. Johnson & Johnson assists causes related to the welfare of women, children, and families who are among the company's key constituencies. For example, one of J & J's premier philanthropic efforts, the Johnson & Johnson Head Start Program at UCLA's Anderson School of Management, has been training child care providers for over a decade in basic business skills to help them run their Head Start Centers professionally and plan for strategic growth.

As companies became more strategic in their corporate giving, they have also professionalized the function within the organization. Corporate philanthropy officers (who often report to senior management in the corporate communication function) have instituted formal procedures for grants that require applicants to demonstrate fiscal accountability, project management skills, significant need for funds, and strategic use for those funds. Corporate staff also monitors the use of funds and project outcomes.

Managed systematically, corporate philanthropy serves global and local communities and, in doing so, enhances corporate reputation. Let's look now at the philanthropy programs of two corporations—Avon and Microsoft—that serve as a benchmark for these activities. Both have programs that exemplify "corporate social investing," or the link between philanthropy and corporate strategy. Each does so by using an approach to planning and executing corporate giving tailored to the company's identity. As you review these stories, consider which elements of their approaches may apply to your own organization's charitable efforts.

Avon: The Created Event and the Sustained "Opportune Moment." Wander downtown in a large U.S. city such as San Francisco or Atlanta during the balmy months of the year and you're bound to see women of all ages sporting T-shirts and sweatshirts announcing Avon's Breast Cancer Walkathon.[36] In each city where the event is sponsored, several thousand women, including breast cancer survivors, walk 20 miles a day for three days to raise funds for the breast cancer cause, resting at the end of the day at predetermined sites where Avon provides them with sleeping tents, meals, hot showers, entertainment, and, if necessary, medical services. Each walker agrees to raise at least $1900. Since the inception of these walkathons in 1998, $65 million has been raised for breast cancer.

What an interesting parallel and contrast these walkathons present to the "Torches of Freedom" Easter Parade of debutantes on Fifth Avenue in New York City that Edward Bernays engineered to encourage women to smoke. Like the "Torches of Freedom" Parade, however, the Avon walkathons are "created circumstances"—scenes involving actions (the walk), actors (the women participants), and props (for example, shirts, banners) that craft an impression in the local community in which the walks occur and in the global community that learns about these noteworthy activities through, for instance, press releases and video clips on TV. The walkathons appeal emotionally to participants who are key players in the event and for whom its entertainment value—even though contrived—and the social bonding that occurs on the walks become important. The Avon walkathons (interestingly enough, part of a campaign to end the diseases that Bernays's "Torches of Freedom" helped to promote by making smoking acceptable—and even fashionable—for women), also draw the attention of those who see or learn about the events through this powerful focus on a cause that deeply affects every woman.

Avon's creation and sponsorship of these events vividly demonstrate—in city streets no less—that the company stands for more than profits, that, in fact, it supports causes dear to women around the world, who are its sole customers. The largest program of Avon's Worldwide Fund for Women's Health, the Avon Breast Cancer Crusade supports research and provides cancer care services, especially to disadvantaged women like the poor, the elderly, and minorities. Why does Avon focus its philanthropic efforts on women's health issues? Because its entire identity is wrapped up in women's concerns. On the Web tour of the company, Avon calls itself "*The* Company for Women." In defining what this means, the company goes on to say, "Avon has evolved over time into a business that keeps company with women of all cultures and age groups—not only as consumers, but as people. We care deeply about their economic well-being and empowerment, their health and the issues that concern them. And we believe in giving back to women and the communities where they live and work." Not surprisingly, the company's sponsored survey of women in 2000 revealed that their major health concerns are ovarian, cervical, and breast cancers.

The company's primary identity, then, fits closely with its philanthropic focus, which it has deepened and extended over time into a full-scale campaign—rather than spreading the company's largesse across several causes less related to its core values. The walkathon belongs to what Avon dubs a "crusade" for women's health that is heavily supported by products and related promotions launched in tandem with the walkathon. There are fundraising pens, pins, candles, stuffed animals, celebrity auctions, and lipsticks with each item meticulously linked to the Crusade's themes. For example, lipsticks bear names like "Courgeous Spirit" (raisin neutral), "Faithful Heart" (creamy berry), "Strength" (warm, bright red), and "Crusade Pink" (shimmery pink), all priced reasonably so that consumers can easily feel a part of the sponsored event through their purchases.

One of Avon's core differentiators—its reliance on a direct sales force of women since its founding in 1886 (when there were very few jobs for women)—boosts its philanthropic program while enhancing the company's appeal to customers by underscoring Avon's long-standing commitment to women in the workforce. As the company's representatives sell these promotional products, a woman employee selling directly to a woman customer, Avon's multifaceted focus on women comes into play—women as employees, as customers, and within communities concerned about vital health issues. Moreover, all of this is conveyed through word-of-mouth, the oldest and one of the most powerful communication channels.

At its best, event sponsorship not only serves the public good but also promotes a company's brands, and, in doing so, its reputation. As brand experts David Aaker and Erich Joachimsthaler explain, "An event experience...can provide a customer with a unique opportunity to develop a link to the brand....Involving a customer in an event can also make that customer part of the same family. ..."[37] Avon is one of the best at this, shaping its self-presentation through its sponsorship of women's health causes. Let's look now at some of the philanthropic efforts of Microsoft to see how they serve the brand as they serve the community.

Like Avon, Microsoft has an approach to corporate giving that is systematic and strategic. Yet, unlike Avon, Microsoft's timing of its campaign to help communities may undermine some of the reputation-enhancing benefits of its philanthropy. During the same period when Microsoft crafted its identity as a corporate giver, it was also under attack by its competitors and the government for being an unscrupulous monopoly requiring restraint and penalties. It may be coincidental that Microsoft's emergence as the world's greatest corporate giver came swiftly on the heels of public scrutiny and negative publicity. Nevertheless, one identity—the giant, greedy monopolist—casts a shadow on the other—the world's greatest corporate giver.

Microsoft: Emergence of the World's Greatest Corporate Giver.   As we saw in Chapter 4, a company's reputation can be quite fragile as it is subject to the changing perceptions of key constituencies. Certainly in the 1980s—and even today—Bill Gates has had his admirers, especially among the aspiring dot.commers who want to follow in the unconventional path to wealth of this Harvard drop-out and—at least until the mid 1990s—this socially inept geek. In some ways, Gates's phenomenal success is yet another example of the American Dream, albeit not a rags-to-riches story but a story of the rise from affluence through genius and unconventionality to enormous wealth. On the other hand, Microsoft's reputation has suffered under the glare of government investigations and media coverage of the case against the company, beginning in the mid-1990s.

Whether or not Microsoft's monumental largess will be sufficient to bolster its reputation and deflect criticism of the company as the supremely arrogant high-tech behemoth is yet to be determined. Critics of Gates's motivation for charitable giving will most likely persist although the facts of his philanthropic efforts may muffle their attacks.

> In January [2001], the Bill and Melinda Gates Foundation edged past Britain's Wellcome Trust to become the largest in the world, with assets of $21.8 billion. Even the greatest philanthropists of the past did not give away as much in real dollars over their entire lifetimes as Gates has at the age of 44. According to the *Chronicle of Philanthropy*, Andrew Carnegie made gifts amounting to $350 million before he died in 1919—a sum that would be worth about $3 billion in today's dollars; and the $540 million that John D. Rockefeller dispensed before death in 1937 would amount to more than $6 billion today—less than a third of the Gates total so far.[38]

Like other multinationals, Microsoft's corporate giving relies on employee involvement. The employee volunteerism program tends to be clustered around local Washington communities where many of Microsoft's employees live and emphasizes a combination of community outreach in the form of tutoring and training and a matching funds program, whereby Microsoft will match employee contributions to their favorite charities dollar for dollar up to $12,000.

In keeping with the firm's core competence in technology, much of Microsoft's giving is in the form of technology training and software. In this instance, Microsoft deals with multiple overlapping constituencies—global and local communities which themselves contain future customers and employees for Microsoft as well as individual citizens who can vote for government representatives supportive of or antagonistic toward Microsoft's agendas. The overriding theme in the area of technology giving is inclusiveness. Steven Ballmer, Microsoft's president and CEO, expressed this as the company's desire to close the "digital divide":

> ...the gap between those who have meaningful access to the tools of technology and those who don't. As a business, Microsoft is committed to empowering people through great software. As a corporate citizen, Microsoft likewise is committed to empowering people and communities by providing the resources they can use to discover a better future through contributions of $34.3 million in cash and $197 million in software....[39]

Opening up access to technology to underrepresented groups like community-college students, Boys and Girls Clubs, the handicapped, and managers in nonprofit organizations, is aimed not only at building a good reputation for the company but also eventually to extending the company's customer base and employee pool to these populations. Philanthropy is, then, a win-win activity.

The company's interest in giving with a high-tech focus gets expressed in short- and long-term efforts. In the wake of terrorist attacks on the World Trade Center buildings and the Pentagon in 2001, Microsoft immediately responded with a direct grant of $10 million and an offer of technical services to assist search and recovery efforts, including help with a computerized database for locating lost family members.[40] As one of its long-term efforts (rather than a response to crisis), the company has assisted in digitizing America's libraries by providing free Microsoft programs and Gateway computers.

Microsoft's assistance to libraries has been controversial: Is its primary aim to help communities or to build business? As Jean Strouse, biographer of another tycoon, J.P. Morgan, explains: "The library-wiring initiative has had critics from the start. It delivers Gateway machines and free Microsoft programs, which led to a widespread perception that Gates was using his philanthropy to expand the market for Microsoft, much the way tobacco companies hook adolescents on cigarettes."[41]

Unlike his contributions to advance technology applications, Gates's sustained initiatives to improve world health seem unblemished by corporate self-interest—which we have argued is not a bad thing anyway—and widely applauded. From the perspective of corporate strategy, we would expect pharmaceutical companies and not a software firm to engage in such giving, yet Gates's foundation has given enormous support to maternal mortality reduction, malaria vaccine, polio eradication, Unicef for neonatal health, and AIDS vaccines and research. He is, then, serving a world community that is unlikely to reciprocate by buying his products, and in an area—world health—that has no direct link to his company's products and services. As Gates has himself said, "We're in this unbelievable era where you could argue, What's the most amazing thing taking place?... Is it software technology stuff and the Internet and new forms of communication? Or is it the revolution in biology?"[42]

Who is talking here? Is this Bill Gates, the sophisticated business leader, who builds a world reputation for his firm by his good works, a reputation that is likely to eclipse the government's attacks in the minds of Microsoft's other constituencies? Is this Gates, the social visionary, who's come upon a set of issues more fascinating and socially important than his company's core business and who, because of his enormous wealth, can crusade against world suffering? Maybe the answer is all of the above.

In many ways, Microsoft's pattern of corporate giving resembles that of other multinationals who are civic-minded: the reliance on employee volunteerism, the attempt to match company strategy and core competencies to corporate giving, the emphasis on giving to the local communities in which Microsoft has a large presence, and the selection of social issues that have global impact and resonance. But, perhaps because of Gates's astronomical wealth and sustained governmental attacks on the company, Microsoft's philanthropy is significantly larger and more wide-ranging.

CONCLUSION

Managing government and community relations has grown in importance and sophistication in the last few decades as companies began to recognize the significant impact these constituencies can have on a business's reputation and strategic goals and as firms emerged from a kind of denial of the importance of government and the public. Begun as makeshift efforts to stave off the impact of government regulation, the government affairs function today brings into play several powerful approaches to managing government relations—coalition building, CEO activism, lobbying, the use of PACs, and the advent of professionally run government affairs units.

One way that companies influence votes is to influence voters, who, as members of both a local and global community, expect businesses to be good corporate citizens. Corporate philanthropy—when strategically focused and well managed—can craft this identity for firms, thereby building corporate reputation while serving the public good.

9
C H A P T E R

THE GOOD NEWS ABOUT
THE BAD NEWS—HOW TO
MANAGE OLD AND NEW
MEDIA STRATEGICALLY

A LHOUGH YOU MAY NEVER RUN your company's media function or directly communicate with the press, your company's management of media communication has an enormous effect on your ability to succeed at work. Unlike all other constituencies, the media is both a constituency and a conduit through which all other constituencies—investors, suppliers, retailers, consumers, and so forth—develop images of your firm. These constituencies might catch a *Dateline NBC* show on your firm, scan an article in an on-line forum, or, even worse, come across an "anticompany" Web site while looking for legitimate information about your products. Think about a reference to your organization that has appeared in the newspaper, on television, or on-line. How well was your firm portrayed? How was your own work affected? Did a client, customer, or fellow employee bring up issues raised in the piece? Could your company have appeared in a better light or strengthened its story? In considering these questions, you can start to see how effectively the media can build or diminish a corporate reputation.

The power of the media hardly needs to be emphasized: The media pervades our lives from waking to sleeping—a result of the technological advances of the last century. In particular, this saturation has produced what Canadian philosopher Marshall McLuhan foresaw decades ago—the creation of a world so intricately intertwined by shared knowledge that it is, in essence, a "Global Village."[1] Today media outlets have vastly expanded, and options, actions, and events are no longer confined to local communities; rather they can and do create reverberations that are felt across the globe.

In this chapter, we will first look at the changing media environment companies face today. We will then track the evolution of the media and its ever-changing relationship with the corporate world and the general public, also considering the media of the future. By exploring new media—in particular, the Internet—you will see its enormous influence on businesses today. We will then outline a media framework your company can adopt in this evolving media environment. After outlining this framework, we'll take a closer look at how two types of companies—a traditional firm such as McDonald's, and a newer e-commerce business such as Buy.com—handled their own media relations. In light of these examples, we will then describe how your own company can implement an Internet strategy to avoid going wrong in the information age.

More than any other constituency, the media has the power to expose a company's flaws. For this reason, strong media relations have become one of the most crucial corporate functions. Owing to their extraordinarily widespread reach, television, print, and the Internet are the primary means by which constituencies attain valuable corporate information—which directly affects the company, its reputation, and, ultimately, its bottom line. And thus, like the muckrakers from the early 1900s whom we looked at in Chapter 2, the media can either make or destroy your company—both in good, but particularly in bad, times. When we take a look at crisis communication in Chapter 10, you will see how invaluable good media relations were to PepsiCO during its 1993 syringe crisis. As Anne Reynolds Ward, spokesperson and manager of Pepsi public affairs at the time of the crisis, explains: "We knew that by cooperating with, not obstructing, the press, we could get our side of the story out there fast."[2]

Day to day, the media relations department—as the chief distributor of information to many of a company's most important constituencies—still has a tremendous influence on a company's overall reputation. In the event of a crisis, the media is an invaluable preestablished network that companies use to share crucial information and calm a distraught public. Thus virtually every company requires and employs some kind of media-relations function. Let's take a closer look at how that function is changing and how the changes in the function have led to more exposure than ever before for companies throughout the world.

UNDERSTANDING THE CHANGING MEDIA ENVIRONMENT

The media of ancient times included everything from epic stories sung by wandering poets to broadcast a culture's achievements, to written documentation providing a tangible record of a culture's achievements. Today the means for broadcasting and documenting culture have expanded dramatically. Faster communication channels, such as breaking-news broadcasts and instantaneous Web-posting, now supplement slower methods of communication such as weekly magazines. The expansion of media channels has given constituencies a chance to gather information and make their own educated decisions. Access to more information has enabled all the constituencies of a company—its consumers, suppliers, employees, and shareholders—to judge it as never before.

Although some people anticipated technology ushering in an era of comfort and increased mobility, navigating the tidal wave of information this technology has brought will not be a smooth ride . Instead, new technologies present rough waters through which you, as managers, will need to navigate. Just as the 1858 introduction of the transatlantic telegraph cable failed to eradicate deeply instilled hostilities and tensions between Europe and the United States, the new media will not offer a panacea for already troubled communications between organizations and their constituents.[3] In fact, as Marshall McLuhan explained, by granting people unprecedented access to all viewpoints at all times, "the global village absolutely insures maximal disagreement on all points....Village is fission, not fusion, in depth....The village is not the place to find ideal peace and harmony. Exact opposite."[4] Fasten your seatbelts and enjoy the bumpy ride that greets the global voyager in the information age.

Extra! Extra! Point, Click, and Learn All About It!

With this information age upon us, anyone with cable television and Internet access has the ability to be remarkably well informed. The unprecedented number of channels and the amount of content available on these channels have caused this shift. Images of early twentieth-century "newsies"—hawking newspapers on city corners to inform all passers-by of the latest scandal—have faded. Today the proverbial news-boy screaming "Extra! Extra!" to make his sales has been replaced by a much more sophisticated and universal technology: the 24-hour television news networks and the on-line news services—offering up-to-the-second access to information.

As a result of this information overload, even the notion of news "headlines" has been altered dramatically. The media that was once dominated by newspapers across the United States and around the world, then by television in the late 1940s and early 1950s and the Internet in the 1990s, has evolved as rapidly as the technology that provides it. In earlier, less media-saturated times, the public eagerly awaited the next newspaper hot off the presses, their anticipation increasing the dramatic and even romantic quality of the latest news.

Yet with the advent of the Internet and 24-hour television news channels such as CNN, the anticipation and the romance have been reduced. The decreased lag time of other media channels has diminished both the power and the electricity of newspapers. Access to news has become so commonplace that the public expects to be informed at all times. The increased accessibility of information has led to a culture less able to be shocked; when you can see and have seen it all, less of what you see tends to come as a surprise. Consider public reactions to the stock market nosedives of 1929, 1989, and 2000, respectively. The initial public response to each event illustrates the decreased shock factor of the news. In 1929 the crash was immediately dubbed "Black Tuesday," in 1987 it was "Black Monday." Yet on Friday, April 14, 2000, the Dow plunged 600 points and made an unprecedented correction, yet no one took the trouble of giving the day a name. It took an event of horrific proportions, the destruction of the World Trade Center in the fall of 2001, to break us out of our torpor.

The apathy and desensitization with which the public approached the year 2000 stock plunge, for example, is a product of a world where media conglomerates and advertising dollars drive a blaring, loud, and excitable media machine. Therefore, today headlines are more prone to jump off the television and computer screen than the newspaper page alone. The speed at which news is delivered, and the repetition of sound bites across communication channels (for example, a CNN news flash at 10 p.m. repeated at 11 P.M., 12 A.M., 1 A.M., and so forth) has increased the likelihood that a company's reputation can be damaged within seconds—with a dramatic sound bite or a glaring, defamatory headline.

The need to adapt and meet the bottom line has propelled most of the changes over the past century in how news is disseminated. Newspapers have given up their strict reliance on headline news because they could not compete with the speed of new media such as television and later the Web. Daily papers adapted by taking over the news analysis that used to appear in weekly news magazines such as *Time* and

Newsweek, as well as by taking this analysis on-line. The news magazines in turn took over the feature writing that used to appear in older magazines such as *Look* and *The Saturday Evening Post.*

In June 2001 the Pew Research Center in Washington reported that a third of American Internet users get their dose of daily news off the Internet,[5] compared with only 6 percent a few years ago.[6] With thousands of health-related Web sites in existence, many people use them as the predominant means to obtain health information.[7] Sports are even more popular to read about on-line, given the time-sensitive and statistical nature of the information.[8] As a result, the Internet presents corporations and journalists alike with a new media game complete with new rules.

The Media's Business Experts

Today so many magazines and Web sites are devoted to business that you'd be hard-pressed to find a topic that is not thoroughly covered by one media outlet or another. In recent years, news of corporations, the stock market, or business personalities has often become the "lead story" on national news television and radio broadcasts. Business correspondents, covering some aspect of the booming or busting economy, are often seen sitting next to network anchorpersons. In addition, business reporters today—particularly those working for national publications and networks—often have business degrees or experience in the industries on which they report, so they can act as qualified experts on their respective subjects. The knowledge of business reporters has surely contributed to the increased credibility of the news that they report. All eyes can now turn to your corporation—its triumphs and failures—like never before in history.

The Lengthening Reach of the Internet

Companies have spent the last five years hurling themselves into the fast-paced stream of the Internet. As a result of this trend, e-commerce is already a $500 billion business, touching the lives of millions with the mere click of a mouse.[9] In 2001 about 61 percent of all U.S. households were on-line,[10] compared with about 27 percent in 1997, according to the New York–based Internet research firm Jupiter Communications.[11] Out of this sea of Web surfers, over 5 million already prefer stock trading on-line through brokers, and their activity accounts for 25 percent of small investor trading.[12] With the Internet explosion now hitting Asia—where the number of Internet users in China skyrocketed from 2.1 million at the outset of 1999 to 8.9 million by the end of the same year—you can expect these numbers to keep soaring upward,[13] in Asia and across the globe.

Just when the average consumer had become acquainted with his or her household personal computer, technology propelled the reach of the Internet to even loftier heights—by providing innovative ways to transfer information globally. Some say that by 2005, 1 billion people will own wireless phones.[14] To speed the information flow even further, technologically advanced Internet-ready phones are making their way into the mainstream marketplace. Fifty million U.S. consumers are expected to own one of these phones within the next two years, literally putting Web microbrowsing capabilities into the palms of these wireless consumers.[15]

WITH KNOWLEDGE COMES POWER

What does all this information, ease of access, and speed mean to you as managers? In brief, you and your organization will need to be vigilant, thorough, and quick to locate and respond to the latest on-line attack on your business. Today's public is perpetually on the lookout for corporations to slip up. In the general-public's view today, the bigger you are, the harder you deserve to fall. Until now, media coverage—newspaper headlines or more in-depth profiles on television shows like *60 Minutes*—has been the primary means for exposing corporate flaws.

Over the last decade, however, wireless communication and the Internet have transferred an enormous amount of power into the hands of individuals. The democratization of the media means that one individual can possess enormous clout. It is almost as though special-interest groups have been handed a high-resolution magnifying glass and a megaphone at the same time—allowing them to see the minutest detail and to react to it with a significantly louder voice. As Patricia Sturdevant, general counsel to the Washington-based National Association of Consumer Advocates, explains, "The Internet is a very effective new weapon for the consumer. Before the Internet, unless you had a lot of time or money, there wasn't any way to get the public's attention to a problem. Now, you can broadcast it to the entire world in an instant."[16] This power in the hands of consumers is a true threat to your company, for, no matter how large or small a mistake you make, someone in cyberspace will catch it and capitalize on it, as we will see in the Buy.com example later in this chapter.

No longer must individuals rely on the press as their sole means to voice concerns, complaints, and opinions. In fact, evidence shows that many people—with the use of their computer—would rather complain to companies themselves. A 1997 study conducted by the Pew Research

Center revealed that the public wanted more reporting on corrupt business practices by a margin of 60 to 28 percent.[17] At the same time, the study also concluded that "public criticism of the press for inaccuracy, lack of fairness, and sensationalism" was on the rise.[18] Logic dictates that if people are losing faith in the press to expose fraudulent corporate behavior, they will increasingly take matters into their own hands through the use of the Internet. Companies, no matter what their industry, must be acutely aware of this increased scrutiny.

Because so many people have instantaneous access to millions of Internet surfers, the powers of public observation have never been so substantial. As crisis management specialist Robin Cohn describes it: "We are a nation of 'watchers.' Even if nothing is happening now, something might. After all, millions of viewers kept their eyes peeled to TV sets watching O. J. Simpson drive down the L.A. Freeway for three hours."[19] Just think about the recent phenomenon of "reality programming," epitomized by hit television shows like CBS's *Survivor*—requiring everyday people to surmount impossible, and often degrading, challenges to win a jackpot prize, while hundreds of viewers look on with glee. Even more voyeuristic, the CBS show *Big Brother* featured 10 strangers cohabiting in a house and being constantly monitored by 28 video cameras and 60 microphones. Over 20 million viewers eagerly tuned in to catch the premiere.[20] Today it seems the more a show exposes, the higher the ratings mount. As Frank Farley, a former president of the American Psychological Association, observes, these shows merely represent "part of a trend in society toward making the private public, toward getting people's inner world out onto the television screen, the computer monitor and the tabloid cover. Walden Pond begone. Welcome Jerry Springer and voyeur TV."[21] Businesses, obviously, cannot avoid this voyeurism. Even the private lives of corporate executives have taken on celebrity notoriety and are fair game for criticism, no matter how irrelevant or inaccurate the information.

Business-minded television viewers seem just as caught up in the need to be as all-seeing and all-knowing as possible. As previously mentioned, the democratization of the stock market generated unprecedented mainstream interest in business. David Brancaccio, senior editor and host of the weeknight public radio show *Marketplace*, explains that the "democratization of the stock market means [businesses and journalists] have to reach out to more people."[22] Half of all U.S. households today own stocks, generating an unquenchable thirst for up-to-the-minute coverage of the stock market's every move.[23]

THE CNBC PHENOMENON: THE WORLD'S EYES
TRAINED ON BUSINESS'S EVERY MOVE

For over a decade, the CNBC cultural phenomenon has answered the public demand for information about business. The Consumer News and Business Channel (CNBC), which debuted in 1989, offers $14\frac{1}{2}$ hours of television programming a day, covering business mergers, quarterly reports, and Dow oscillations. The economic boom of the 1990s and the introduction of astronomical Internet stocks caused a veritable explosion in the realm of day trading—not to mention the demand for instantaneous business information. This demand was exemplified by CNBC's ratings. The show attracted 35,000 viewers per day in 1990; on April 17, 2000—the day following one of the market's most tumultuous weeks in history—it attracted an estimated 800,000 viewers. In the last quarter of 1999, CNBC beat CNN in numbers of daytime viewers. As if these numbers weren't impressive enough already, CNBC estimates that it has about 40 percent more viewers than cited by Nielsen, which fails to tally office and restaurant viewers.[24]

Thousands—from retirees to housewives to market pros and amateurs alike—have become hooked on getting the daily inside scoop, live from the trading floor with a locker-room feel. This democratization of business news has caused a strong majority—67 percent of those surveyed in Scudder Kemper Investments (March–June 2000)—to believe that the media has turned investing into a form of popular entertainment.[25] In a way, then, big businesses and their leaders have acquired a quasi-Hollywood status and, accordingly, must be prepared for the glare of the spotlight.

Through 24-hour networks and all-day business coverage such as that offered by CNBC, today's media bombardment is impossible to ignore. Business programming is a cultural fixture that echoes the priorities of today's culture—on CNBC's news broadcasts of the devastation at the World Trade Center in 2001, a stock ticker could still be seen perpetually ticking across the bottom of the screen.

As cyberspace and public interest in business grows, so do the number of anticompany Web sites and discussion groups on-line. Consumers are quickly realizing that the Internet is an unregulated space where they can reach people worldwide instantly at very little cost. At the same time, you, as managers, must become acutely aware of the dangers such negative on-line publicity can pose to your company's bottom line. Darryl Peck, chairman of Cyberian Outpost, an on-line computer retailer, notes, "In the Internet universe, nothing replaces word of mouth and word of mouth can spread fast. You can't ignore what is being said out there."[26]

DEVELOPING A MEDIA RELATIONS FRAMEWORK

Instead of ignoring this potential threat to your business's reputation, you as a manager must learn to listen—and not only that, you should go on the offensive. We recommend that your company approach its media relations by adopting the following three-step framework, which we will discuss in more detail:

- Begin by establishing a media department that is aligned with company strategy and by employing the best mix of in-house and outside expertise.
- Keep score of all your media successes and defeats.
- Research which reporters cover your beat, so you can try to anticipate responses before your company is caught off guard.
- Prepare for intimidating media interviews by researching past interviews and anticipating possible questions.

In following each of these crucial steps, however, it is just as important to keep your eyes trained on your company's greater goal—the development of strong and lasting relationships with the media.

Establish a Media Department Aligned with Strategy

In this fast-paced age, how exactly can these steps help your company generate a successful media relations program? First, your organization must be willing to invest resources in all of its media efforts. This doesn't have to imply spending large sums of money; an executive's time can be just as valuable. For most larger-sized companies, however, a strong media relations effort will entail devoting personnel to the effort, and, frequently, using outside counsel as well.

Companies also need to involve someone—preferably the most senior corporate communication executive—in the strategic decision-making process. In this way, as company strategy is formulated, the challenges of communicating strategy to key constituencies becomes part of the conversation. Often, if communication issues such as "How do we get buy-in from stockholders?" are voiced when strategy is being formulated, senior management will be better able to shape strategic decisions in a way that will be more acceptable to key constituencies than if communication is brought into the discussion as an afterthought.

Communication professionals who are involved in the decision-making process will also feel more ownership of the ideas that they must then present to the media. While the communication point of view will not always win in the discussions that take place at top-management meetings, through hammering out the issues both the other executives involved and the communication experts will understand the likely reaction of the media to the company's announcement of its strategy.

Although consultants and public relations firms can provide good advice in managing the media, your company can save money and build invaluable in-house expertise by using an internal staff and investing in the right databases to conduct research for analyzing the media. Avoid the common mistake of not considering media relations to be important enough to require hiring a professional. Many companies make the unfortunate assumption that anyone can communicate, and, therefore, it doesn't matter who is given the assignment. As a result, lawyers, secretaries, accountants, and even former securities dealers are often assigned the task of handling communication. Although it may not be rocket science, building relations with the media requires skills, which are built through training and experience.

Keep Score by Quality, not Quantity

Today, because constituencies are sophisticated, quality coverage has undoubtedly replaced quantity. For years, simply generating a huge amount of "ink" (or coverage) indicated that in-house professionals or outside consultants had done a good job. Quantity was inherently good. Yet no one ever stopped to figure out what value a "hit" (as they are called in the business) in a relatively unimportant publication has in terms of a firm's overall reputation. The quality of coverage—including who the audience is and whether the desired message is being strategically conveyed—is what counts. Getting lots of ink has no value if you aren't achieving your communication objective. Remember that the blizzard of messages hurled at consumers in this age of information is numbing if astuteness and focus don't figure in the effort. A perfect example of this is the e-mail phenomenon of "spam," or unsolicited junk e-mail. While thousands of people may receive your message, it only elicits irritation.

Choose the Right Channel

The main lesson of media relations is to respect your constituencies (journalists as well as consumers, employees, governmental representatives, and shareholders). Just as you don't want to be bombarded by spam mail in your inbox and junk mail at the post office, neither do journalists. Accordingly, be sparing in your use of mass-mailed releases of any kind. Companies should avoid sending full press releases by e-mail; instead send a brief, succinct e-mail to the reporters that someone in your media relations department knows personally. Offer to speak with each reporter on the telephone or to meet with him or her. Then follow up with a phone call. Lengthy, unsolicited messages breed frustration. Only in a time of true crisis should your company send messages across multiple channels. If mass mailings are released in noncrucial times, their effect is greatly diminished in the times when they are needed most. Companies should use this high-quantity tactic only for stories that they are sure will have a wide audience. Also remember that you can achieve the same result by placing the story on Bloomberg or convincing the Associated Press to run the story on its wire for you.

Part of respecting your constituencies is sending messages tailored specifically for each one of them. Instead of sending a mass communication that conveys information to employees and shareholders (about a merger, perhaps), send two similar messages through different channels. One message could be posted on an employee Intranet and another message could be sent to a selected business news organization (for example, *Business Week Online*, *WSJ*, and *WSJ* on-line), instead of sending all constituencies a long e-mail.

If, for example, the story involves job creation, something that will lead to a drop or increase in stock price, or a major merger, accident, or scandal, it's probably newsworthy and worth pitching—in whatever channel you feel is most appropriate to convey the message effectively. You might use different channels, such as *The Financial Times* for investors, or *Time* to reach a more mainstream audience. If you don't pitch your message directly, the rumor mill—particular via Internet sites that do not require authorization for their postings—will surely cook up some version of the story to circulate.

From keeping your investors apprised of your company's latest mergers and significant happenings, to keeping the public informed and appeased in a time of crisis, the press release can be your first, rudimentary step on the path to communicating successfully with the public via media channels.

What story will best promote your company and how can the company plan it? Planning begins with knowing the scoop on the journalists with whom your company will be dealing directly. Such understanding involves meticulous research as well as keeping a measurement of past successes and failures with the media.

Verizon, for example, keeps records of all its hits, looking at not only where the ink has landed but also how well the company's key messages are communicated. Nancy Bavec, former director of media relations at Verizon, explains, "My entire department's compensation is tied to our ability to elevate our media scores."[27] Part of elevating Verizon's media score is finding out where the media hits have landed (with what constituencies), not just determining that the media carried a story on the company. Verizon isn't alone in recognizing the importance of being heard the way the company wants to be heard.

AT&T, another example of a company that actively keeps track of its media score,[28] launched a new measurement initiative in 1996 to discover how effective the company was at communicating with the media. Because of the magnitude of the task, the company hired help to find "the scoop" on its media coverage. The research was focused on the organization's trouble spots and used clipping services to track media coverage. In addition, AT&T contracted Yankelovich Partners (a research and consulting firm) to conduct an annual survey of business journalists to gauge perceptions of AT&T and its media relations staff.

Not only was this information useful for improving the company's media relations within the company, but the information provided by all the measurement research also allowed AT&T to benchmark its results against those of its competitors. In the end, according to John Heath, a media relations manager at AT&T, "the media tracking ignited changes and improvements in AT&T's media relations department."[29]

Research the Reporters on the Beat

In addition to such measurement tactics, research and analysis are crucial to understanding the views of journalists who write articles on your company, because these views build your company's image with the public. With this seemingly daunting task before you, how should your corporate communication professionals proceed? They should identify what publications and, more specifically, which reporters and publications cover your industry and company. This isn't hard to do since the same reporters typically cover the same beat for a period of time and have some sort of established relationship with companies. The corporate communication department should keep records to determine at a glance who is most likely to cover a story and, even more important, who is likely to write a "balanced story" (code words for a positive piece) about your organization.

But how will your organization determine who is going to write a positive story before rather than after you pitch a story? This is where ongoing research can really pay off for your firm. Each time a journalist covers a firm in your industry, your communication professionals need to determine what angle the reporter has taken. Suppose a look at the records shows that *The Wall Street Journal* reporter who covers your beat wrote a piece recently about a competitor firm moving into a different market as part of its new global strategy. Chances are that this reporter is not going to be interested in writing the same story about your firm. You can, therefore, scratch this journalist off your pitching list for this story.

If your records are well documented, your communication professionals should be able to determine who among the list of many reporters is due to write such a piece and who is not. Give a reporter information that he or she cares about, and that reporter is likely to be receptive. While this system is by no means foolproof, it makes far more sense than sending out a story to 300 reporters hoping that four or five may pick it up—with no idea of who these reporters are or whether you want the story placed with them or not. And don't use e-mail or a blast fax to distribute the message. One journalist participating in a 1996 survey conducted by *Interactive PR* states, "Just because you can e-mail 100 people as easily as one doesn't mean [that you should] send releases to any editor you have an e-mail address for."[30] Ron Alridge, publisher and editorial director of Electronic Media, also makes this point in his article "A Few Tips on Having Good Media Relations." He emphasizes: "Understand the news organization you are dealing with. I wouldn't bother to list this seemingly obvious rule if so many media relations types didn't break it so often.... Ignorance is always a turnoff."[31] Don't let the ease of new technology lull you into substituting mass quantity for quality.

How difficult is it to conduct this kind of valuable research about various media figures? Most companies today can easily access information about journalists who cover them. In-house experts or consultants can generate computer analyses of reporters' articles, ask industry sources to provide critiques of writers they know, and find out personal information. While earlier generations of PR professionals worked hard to get such information at long lunches with reporters, the new technology allows corporate communication professionals to access such information through electronic databases.

Research the Individual Reporter

In addition to figuring out who is covering your beat, your firm needs to determine what kind of a reporter you are dealing with. This is easier to do than you might realize. For a television network like CNN, one needs to know who the producer for the piece will be. Then a communication professional from your company can call the head office in Atlanta and purchase the producer's last two or three stories. For a business magazine such as *Forbes*, electronic databases—such as LexisNexis Universe or eLibrary—contain stories that reporters have written over a period of time. Those written in the last two years are most likely to be useful to your company.

What exactly can you learn by looking at previous stories the *Forbes* reporter has written and the CNN producer has filed? An individual journalist tends to write about things or put together reports in a consistent manner. Very few reporters change their style from one story to the next. In all likelihood, they have found an approach that works for them—a sort of formula—and they tend to stick with it. For example, an analysis performed for a company on a *Forbes* reporter's work showed that he liked to write "turnaround" stories. Essentially, he tended to present the opposite point of view from what everyone else had written. So if you're looking to make a case for such a turnaround, this reporter would be more likely to write the kind of article that would be helpful for your company. When observing the CNN producer's work, pay attention to how that person conducts interviews, how the stories are edited, whether he or she likes to use charts and graphs as part of the story, and so on. Let's say that the producer seems to present balanced interviews, as opposed to antagonistic ones, and likes to use charts and graphs. This is pertinent information to have; not only do you know that this producer could easily generate a positive story for your company, but you also know what sort of data and information to supply that producer.

Your corporate communication department should perform this kind of analysis for each call that comes in—particularly from important national media organizations. Although a certain amount of time needs to be devoted to such examinations, the rewards can be tremendous for a company that is trying to get its views out to a particular constituency.

Besides conducting research and analysis, another key stepping-stone to building good relationships with the media is to be responsive to their requests for information. Many companies willingly spend hundreds of millions of dollars on advertising but are unwilling to staff their media relations group with enough personnel to handle incoming calls.

Typically, a company can expect a call to come in for an interview with the president or CEO from a reporter looking to write a major piece in a national publication. The organization's response to such a request can make a huge difference in how the company is represented in the story. Let's say, for example, that a company has received negative press over the last couple of years because it hasn't kept up with cultural changes—such as today's standard of equal opportunity hiring practices—but it is now in the process of updating its employee practices. A call comes in from a reporter at CNN, and another call comes in from a reporter at *Forbes*. What should your company's communication staff do to ensure that both of these requests are met in a timely manner and to the best advantage of the company?

To begin with, the company should ensure that calls come into a central office that deals with all requests for information from important members of the media. While this sounds like common sense, often the phone is answered by a front-desk receptionist who has no idea which calls from the media are important and which are not. To avoid losing valuable opportunities, all media requests should be automatically routed to a knowledgeable person in the corporate communication department.

Here familiarity with a journalist's history and reporting style become important. To ensure that the company is portrayed in a way that will elicit the most positive story from the reporter in question, your company's media expert needs to assess the journalist's angle before responding to the request. Returning to our earlier example, let's say that CNN wants to look at your company as part of a developing trend in the industry: "organizations are all trying to position themselves as aggressively entrepreneurial." The *Forbes* reporter, on the other hand, seems to imply from the conversation that she will dub the company's new approach as "rash and overly aggressive."

First, because each reporter calls your organization, the media relations staffer who is responsible for handling these telephone calls should get as much information out of the reporter as possible while, in return, giving out little or no information that is not already common knowledge. The tone of the conversation should be friendly, and the media relations professional should try to communicate honestly about the possibilities of arranging an interview and so on. He or she also needs to find out what kind of deadline the reporter is working under. Media relations professionals should end the dialogue by agreeing to get back to the reporter within the allotted time. After making some inquiries and doing some research, a choice has to be made to either grant an interview or not. There are times when the decision not to grant an interview is the right one—when a reporter has a history of sleazy reporting, or if the person who is to be interviewed simply isn't prepared to answer the questions posed. In that case, the company should issue written answers to questions, or give a statement to the reporter.

Prepare for the Media Interview: Facing the Music

Let's assume it's your time in the media spotlight. How should you prepare for this interview, which is often felt by managers to be one of the most difficult communication challenges?

First, you should get your hands on a short analysis, with cited examples, of the reporter or producer's favored style, from the media relations professionals you are working with. Former Kmart CEO Joseph Antonini prepared for an interview with CNN by watching the last two or three major stories the producer had filed. He began the session with a compliment about one of the pieces. This made the reporter immediately comfortable, and the rapport Antonini established was carried throughout the interview. From watching the tapes, Antonini had also noticed that the producer generally liked to use a list of bullet points as part of each story. Antonini came up with a series of bullet points—essentially his key talking points that conveyed his message during the interview—and handed them to the producer at the end of the interview. The story ran, was very positive, and the list of bullet points was posted right up there on the television screen. Even this small amount of research provides a tremendous amount of leverage for positioning your company in the eyes of the media.

Next, make sure that you, or whoever is being interviewed, clearly grasp the point of view of the reporter. In this way, you can practice your responses with an eye toward meeting the reporter's goals as well. Equipped with this knowledge, you can help steer the interview to cast favorable light on your company. If the interview is to be conducted by phone—as is often the case with print reporters—a media relations professional should plan to sit in on the interview.

Third, you should devise a list of possible questions that the reporter is likely to ask, and most important, prepare answers for these questions. Media relations professionals can compile this list based on previous conversations with the reporter, from an analysis of the reporter's work, and from what you personally know to be the crucial issues on the subject of the interview. If possible, arrange a mock interview. If you're headed for a television interview, a full dress rehearsal is absolutely essential. The interview should look as if it is totally natural and unrehearsed, but you should, in reality, be prepared well in advance; in fact, careful preparation will allow you to appear spontaneous and relaxed at the actual interview. To prepare, determine what to communicate during the interview, no matter what the reporter asks. Although you cannot change the agenda for the interview, you can make sure you get certain points across as you bridge from one idea to the next.

What to do when it's show time…

Remain Calm: As Stephen A. Greyser, a professor at the Harvard Business School, advises: "take care to avoid a 'sky is falling' attitude."[32] Leave panic and distress at the roadside. If you are shocked by an unanticipated phone call from Mike Wallace and *60 Minutes*, take the call, even if only to arrange a time to call back later, to allow for some preparation time.

Think About the Consequences: Be very aware of what the ramifications of your interview can be. As Sandi Sonnenfield notes, "if reporters from the Associated Press, Bloomberg, or Dow Jones get wind of the story and call the company, the news may reach the investment world. That could result in temporary pressure on the stock, which will upset faithful institutional investors and may prompt lawsuits by shareholders."[33]

Know Your Stuff: If an interview request comes in the wake of some negative customer comment, research the complaint, its legitimacy, and the complainant, and formulate an articulate defense.

Don't Fake It: Be honest about not having all the answers, but assure the press and public that you are trying to provide answers as soon as is humanly possible. Be honest, or else it will appear that you're trying to evade important issues. Also don't be afraid to admit to areas of weakness and other shortcomings. The public is much more likely to be forgiving toward a company that is able to say it's sorry than one that is adamantly denying blame.

Know Who You're Talking to: Conduct research to become well versed in a particular reporter's style and typical angle so that in the event of an interview, you'll be able to anticipate the types of questions you will be asked and prepare your answers in advance.

Set the Record Straight: Emphasize your firm's intentions and motives. Be firm and articulate, or a negative media barrage may very well continue. Reiterate any well-established company philosophies. Offer crucial information, even if a reporter does not explicitly ask.

Learn from Experience: Consider your media policy—if you have one in the first place—and how it can be improved to handle media relations better next time around. If the company did not function like clockwork in reaction to the media scandal, then get a game plan in gear for next time. Always be prepared for a similar incident to recur.

In addition to thinking about what to say, you also need to think about how to say it. Using statistics and anecdotes helps bring ideas to life in an interview. The selection of "interesting" anecdotes and statistics is ultimately determined by who your audience will be. Managers often mistakenly assume that the reporter is the audience, but—in reality—the people who watch the interview should be the focus of your communication.

You must to be prepared to state your most important ideas as clearly as possible at the beginning of the interview. In addition, your answers to questions need to be as succinct as possible. Long-winded responses have no place in any media interview, and will end up on the cutting-room floor anyhow. Especially in television where "sound bites" of three or four seconds are the rule rather than the exception, you need training to put complex ideas into a compact form that the public can easily understand.

LOOKING AT THE BIGGER PICTURE

While each of these individual steps—establishing an internal media relations department, conducting thorough research and analysis, carefully interacting with media figures when fielding calls or being interviewed—are crucial aspects of media relations, don't forget to look at the bigger picture. By far the most important component in media relations is developing and maintaining a network of contacts with the media. After all, building and maintaining close relationships is a prerequisite for generating coverage. Beware that not all journalists command respect. There is a segment of the media that can only be described as sleazy. The majority of legitimate, national media journalists automatically command attention and respect because of their power to convey authoritative information to a wide audience.

Remember, your company cannot simply turn its relationship with members of the media on and off when a crisis strikes or when the company has something it wants to promote with the help of extra publicity. Instead, your company needs to work to develop long-term relationships with the "right" journalists who cover the industry. This usually means being aware of and meeting with these reporters just to build goodwill credibility. Your company's media relations director should meet regularly with journalists who cover your industry and should also arrange yearly meetings with key reporters and the CEO. The more private and privileged these sessions are, the better the long-term relationship is likely to be.

Since meetings with reporters have no set agenda, they have the potential to be awkward for all but the most skilled communicators. The meeting only presents an opportunity to share information about what is going on at the company, so don't expect that a story will necessarily appear any time soon. Before meeting with the press, skilled communicators try to find out what is most likely to interest the reporter as a possible story.

Don't be discouraged by occasional rejection. Your company's media relations professionals may find themselves turned down for lunch several times by reporters who are particularly busy, only to find sometime later that these same journalists are receptive to a long telephone conversation. And, of course, there may be journalists your company encounters who simply don't get along with your media relations expert. This is a problem only if the reporter is the only one covering your organization's beat at an important national media outlet.

To see how invaluable implementing such a media framework can be, let's take a look at several real-life examples of companies' media successes and failures. First, we'll look at Easyjet and Matalan clothing and then at McDonald's handling of growing environmental concerns in the 1990s. These examples demonstrate the need for companies to adapt to evolving public interests—before media channels fatally expose a company as failing to do so. Next, we'll venture into the realm of e-commerce through an analysis of Buy.com—revealing the need for computer-savvy companies to be just as savvy in their handling of consumers. These examples will demonstrate the importance of adopting an informed, proactive approach to dealing with the media, and, as a result, the public at large.

Taking a Proactive Media Approach

As with all relationships, media relations is a two-way street, requiring proactive efforts on your company's part to ensure success. The media typically does not get excited about the good things that companies do; in fact, companies are *expected* to back admirable philanthropic causes or advocate positive messages such as Shell's driver safety PSAs. In the event that negative media interest develops, solid relationships and open lines of communication with various messengers of the media will be of great use to your company.

A hallmark of good relationships with the media is your awareness that your company is communicating the way it intends to, and promoting the messages it desires. With this in mind, it can prove helpful to approach journalists after imagining what the next day's headline will be if you could write it. The chairman of the low-cost airline EasyJet, Stelios Haji-Ioannou, achieved the headlines he desired by actively taking advantage of today's media-obsessed public, and, consequently, he reaped impressive rewards. When the Swiss government vetoed EasyJet's route from Geneva to Barcelona, not only did Haji-Ioannou refund all passengers upon check-in, but he also spontaneously decided to convert the journey into a private flight. EasyJet broadcast the message by emblazoning "No to Swiss Air monopoly" on the side of the chartered aircraft.[34] A veritable sea of flattering press ensued. Similarly, after British Airways' announcement of its merger talks with its Dutch rival KLM, EasyJet posted a press release on the event on its Web site within minutes—proclaiming that the merger would stifle much-needed competition in the industry. Through such moves, EasyJet has self-produced an image and message typically advocated by antibusiness groups and, in doing so, won the hearts of many.

James Rothnie, director of communications at EasyJet, says the key is knowing your audience and targeting them appropriately. He explains, "You need to know whether you are trying to reach the old lady with the cat or the man in the business suit."[35] Rothnie illustrates that, in the United Kingdom, getting coverage in tabloids can win over a certain type of everyday consumer, while exposure in the *Financial Times* or on the BBC is crucial to target a more cosmopolitan London audience. By using the right media channels and crafting the appropriate messages, even the smallest companies can target the right constituencies and achieve national press.

An example of a smaller-scale success story is Matalan Clothing Retailers in the United Kingdom. The company offers tours of its company headquarters, giving journalists the opportunity to sample its clothing in changing rooms, and, most surprisingly, fully analyze its distribution network. Chris Lynch of Ludgate Communications, a representative of Matalan, explains, "We tactically avoid granting phone interviews in order to get journalists to meet us face-to-face. Otherwise it ends up being just about the numbers."[36] By taking such a personalized approach, Matalan has become a favorite among journalists.

Consider success stories like Matalan and EasyJet. Taking a proactive rather than a reactive approach would undoubtedly increase customer satisfaction and the overall success of your company.

McDonald's and the Media—Food for Consumers' Thoughts

Let's shift to a larger-scale media relations example now— McDonald's reactive and proactive moves of the past 15 years—to see the benefits of recognizing the power of consumer opinion. McDonald's stands as a particularly interesting case study, not only as a hamburger retailer but also as a cultural institution. Earning the title of the most visible American fast-food chain, serving over 22 million customers a day worldwide, McDonald's has perpetually found itself in a vulnerable position for a number of reasons. The giant company is a symbol not only of America's "cultural imperialism" but also of American industry's environmental misdeeds.

With this visibility comes greater accountability to the needs and concerns of consumers. By the 1990s, plastic packaging was coming under fire; in 1989 over 12 billion pounds of plastic packaging was designed to be thrown away as soon as the package was opened. Because McDonald's is the leader of the fast-food giants, its sea of Big Mac, Quarter Pounder, and Egg McMuffin polystyrofoam boxes earned it an equally vast sea of criticism. The "clamshell" packaging had become a symbol of our wasteful, rubbish-laden society.

Americans' growing sense of responsibility to the environment stems in part from the excess and pollution of corporate America. Environmental organizations such as Greenpeace and the World Wildlife Fund increased their memberships by 50 and 100 percent, respectively, in the late 1980s and early 1990s. While only 14 percent of respondents to a May 1989 Gallup poll considered themselves "active in green organizations," a whopping 75 percent dubbed themselves "environmentalists."[37] Business-oriented publications even began to forewarn businesses that turned a blind eye to environmental concerns. As well they should have—by 1990 various pollsters determined that "between one-third and three-quarters of consumers had made, or would make, purchasing decisions in favor of 'green' products."[38] These were numbers that McDonald's—the largest single user of polystyrene in the United States— could not afford to ignore.

The mounting protests added to the visibility of the issue. Schoolchildren picketed outside of franchises. Disapproving customers mailed "clamshells" to the company's Oak Brook, Illinois, headquarters, in addition to thousands of hostile letters. McDonald's, well aware of its culturally visible positioning, started paying attention. And so, in August 1990, the Environmental Defense Fund (EDF), an environmental research and lobbying group headquartered in the United States, and McDonald's forged an agreement to form a joint taskforce and brainstorm ideas to reduce the company's annual solid waste production. The decision tapped into the company's awareness of growing consumer concerns. Edward H. Rensi, the president of McDonald's U.S.A. at the time, explained that the company had adamantly insisted that its foam packaging was not environmentally detrimental, only to realize that "our customers just don't feel good about it. So we're changing."[39] Changes involved eliminating the notorious plastic "clamshell" and replacing it with a more environmentally friendly quilted paper wrap.

How did the public perceive McDonald's cooperation with the EDF and the rapid change from plastic to paper packaging? The EDF agreement generated an image of McDonald's as a company ready and willing to take into account the concerns of environmentally aware consumers. The pressure applied by the EDF is one of the reasons that McDonald's switched from foam to paper packaging in 1990, reducing packaging bulk by a whopping 90 percent. But what exactly gave the EDF's voice so much clout? Frederic Krupp, the executive director of the Fund, explained that had McDonald's merely stuck with recycling initiatives, the Fund would have turned to media sources to publicly oppose McDonald's decision. With the prospect of negative press looming, McDonald's was coerced into recognizing that, as Mr. Krupp so eloquently puts it, "the future is green."[40] The company could not ignore the widespread influence of public sentiment and advocacy groups—all important constituencies.

Favorable press was generated largely because of McDonald's joint efforts with the EDF—identifying itself with a sensitive issue, and actively making self-adjustments before McDonald's packaging spun into a large-scale scandal. In July 1991 a *Wall Street Journal*/NBC poll revealed that 53 percent of nationwide respondents avoided purchasing products because of a manufacturer's questionable environmental reputation. McDonald's anticipated such consumer sentiments and publicly changed its ways.[41]

McDonald's environmental image attained rosier hues; the influx of hostile mail was replaced by congratulatory tidings. The change can be viewed as a glowing testimony to the triumphs of consumer pressure. As Joseph W. Bow, president of the Foodservice and Packaging Institute, explains: "This is a big deal to us because of the fact that McDonald's bowed to public pressure. We want to see a free economy where materials are used based on their advantages, not on the wishes of powerful groups."[42] Bow saw the company's efforts as proof of the effect constituencies can have on corporations. It is no coincidence that in October 2000 McDonald's advertising campaign focused on a new "Made for You" cooking system that aimed to serve fresher, hotter fast food, exactly how the customer wants it.[43] The company injected $500 million into promoting this "made-to-order flexibility."[44] Forty-five years after its founding, the McDonald's way has officially yielded to the customers' desires, as part of a greater cultural trend.

The ability of the public to put such pressure on companies has intensified with the advent of a new channel of communication between consumers and customers: the Internet. The Internet has proved to be a double-edged sword. While companies have increased knowledge of, and communication with, consumers, companies are also being held accountable in more ways. The lessons to be drawn from the next case—Buy.com's lack of strategy to handle computer glitches—will reveal both the hazards and the possibilities of this new media.

The Buy.com Fiasco

Even if you are certain that your company is the Web-savviest on the block, the Internet and the new media can still pose a threat to your well-being and security—not to mention to your customers' satisfaction. In fact, if you are the manager of an Internet-based business, you may find yourself situated in even riskier territory. Consider the 1999 case of Phil Van der Vossen's launching of a Web page to voice his fury against Internet retailer Buy.com. Look for Buy.com's hasty reaction to the dilemma and consider preventive tactics the company could have—but did not—adopt prior to the uproar.

When Phil Van der Vossen, a 20-year-old University of Maryland student, unleashed his Web site, www.buycrap.cjb.net, it was in response to Buy.com's pricing error for the Hitachi SuperScan 753—a high-end computer monitor sold on the company's Web site. On February 6, 1999, the item was accidentally marked at $164.50—hundreds of dollars below its regular retail price of $588. Internet newsgroups spread news of the phenomenal deal, and after 48 hours, 1600 customers had already placed orders before Buy.com realized its error.[45] In reaction, Buy.com issued a statement to the public, announcing that the company would honor the accidental discount for the 143 monitors currently in stock, but would cancel all remaining orders—leaving a total of 1457 customers with the sense of being cheated. Pricing was a particularly sensitive issue for Buy.com, whose marketing campaign boasts that the vendor offers the "lowest prices on Earth."

Although the company expected an outcry from customers, it reacted with ambivalence. Founder Scott Blum fumbled with a lame apology, explaining that "it was an unfortunate, honest mistake, and companies are allowed to make mistakes."[46] Consumers could not figure out whether they would indeed receive the discount, and some even had their credit cards charged without ever receiving a monitor.[47] Boycotts were threatened. A total of 46 complaints were filed against Buy.com to the Better Business Bureau of Orange County, California, as a result of the error.[48]

So what better way for an angry customer to instantaneously vent frustration than via an Internet newsgroup? Van der Vossen apparently complained in the honest hopes of initiating change. "I wanted people to know that there had been many problems with Buy.com and that they couldn't be trusted," he explained, peppering his Web site with hotlinks to other anti-Buy.com sites, company information—and perhaps most important to managers—a direct e-mail link to Buy.com's CEO.[49] As an attempt at future defense, Buy.com posted a new legal addition to its Web site: "In the event a product is listed at an incorrect price due to typographical error or error in pricing information received from our suppliers, Buy.com shall have the right to refuse or cancel any orders placed for the product listed at the incorrect price." The Federal Trade Commission has not stated whether this statement would release Buy.com from legal liability in the event that such an error occurs in the future.[50]

What was the final price of this scandal for Buy.com? Prior to the error, the company was rated 5.5 out of 7 by ResellerRatings.com—a Web site that ranks computer product retailer performance based on customer evaluations. After the pricing fiasco, Buy.com's rating plummeted to 3.5.[51] Similarly, after the scandal, Shopping100.com, another on-line ranking service based on consumer opinion, ranked Buy.com last of all 53 on-line hardware retailers. With these altered ratings in mind, it is not all that surprising that two months later Van der Vossen found himself flying to the West Coast on an all-expenses-paid trip to California to meet with all of Buy.com's top executives. As he explained, "I never imagined that they would ever care enough to even look at the site, no less fly me out there to talk about how to improve their business."[52] With the customer loyalty and the company's bottom line at risk, more and more businesses are realizing the value of granting an open ear to disgruntled consumers—even if it means flying them across the continent.

Yet in recent years, similar scandals have erupted. Recent fiascoes include the E-Trade Group facing class-action lawsuits after its computer system crashed repeatedly, impeding numerous investors from ordering and placing trades. Amazon.com Inc. was also censured for editorial partiality after charging publishers for book endorsements.[53] In light of all these examples, managers must implement and adhere to a clear-cut Internet media strategy.

DEVELOPING AN INTERNET STRATEGY

Given the advent of the Internet and an array of new technologies, companies today must face an even greater number of new challenges. Not only does technology mean new types of companies; it also means a new media approach for your company. This approach should include establishing a forum for discussion between the company and its constituencies, proactively paying attention to information circulating about your company in various media channels, managing the flow of information in and out of the company successfully, and handling negative press effectively.

Establish a Forum for Discussion

First, companies must provide an avenue for customers to vent their frustration—particularly on the Web—before they take matters into their own hands. Perhaps the whole Buy.com episode could have been avoided if the company had had its own arena for handling customer complaints immediately. As James Alexander, president of Ewatch Inc. in White Plains, New York, states: "Sometimes a customer won't be able to get through to the customer-service department and starts to use the Internet as a more direct (avenue) to a company."[54] If customers have been denied a venue to complain, overcompensate them for your company's shortcomings or mistakes. We can look to Blockbuster Video stores, a subsidiary of Viacom Inc., as an example of how a company turned a wrong into a right by following this approach. Similar to the Buy.com fiasco, a customer posted an "I-hate-Blockbuster" site when the company sent a collection agency after her for not paying a $5 late fee. Blockbuster's vice president heard about the site, negated the fine, and personally sent the woman a Blockbuster gift certificate.[55]

Pay Attention Proactively

Receiving comments and criticism directly does not mean your company should limit its media strategy to a defensive approach. Because of the widespread reach of the Internet, a growing number of companies are paying more attention to Web content, realizing that bad publicity online can legitimately threaten their bottom line. Some firms have taken independent initiatives, assigning employees or obtaining external specialists to perform a range of on-line espionage services—from chat room eavesdropping to tracking unflattering Web pages.[56] Search engines such as Yahoo! are good places to start investigating. The "consumer opinion" section on Yahoo!'s site alone (http://dir.yahoo.com) lists over 300 consumer opinion sites—all criticizing companies such as American Express, Ford, Nike, Wal-Mart, and even Yahoo! itself.[57] To intensify your search, firms such as eWatch index more than 1000 Web-based newspapers, magazines, and other news sources. eWatch even has a feature called CyberSleuth that can search for the specific individual responsible for the rogue Web site.[58] IdNames, a subsidiary of Network Solutions, searches, registers, and secures companies' Web addresses worldwide, to keep invaders from harmfully infringing on the companies' Web addresses. A summer 2000 idNames ad campaign featured a newspaper clipping reading, "New Jersey man attaches sucks.com to over 500 respected domain names." While such a headline may at first seem laughable, the Buy.com scenario shows that such a crisis could be lurking just around the corner for any company in today's global village. To increase security, some companies are even taking preventive measures themselves by self-registering negative domain names, to reduce the likelihood of external attack. For example, the former Chase Manhattan Bank owned ihatechase.com, chasesucks.com and chasestinks.com.[59] Other large corporations, such as Verizon, Levi-Strauss, and Dell Computers spend between $30,000 and $1 million annually on monitoring the Web. These numbers indicate the importance of staying atop the wave of Internet information that can otherwise, all too easily, drown a company's reputation with the click of a mouse.

Manage the Flow of Information

Tapping into the information circulating on the Internet can also give companies extraordinary access to information about customer needs and complaints. Even though you cannot please all constituencies at all times, monitoring Internet discussions of your company will enable your company to learn about current constituency needs and tailor actions to meet those that are most vital to the company's reputation and bottom line.

Keep in mind that while the Internet can present perils, it can also open vast opportunities. Information harnessed from the Internet can yield substantial gains in a company's customer, employee, investor, and government relations sectors, as well as general improvements in the products and services a company offers. By using the Internet proactively, your company can glean valuable insights about constituency attitudes, sentiments, and reactions to which you might otherwise be oblivious. In many ways, a company should view the Internet as an unprecedented and ideal survey group. Thus, effective Internet use will enable your company to gauge the sentiment of constituencies toward your company and, in turn, to respond quickly to any substantive or communication dilemmas that might arise. As Alan Shea, head of the Internet monitoring firm Eclipze, comments, "Watching the Web is like competitive intelligence. You need to keep track of who is saying what to stay ahead."[60]

Gauging the effects of comments about your firm that circulate on the Web presents substantial challenges. Despite the best tracking system, your company will never be able to fully identify the actual motivations of a creator of a Web site that is critical of your company. Some may be legitimately dissatisfied with your product or service, or may have been victimized in some way, yet others may be spreading rumors on-line merely to manipulate stock prices. In 1998, the Securities and Exchange Commission formed a group to investigate such potentially manipulative sites and was taking a closer look at 30 cases.[61] Just as rumors of an innovative discovery can send stocks skyrocketing, so can tales of internal lawsuits send them into a nosedive. While it may be difficult to discern when and when not to act, the important thing managers can do is to make sure their company's eyes are wide open.

Handle Negative Press Effectively

If you do stumble upon bad news circulating about your company—be it a condemning Web site, environmentalists picketing, or a hostile op-ed article in the daily newspaper—your communication department should determine the potential damage that the news might cause. Who is the person who has issued the complaint and are his or her comments valid? Is the person alone, or is the dissatisfaction pervasive? If so, how widespread are the complaints? Is the person speaking for him- or herself, or does the person represent a constituency such as investors or employees? If a rogue Web site has been constructed, how many hits per day has it received, and how have people generally responded to the negative message? If an unflattering newspaper article has been printed, how wide is the paper's circulation? Once these questions are answered, a company's task force or permanent crisis communication team—including members of senior management— must brainstorm some potential actions. Several options are usually available, ranging from doing nothing to challenging the opposition. Company lawyers should be consulted to discuss what legal stance the company might need to take. Lawyers will be able to offer advice about whether statements or Web sites are defamatory, warranting a lawsuit against the perpetrator.

Internet-related problems are especially difficult to undo; once a page is up and running, millions have instantaneous access to whatever message is posted, presenting the possibility for those same millions to take the message the wrong way. For this reason, your company should carefully select the most appropriate action.

Remember the Power of Traditional Media

On-line monitoring can help companies gauge the sentiments of constituencies, respond to them effectively, and stay on top of the information surge before us today. Yet, when keeping these things in mind, companies should not become so consumed with the power of the Internet that they completely ignore other important media channels, such as newspapers and television.

Whether your company is dealing with the new or more traditional media, actively communicating a desired image to the media and general public—instead of blindly accepting what the media throws your way—is crucial. With so much power in the hands of constituencies, as we noted earlier, businesses must take advantage of actively wooing the media for positive press. In doing so, you should not underestimate the power of anecdotes. Andrew Grant, head of Tulchan Communications and a 10-year veteran of Brunswick Public Relations, advises: "A chief executive must distill the company into a story he or she can tell over lunch and a journalist should be able to walk away and write it down on the back of a cigarette packet."[62] The message here is simple: Know your company's talking points and message as well as which media outlet can get maximum positive coverage for your company.

CONCLUSION

As technology develops new mechanisms to disseminate information and communication professionals develop databases by using sophisticated software, the media-relations function will continue to evolve from the old PR "flack" into a proactive professional group, delivering a company's message honestly, quickly, and to the right media. As we have seen throughout this chapter, your company exists in an age of unprecedented scrutiny on the part of constituencies. A demand for instantaneous information accompanies this public watchfulness, and the pressure is increasing with each new technological innovation. As a manager, you must readily answer this demand by considering all constituencies—on- or off-line—when dealing with the media agents that inform them. As cases such as the Buy.com dilemma demonstrate, the new media has granted all your company's constituencies—even individual members of each group—a voice that is so loud that you cannot afford to overlook any individual. By crafting messages with care and paying attention to the channels that grant individuals corporate access, your company can confront today's daunting glut of information successfully. To protect and even enhance your company's reputation, your company must manage relations with the media rather than react to calls as they come.

10

MANAGING COMMUNICATIONS IN A CRISIS: EXPECT THE UNEXPECTED

NEWS MEDIA HAVE TRADITIONALLY derived a high percentage of front-page or prime-time news stories from crises occurring in the corporate world. And Americans have been eager consumers of the stories the media throws our way. A crisis has everything journalists and readers alike crave: high drama and the catharsis that accompanies witnessing such events. Moreover, well-known personalities are often involved—such as Bill Gates of Microsoft and Douglas Ivester of Coke—which adds to the potential for a juicy story.

Why do managers need to understand crisis communication? Because organizations face crises, ones often capable of reaching huge proportions and substantially influencing your ability to work—no matter where you are located on the organizational chart. The most widely reported corporate crises even become international events: Exxon's *Valdez*, Ford Motor Company/Firestone's tire problems, Coca-Cola's product recall in Belgium after hundreds of reported illnesses, and Perrier's contaminated water—all became big media events as well as crises for the companies and people involved. Regardless of the event, we cannot forget that for those in its throes, a crisis contains a highly emotional component that a company's management cannot ignore without facing dire consequences to the company's reputation and—ultimately—to its bottom line. If you are someone who insists that major corporate crises are few and far between, scan this list of only a few of the crises in the last decade that captured the attention of millions:

- Ford Motor Company recalled 6.5 million Firestone tires in August 2000, seven months after a CBS affiliate station in Houston broke the story of significant numbers of deaths and lawsuits surrounding Firestone tires on Ford Explorers.
- The "I Love You" computer virus was unleashed in May 2000—devastating computer systems in more than 20 countries and causing an estimated $10 billion in damages.
- Coca-Cola issued a recall of its soft drinks in Belgium, France, the Netherlands, and Luxembourg in June 1999, after over 200 people reported illnesses.
- Swissair Flight 111 bound for Geneva crashed off the coast of Nova Scotia, killing all 229 passengers and crew aboard in September 1998.
- After annual prescriptions for the miracle weight-loss drug Fen-Phen had risen to 20.6 million by 1996, in 1997 FDA data suggested that as many as 30 percent of the Fen-Phen users may have holes in their heart valves or other valve damage as a result of taking the medication.[1]

As recently as 30 years ago, such events might have received some national attention, but the news would more likely have been confined to the local and regional area where the events actually occurred. Today, because of changes in technology and the makeup of the media itself, any corporate crisis is covered in a matter of hours by the national and international media as well as Webcast over the Internet. Thus, a more sophisticated media environment, as well as a new emphasis on technology in business, has created the need for a more sophisticated response to crises.

In this chapter, we will first take a closer look at what characterizes a corporate crisis, considering several examples of such crises. We will then describe how you can prepare for a crisis, including how to assess the risk of your organization, how you should centralize if and when a crisis hits, and, finally, how you can communicate in the midst of a crisis—by pointing to some of the right and wrong paths taken by the companies discussed earlier in the chapter. As you read the chapter, consider these two questions:

- How might crises like the ones described here affect your organization?
- How prepared are you to address such crises successfully?

WHAT CHARACTERIZES A CRISIS?

We have all experienced crises. By the time we reach our twenties, for instance, most of us have faced the unexpected death or illness of a loved one; a breakup of a long-term relationship; or a natural disaster like a flood, earthquake, or tornado.

Such unpredictable, *natural occurrences* are clearly crises for the individuals involved. Like individuals, corporations face crises that occur naturally: A hurricane rips through a town, leveling the local waste management company's primary facility; an earthquake turns the three biggest supermarkets in the area into piles of rubble; a ship is battered at sea by a storm and sinks with cargo destined for a foreign market. For crises that the organization had no control over, such as the destruction of supermarkets during an earthquake, the general public's perception is more likely to be positive, as opposed to crises that could have been avoided, such as the massive Exxon *Valdez* oil spill in Alaska. The public may more readily react with a measure of forgiveness for naturally occurring disasters but generally reacts severely to crises born of human error.

Although you can't avoid natural disasters, there are many crises—those caused by human error or negligence—that planning could have prevented in the first place. In fact, most of the crises described later in this chapter were human-induced crises rather than natural disasters. Today such human-induced crises can be bigger than natural disasters in terms of costs to companies in both dollars and reputation.

All human-induced crises cannot be lumped together, however. One type includes cases in which the company is clearly at fault, for instance, in cases of negligence—such as the June 2000 sinking of a Panamanian tanker, the *Treasure*, which spilled 400 tons of heavy bunker oil off the west coast of South Africa. The second type includes cases in which the company becomes a victim, such as when CD Universe was a victim of cyber-blackmailing, a case we will examine later in the chapter. Once again the company becomes the prey to circumstances, just as when natural disasters hit unexpectedly. A company's role as perpetrator or victim is the distinction upon which public perception often hinges.

Regardless of a company's role in a crisis, there are some characteristics that are common to all crises. Keep this list in mind as we look more closely at the crises described in this chapter. Most crises demonstrate the following elements:

- A rude awakening—Clearly, Diet Pepsi management never anticipated a flurry of false reports of syringes and other foreign objects lodged in their cans in 1993.

- The rapid speed and escalation of events—In 1989, even before Exxon's crisis center was set up in Valdez, the state of Alaska and several environmental groups had command centers up and running.

- The presence of panic—Without sufficient explanation of why benzene was present in Perrier bottles, chairman Gustave Leven explained the worldwide recall of the product by declaring: "Perrier is crazy!"[2] The comment was in reference to a French ad campaign, but it demonstrates how panic-generated statements can make matters worse.

- The tendency to act irrationally and precipitously when feeling intense emotions—When three children died and 144 customers were hospitalized from eating Jack in the Box hamburgers in the early 1990s, management first addressed the financial effect of the crisis, without mentioning any concern for the victims or their families. Only a week later did the company make a public apology and announce it would cover all the medical costs of the victims.[3]

- Chaos in internal communication, even if a company has a crisis communication plan—But especially in the absence of one. TWA's handling of the 1996 crash of Flight 800 off the coast of Long Island generated public fury after victims' families reported that toll-free telephone lines went unanswered, crash information was disseminated poorly, and insufficient attention was paid to the families' travel and accommodation needs when they attempted to visit the crash site.

- The omnipresent press—Executives are often unprepared for the media spotlight, which is immediate, whereas the company normally needs time to take effective action or resolve the crisis. It took Coca-Cola over a week to figure out the source of the problem in May 1999, when four adults in Belgium became ill after drinking Coke. Coca-Cola's lack of initiative cost the company much goodwill. And company CEO Douglas Ivester himself paid an even higher price: The poor handling of this incident cost him his job.

- A threat to the company's reputation and, ultimately, to its bottom line—the highly disconcerting imagery of used syringes floating in

Pepsi cans in 1993 posed a serious threat to people's positive impression of the company and, as a result, their willingness to consume the product. PepsiCo's seamless handling of the crisis saved its market share from plummeting and actually strengthened its brand reputation.

What lessons should you take away from all of this? You are likely to become a key player in a crisis, or even a spokesperson for the firm, simply by being a member of a corporation. And the likelihood that you will become a key player in a crisis increases the higher up you are on the organizational chart. Even if you are not a key player, you will need to be sufficiently versed in crisis communication issues to judge the performance of your in-house and outside experts. And so—for everyone—the price of poor crisis communication can suddenly become personal.

If the price is so high, why do so many managers have trouble achieving a clear understanding of crisis communication? Let's think about the characteristics of crises, which we listed earlier. What makes crises difficult for executives is that because crises usually come as a surprise, there is a perceived loss of control, which is often compounded by the rapid speed of events. This high-pressure combination can generate panicked, error-prone, and irrational behavior on the part of managers. It's hard to think strategically when outside events take over.

To add more fuel to the fire, the ever-watchful media often prompts the development of a siege mentality, which leads to management working with a short-term focus. Thoughts shift from the business at large to the crisis alone, narrowing all decision making down to the shortest time period. This short-term perspective encourages precipitous behavior—more defensive than offensive—even more so when a company has insufficient information at its fingertips. For example, in the early 1990s, the public relations firm Burson-Marstellar was hired six days after the Perrier benzene scare began, and already they had to counter three different explanations the company had put forward, none of which were true. Perrier's off-the-cuff explanations only increased the likelihood that the company would provide erroneous information which it later had to account for again and again. Ultimately, the company's scattershot responses only served to expose the greater communication flaws that riddled the internal structure of the company. In such cases, when panic ultimately sets in, it only leads to escalation in the crisis within the company. As we look at three of the major corporate crises in recent history—the Perrier benzene crisis of 1990, Johnson & Johnson's Tylenol recalls of 1983 and 1986, and

PepsiCo's syringe hoax of 1993—keep this list of crisis characteristics in your mind:

- A rude awakening
- The rapid speed and escalation of events
- The presence of panic
- The tendency to act irrationally and precipitously when feeling intense emotions
- Chaos in internal communication even if a company has a crisis communication plan

Although certain characteristics will be more pronounced in different cases, in every crisis we explore you will see how preparation, and the ability to expect the unexpected, can make all the difference in addressing the situation successfully. First, let's take a closer look at the Perrier case to see these characteristics in action. Notice how easily the rapid speed of events and the vigilance of the media precipitated panic and inconsistent behavior on the part of Perrier.

PERRIER AND BENZENE

Every crisis poses the threat of robbing the company it strikes of its sparkle—temporarily or permanently. Riding on the crest of 1980s health-consciousness, this was an all-too-literal reality for Perrier Sparkling Water. In February of 1990, Perrier issued the following press release:

> The Perrier Group of America, Inc. is voluntarily recalling all Perrier Sparkling Water (regular and flavored) in the United States. Testing by the Food and Drug Administration and the State of North Carolina showed the presence of the chemical benzene at levels above proposed federal standards in isolated samples of product produced between June 1989 and January 1990.[4]

This press release marked the beginning of the end of Perrier's untainted reign over the sparkling water industry. In 1989 Perrier, one of the most distinguished names in the bottled-water industry at the time, sold 1 billion bottles of sparkling water. Then, in January 1990, a technician in the Mecklenberg County Environmental Protection Department in Charlotte, North Carolina, discovered a minute amount of benzene, 12.3 to 19.9 parts per billion (less than what is present in a non–freeze-dried cup of coffee) in a bottle of Perrier being used for research. After receiving confirmation from both state and federal officials, Mecklenberg briefed Perrier Group of America about the contamination.[5]

Two full days after the crisis broke, after recalling over 70 million bottles from North America, but before identifying the source of the contamination, Perrier America president Ronald Davis confidently announced that the problem was limited to North America. Apparently, officials reported that a cleaning fluid containing benzene had been mistakenly used on a production line machine. As was later learned, Perrier was jumping the gun with faulty information—a cardinal sin in effective and efficient communication with constituencies. Despite the false confidence Perrier assumed in the public eye, at the time that the company offered its first explanation, it still had not pinpointed the specific source of the contamination. The real cause was discovered less than three days later, and contrary to what Ronald Davis had previously announced, six months' worth of production would be affected, encompassing Perrier's entire global market, not merely the North American market. The firm was forced to change its story.

Perrier had worked too hastily with insufficient information, and had been unprepared for both the rapid pace of the crisis and the prying lenses of the media. Instead of mounting a solid public relations campaign to inform Americans what exactly had gone wrong, Perrier had panicked.[6] The company took what it erroneously assumed to be the easy way out, "rely[ing] exclusively on media reports to communicate with consumers."[7]

The company's lack of an official crisis plan and its reliance on the media to communicate the company's point of view were fatal miscalculations. The omnipresent press only served to expose the greater problems lying at the heart of the crisis—namely, the lack of internal communication and cross-border coordination. When Perrier first announced the recall of its estimated 72 million bottles of sparkling water in the U.S. market, chairman Gustave Leven claimed that the recall was the only way to maintain the faith of U.S. consumers—implying that U.S. consumers were more hypersensitive than their international counterparts about such issues.[8]

Perrier's lack of internal coordination was exposed at a news conference in Paris, when Perrier-France announced that it was also issuing a recall, owing to the presence of benzene. The president of Perrier's international division, Frederik Zimmer, then offered the explanation that "Perrier water naturally contains several gases, including benzene."[9] From the contradictory messages released to the press, it was clear that U.S. operations were not communicating well—if at all—with the international division. Moreover, yet another story emerged that contradicted the previous explanations: According to Perrier officials, "the benzene entered the water because of a dirty pipe filter at an underground spring at Vergeze in southern France."[10] These contradictions badly hurt the company's credibility. On top of everything else, Perrier's advertising claims of being naturally pure were exposed as untrue. As Anne Mougenot, an analyst with Didier Philippe brokerage in Paris, commented at the time, "I think it is fairly clear that they rearranged the truth. At first they grabbed for anything, and now they have this theory of saturated filters."[11]

What did this crisis mean for Perrier's management and overall performance? The company's chairman and founder, Gustave Leven, was quickly replaced, and Perrier's stock price fell by one-third within the year. The 18 percent fall in stock turnover in the 1990s was accompanied by a 21 percent decline in the group's operating profits. But the lasting legacy of the benzene crisis can be seen in Perrier's withered market shares. America, Perrier's biggest overseas market, saw a 13 percent pre-crisis share of the market for sparkling waters drop to 9 percent.[12] These numbers show how the inept handling of the benzene crisis affected Perrier's management structure and its bottom line. The firm's tendency to panic when faced with surprise, insufficient information, and the media's intense scrutiny highlight the importance of developing an active—not merely reactive—strategy to deal with crises.

By the time Perrier had learned its lesson about the importance of taking an offensive approach to crisis management, it was too late. In 1991, newly appointed chairman Jacques Vincent vowed "to create better coordination between colleagues at all levels."[13] Yet despite these plans to restructure, Perrier's twisting of explanations during the crisis, along with the revelation that "natural" Perrier water was in fact processed, created a lasting dent in Perrier's reputation. The cost of the recall and eventual relaunch of the product—ushered in by a pricey advertising campaign—meant customers found the new 750-ml bottles selling at the same price as the old 1-liter ones. Nestlé swiftly scooped up the company in a takeover bid in 1992, and Perrier's precrisis 1989 market share of 44.8 percent had plummeted to 5.1 percent by 1998.

Many companies run the risk of suffering a similar plight because they do not realize just how vulnerable they are to a major crisis until one occurs. Moreover, being unprepared for potential crises, such as Perrier's, can also lead to a further crisis, as we have seen. And so the downward spiral continues to engulf an organization until someone finally realizes that mitigation is necessary to pull out of the crisis.

JOHNSON & JOHNSON'S TYLENOL RECALL

If effective mitigation occurs soon enough, even the most dismal corporate crisis can have a happy ending. Let's turn to Johnson & Johnson's Tylenol recall to see how such seemingly miraculous turnarounds can come about. In 1982 the product-tampering crisis for Johnson & Johnson captured the imagination of the American public. The company's successful handling of the crisis was characterized by its rapid and unified response, and its ability to care for its consumers, without letting emotions overwhelm its crisis strategy.

In late September and early October of 1982, seven people died after taking Tylenol capsules. The capsules were laced with cyanide; the perpetrator was never caught. At the time, Tylenol had close to 40 percent of the over-the-counter market for pain relievers; within days, sales dropped by close to 90 percent. Johnson & Johnson recalled over 22 million bottles soon after the tragedy came to light, and began to rebuild the brand almost immediately. Unlike Perrier's removal of the brand from the shelves for three months following their benzene crisis, J&J's immediate relaunch emphasized the company's unwavering faith in the Tylenol brand's integrity.

Did this tactic pay off with the panicking public? Certainly the irony of a painkiller medication turning into a killer was responsible for this event becoming so infamous in the pantheon of crises. But many experts on crisis communication, marketing, and psychology feel that it was Johnson & Johnson's caring response that was primarily responsible for turning this disaster into a triumph for the company. Despite losses exceeding $100 million, the Tylenol brand came back stronger than ever within a matter of years.

So what did Johnson & Johnson management actually do? First, they didn't just react to what was happening. Instead, they took the offensive—which the Perrier misfortune proved is key—and removed the potentially deadly product from shelves. Second, they leveraged the goodwill they had taken years to build among constituencies ranging from doctors to the media and decided to try to save the brand rather than simply coming out with a new name for the product. And, third, they acted like responsible human beings concerned with life rather than simply looking at the incident from a purely legal or financial perspective. Thousands of Johnson & Johnson employees made over a million personal visits to hospitals, physicians, and pharmacists around the nation to restore faith in the Tylenol name.[14]

How did this thoughtful reaction enable Tylenol to bounce back so successfully? For one, J&J reacted instantly and seemingly without panic. Top management and PR teams issued full-page ads and videos to newspapers and television networks to keep the public informed; they also promptly designed tamper-proof bottles to further calm the distressed public psyche. Essentially, Johnson & Johnson knew its constituency and was well aware of the emotional nature of the crisis. The company's strategy took emotion into account. By caring, the company was praised for its commitment to ethics and regarded even more highly than it had been before the crisis.

Why did they care? And how did management do such a good job? The answer was literally carved in stone. Despite its decentralized structure, Johnson & Johnson's management is bound together by the Credo—a 308-word companywide code of ethics—that was first used in 1935 to boost morale during the Depression, and is carved in stone at company headquarters in New Brunswick, New Jersey, today. The Credo contains a hierarchy of who managers should care about most—consumers first, employees and the greater community second, and stockholders last. Because the Credo is a living document that is discussed and reaffirmed periodically by Johnson & Johnson's management, the principles of the Credo shifted to the forefront during the Tylenol crisis. These principles provided a written priority code for the company to follow—galvanizing action despite the absence of an official crisis team. As then CEO James Burke—who was brought in early as the lead person handling the crisis—explained, "We had to put our money where our mouth was. We'd committed to putting the public first, and everybody in the company was looking to see if we'd live up to our pretensions." Johnson & Johnson management did just that, and the public duly rewarded them. Within three months of the crisis, the company had regained 95 percent of its previous market share.[15]

The nightmare returned in 1986, when a New Yorker died after taking cyanide-riddled Tylenol capsules. But as a newly seasoned veteran to crisis, Johnson & Johnson was poised to handle the situation. The company rapidly implemented a crisis plan—establishing a toll-free telephone hotline to field questions and offer refunds or exchanges; canceling all Tylenol television ads; and, a few minutes after another defiled bottle was found, issuing a nationwide warning not to use Tylenol capsules. Following the proverbial Boy Scout motto of "Be prepared," J&J's response curbed the panic and organizational chaos that are all too often synonymous with the shock of a crisis.

PEPSICO'S SYRINGE CRISIS

PepsiCo's learned the value of preparation firsthand. Just as Johnson & Johnson's senior management combined strategic thinking with an

Our Credo

We believe our first responsibility is to the doctors, nurses and patients,
to mothers and fathers and all others who use our products and services.
In meeting their needs everything we do must be of high quality.
We must constantly strive to reduce our costs
in order to maintain reasonable prices.
Customers' orders must be serviced promptly and accurately.
Our suppliers and distributors must have an opportunity
to make a fair profit.

We are responsible to our employees,
the men and women who work with us throughout the world.
Everyone must be considered as an individual.
We must respect their dignity and recognize their merit.
They must have a sense of security in their jobs.
Compensation must be fair and adequate,
and working conditions clean, orderly and safe.
We must be mindful of ways to help our employees fulfill
their family responsibilities.
Employees must feel free to make suggestions and complaints.
There must be equal opportunity for employment, development
and advancement for those qualified.
We must provide competent management,
and their actions must be just and ethical.

We are responsible to the communities in which we live and work
and to the world community as well.
We must be good citizens — support good works and charities
and bear our fair share of taxes.
We must encourage civic improvements and better health and education.
We must maintain in good order
the property we are privileged to use,
protecting the environment and natural resources.

Our final responsibility is to our stockholders.
Business must make a sound profit.
We must experiment with new ideas.
Research must be carried on, innovative programs developed
and mistakes paid for.
New equipment must be purchased, new facilities provided
and new products launched.
Reserves must be created to provide for adverse times.
When we operate according to these principles,
the stockholders should realize a fair return.

Johnson & Johnson

Figure 10-1   *Text of Johnson & Johnson's credo.*

awareness of public emotions, so did PepsiCo's management during the
1993 syringe hoax—but PepsiCo's management took it one step further.
While J&J successfully braved its crisis by adhering to its value system
and caring for the public, PepsiCo did the same but added an awareness
for two other crucial groups—the government and, most important, the
media. Notice how good relations with the FDA and journalists curbed

panic and allowed the company not only to address the crisis success-fully but also to emerge from the crisis even stronger than before.

On the evening of June 14, 1993, in Fircrest, Washington, Earl and Mary Triplett drank half a Diet Pepsi. The next morning Earl reported that he had discovered a syringe in the can when he shook out the rest of the contents into the sink.[16] This was the beginning of a major crisis for PepsiCo.

The CEO of PepsiCo North America, Craig E. Weatherup, was at home, gardening, that evening, when he received the news of the syringe incident from FDA commissioner David Kessler. Immediately both men recognized that the claims were illogical. They went into action—with Kessler pursuing the criminal side of the investigation, and Weatherup dealing with the corporate side of the crisis.

Weatherup didn't let the effect and surprise of the crisis overwhelm him for a second. Instead—just like CEO James Burke's proactive response to the Tylenol crisis—Weatherup channeled his energy into devising a strategy to save the company. His first action was to engage PepsiCo's crisis management team. PepsiCo's core four-person crisis team—made up of "experienced crisis managers from public affairs, reg-ulatory affairs, consumer relations, and operations"[17]—responded to the crisis swiftly. The response included clear communication with FDA reg-ulatory officials, the media, and, of course, consumers. Internally, the team prevented organizational chaos by updating employees with daily advisories to over 400 PepsiCo facilities nationwide. The communication flow—internally and externally—never slackened its pace. As PepsiCo's manager of public affairs Anne Reynolds Ward explained, "The sooner you present the facts clearly to the public, the sooner the issue will be resolved." This is a radical shift from Perrier's evasive comments and unconvincing half-truths.[18]

How did PepsiCo manage to keep control? Thirty-six consumer affairs employees and a dozen spokespeople responded to consumers and the media, and PepsiCo also mobilized its legal, government rela-tions, and science departments. Unlike Johnson & Johnson's decision to recall Tylenol from the shelves immediately, by the next morning Weatherup had decided *not* to recall the product—despite more reports flooding into the FDA's office that the products had been contaminated with dangerous objects. As would be expected, television networks were calling to see if PepsiCo officials wanted to respond or issue any formal statements. They did. More important, PepsiCo had a lot to *show*. Realizing that the crisis began with visuals—and the disturbing imagery of syringes in cans—Weatherup beat the crisis at its own visual game. He had his staff prepare video footage demonstrating the canning process at PepsiCo, showing how it was virtually impossible to insert a syringe into the cans. As Weatherup explained, "We sent the footage up by satellite by 3 o'clock Tuesday."[19] To add even more visual punch, PepsiCo later distributed a grocery-store surveillance tape of a woman stealthily dropping a syringe into her Pepsi can. After the footage appeared as the lead story on three major networks Thursday night, no new reports of syringes were made.[20]

PepsiCo North American CEO also made several television appearances throughout the day, on *The MacNeil/Lehrer News Hour* and *Larry King Live*. In Weatherup's last appearance, Kessler accompanied him. Representing the FDA, Kessler added the necessary authoritative power to legitimize all of PepsiCo's defenses. Both men stressed the implausibility of the claims and the criminality of making false statements (five years in prison and up to $250,000 in fines). In addition, the Federal Anti-Tampering Act—dubbing it a felony to tamper with foods, drugs, devices, cosmetics, and all consumer products—was on PepsiCo's side. As a result, Weatherrup could say with certainty on NBC's *Today Show*: "I can't give you a 100 percent guarantee, but I would assure you it is 99.99 percent assured that nothing is happening in the facilities themselves, in the plants. It's literally, physically impossible." Some bottlers even tried to calm local jitters themselves. "Hell, we opened our plant up to everybody," says James C. Lee, Jr., chairman of the Buffalo Rock Co. in Birmingham, Alabama. "The TV stations came over, and we showed 'em we got 2S people doing quality control 'round the clock."[21]

Regardless of all these efforts, it was the FDA's recurring voice in the crisis that stamped all of PepsiCo's statements with the necessary authority. PepsiCo—when united with a U.S. government agency—seemed much more credible to consumers than it would have been standing alone. Without an investigative reporting team of its own, PepsiCo found that the government agency was invaluable to the company during the crisis. In 1989 the FDA established a center in the wake of the Tylenol tampering incident to provide the agency with a team of forensic science experts who can respond immediately to all tampering incidents and provide expert advice and scientific evidence to FDA officials. Through careful observation and the use of high-tech instruments, 30 chemists and three biologists solve tampering mysteries and other criminal activities involving FDA-regulated products. It was FDA sleuthing that provided the evidence used to convict a tamperer who had falsely claimed she found a mouse inside a Pepsi can when she opened it. From there the hoax began to unravel. Several days later, the FBI arrested four individuals for making false claims, and the crisis appeared even more like a hoax. In the end 20 arrests were made, and the crisis was resolved.

PepsiCo did not stop there, however. To ensure that consumers knew the case was a scam and the company was in no way at fault, as a classic follow-up, Weatherup took out an ad to address the concerns of employees and customers. As he explained, "On Monday, Pepsi will run full-page advertisements in 200 newspapers around the country, including the *Washington Post*. The ad reads: 'Pepsi is pleased to announce...nothing. As America now knows, those stories about Diet Pepsi were a hoax. Plain and

Pepsi is pleased to announce...

...nothing.

As America now knows, those stories about Diet Pepsi were a hoax. Plain and simple, not true. Hundreds of investigators have found no evidence to support a single claim.

As for the many, many thousands of people who work at Pepsi-Cola, we feel great that it's over. And we're ready to get on with making and bringing you what we believe is the best-tasting diet cola in America.

There's not much more we can say. Except that most importantly, we won't let this hoax change our exciting plans for this summer.

We've set up special offers so you can enjoy our great quality products at prices that will save you money all summer long. It all starts on July 4th weekend and we hope you'll stock up with a little extra, just to make up for what you might have missed last week.

That's it. Just one last word of thanks to the millions of you who have stood with us.

**Drink All The Diet Pepsi You Want.
Uh Huh.**

Figure 10-2   *Diet Pepsi ad run after hoax.*

Simple. Not true.' It ends with an invitation: 'Drink All the Diet Pepsi You Want.' 'Uh Huh.'"[22] Pepsi remains one of America's leading soft drinks, with 32 percent market share[23] (with Diet Pepsi making up 5.3 percent of that[24]), demonstrating that negative publicity and crisis situations can be overcome when the crisis is successfully handled.

What conclusions can we draw from the Perrier, Tylenol, and PepsiCo crises? A well-thought-out, efficiently executed, communications-based crisis management strategy can make all the difference in the outcome for a corporation facing any disaster. Where Perrier floundered, even lying to an extremely important constituency—its consumers—PepsiCo went all out and with a mass-media blitz, denied the charges, and took control, emphasizing that it was going to find a solution. PepsiCo's cooperation with and cultivation of a relationship with the FDA were the keys to the company's success. The FDA's solid track record of protecting consumers made it a better voice than PepsiCo's for exonerating the company of any blame. Johnson & Johnson took a similarly proactive approach in its handling of the 1982 and 1986 Tylenol crises. The value system binding the company together through the Credo made it clear that for Johnson & Johnson, the consumer comes first. This pledge essentially restored customers' faith in the credibility of the organization and its products. When you compare these careful responses to Perrier's panicked reaction, the aftereffects of each company's crisis should not be surprising. Perrier's market share fell through the floor, but both Tylenol and PepsiCo strengthened their brand and corporate reputations.

CRISES AND THE AMERICAN PSYCHE

Through the use of good or poor crisis management, we have seen how the Perrier, Tylenol, and Pepsi crises all wound their way—directly or indirectly—into the everyday lives of the American public. Even more crucial is the way these crises managed to infiltrate the American psyche. Why do these episodes have such a powerful effect on the average consumer? And, more generally, do such crises have lasting power in the public's memory as well as on the fortunes of the companies involved? We can all agree that we remember and are moved by negative news more than by positive news.

Just take a look at the nightly television news. You rarely see positive news pieces because they just don't sell to an audience accustomed to the more dramatic events that come out of the prime-time fare on television.

Second, the human tragedy associated with a crisis pulls at the heartstrings of us all. The terrorist bombing of the World Trade Center and the

Pentagon in 2001, a cable car detaching over the French Alps in 1999, a New York–bound Air France Concorde exploding northeast of Charles de Gaulle airport in July 2000—such events make people realize how vulnerable we all are and how quickly events can engulf innocent victims. Whether a company's error prompted the crisis—as with Perrier—or the company became a victim in its own right—as we saw with both the Tylenol and Pepsi crises—often determines the emotional response, and most important, the ability of the public to both forgive and forget.

Finally, corporate crises often do manage to stick in people's minds because business has such low credibility in the first place—reinforced by incessant media images of ruthless and profit-hungry corporations. A public that was already predisposed to hate big companies could not be completely surprised by what happened to the Exxon *Valdez*. People almost expect these events to happen and delight in the subsequent misfortunes of these large companies. If the crisis happens to overlap with already controversial cultural topics—like diversity in the workplace or threats to personal security on the Internet—the public's reaction will be all the more animated. As a result, your company needs to become an astute "reader" of the culture, to observe, in particular, those aspects of the culture that can influence how your organization is perceived and how best to get your company's image seen and its voice heard.

As we look at two other major crises—the Merrill Lynch discrimination suit in 1997 and the CD Universe security breach of 2000—consider the effect of cultural norms and trends. Then consider what effect cultural norms and trends have on your own organization. You will begin to recognize why these events linger in the American psyche for more than a short period of time. In this age of information, the average person is bombarded by more images—both skewed and realistic—than ever before. For this very reason companies must tread more carefully and cast a broader net when observing existing cultural trends. In the two crises we are about to explore, two major trends came into play—equal opportunity in the Merrill Lynch discrimination case and personal privacy in the CD Universe cyber-blackmailing episode. Let's take a closer look at the Merrill Lynch case, paying particular attention to how the company's failure to recognize cultural trends escalated the crisis.

MERRILL LYNCH AND GENDER DISCRIMINATION ON WALL STREET

Given the persistence of the American public's memory, we can all see how important it is for companies to recognize the continuing evolution of

American culture. Since the feminist movement gained substantial momentum in the early 1970s, gender equality in the workplace has been a notable hot spot on America's cultural radar. Public dissatisfaction persists. "There is so much that needs to change....It's kind of like trying to melt a glacier with a blow dryer." That is how Mary Stowell, an attorney at the law firm representing 947 women who filed gender discrimination cases against Merrill Lynch, described the need for change at the brokerage firm. To start the process, Stowell's law firm brought a class-action suit against Merrill Lynch in 1997. The suit catapulted Merrill Lynch's treatment of women into the limelight and brought the firm into a crisis situation.[25]

Like many other investment banks, Merrill Lynch has never had a great reputation for its treatment of female employees. In the early 1970s Merrill Lynch described its prototypical employee as "a man, who among other things, did not have a wife who works, for his ego requires that he be the full supporter of their family."[26]

Although the times have changed significantly since those days, Wall Street is often still considered "one of the last bastions of discriminatory treatment and unequal standards in the country," according to Laurel Bellows, former head of the American Bar Association's Commission on Women.[27] Thus the Merrill Lynch case is viewed in both the private and the public spheres as a landmark case whose conclusion affected the industry as a whole.

Shouldn't Merrill Lynch have seen this coming? The original case against the brokerage firm was filed in 1997 by eight female employees who claimed that the firm systematically discriminated against women in wages, promotional opportunities, account distribution, resources, training, and other areas that were crucial to achieving success at the firm. Linda M. Conti, one of the original eight plaintiffs, claimed there wasn't a level playing field for employees. She described the roadblocks faced by female employees, such as the passing of leads or references on to male brokers.[28] Angela Covo's experience echoes that of Conti's. Covo started out at a lower salary than her male colleagues did. When she transferred from the Manhattan office to the San Antonio office, her career "hit a serious wall."[29] Covo asserts that she didn't get the same opportunities as the male brokers in her office, wasn't given the same partnerships and help, and was socially ostracized.[30] Lower salaries were justified by " 'Well, you have a husband,' or 'Men have a family to support,' " explained Stowell, a partner in Stowell & Friedman, the law firm representing the plaintiffs.[31] In addition, the women charged that Merrill Lynch penalized women who took maternity leave.[32] As one woman summed it up, "They scare you so badly and beat you down."[33]

Although Merrill Lynch's spokesperson continually denied any systematic discrimination by the firm, the firm settled the suit in September 1998. It rewarded the eight original claimants $600,000 to be distributed among them because they were first to come forward with the case, and $5 million to the law firm involved in the class action suit. More significantly, the class-action settlement was opened to financial consultants who worked for Merrill Lynch between January 1994 and June 1998. These employees were now eligible to redress any complaints of discrimination and to have their case heard through mediation and arbitration. This effectively opened the floodgates. To Merrill Lynch's dismay, about one-third of both former and current eligible employees filed suit against the firm, three to four times more complaints than the firm had expected.[34] A Merrill Lynch vice chairman evaluated the programs and outreach Merrill Lynch had organized for the previous five years: "Clearly the numbers are both quite distressing and disappointing to me....This indicated that either we didn't do enough or the message didn't get around."[35]

Merrill Lynch had 60 days to review and respond to each of the 947 claims it received. Women who were not pleased with Merrill Lynch's assessment could pursue further mediation.[36] Those who proved their case were entitled to financial compensation, estimated to cost Merrill Lynch $250 million.[37]

Through all of this, the firm continued to deny all accusations. Susan Thomson, a Merrill Lynch spokesperson, asserted that after investigating all the allegations, the firm could find no evidence of widespread or systematic discrimination at the firm.[38] CEO David Komansky, President Herb Allison, and John Steffens, vice chairman and head of the company's retail division, sent a memo to all employees announcing these findings.[39] The memo also denied reports that the settlement would cost the company over $250 million and added that without any court decision, the firm couldn't even know "how many, if any, of the individual claims have merit."[40]

After so much staunch denial, Merrill Lynch was eventually forced to eat its words. By June 1999 the firm conceded that 900 of the now 2900 complaints against the firm had merit or at least deserved further investigation.

Is it surprising, then, that the case resulted in such a public outcry? Perhaps Merrill Lynch's defensive approach and constant denial of fault prevented the firm from having a positive experience with the plaintiffs and the public at large.

But the icing on the cake—further damaging the firm's reputation—was the company's untimely attempt or complete failure to fulfill the terms of the settlement. Stowell & Friedman have accused Merrill Lynch of dragging its feet on the promises of change within the firm and of not yet settling any of the 900 claims. A former Merrill Lynch employee who is one of the plaintiffs said, "I know dozens of women, including myself, who have not had their claims negotiated in good faith by Merrill Lynch."[41] In addition, the lawyers for the plaintiffs claim that "retaliation against class members who filed claims has become commonplace and widespread."[42] Once again, Merrill Lynch disagreed with the accusations and highlighted that 70 percent of those receiving promotions in 1998 were women, and that in the same year there were 7 percent more female financial consultants than in the previous year, as compared to only 1 percent more among male employees.[43]

Given society's awareness of workplace discrimination, the public was watching the case proceedings intently. Women's groups followed the case with an especially keen interest, and advocacy groups were pleased with the threat of legal action posed to firms, which could bring both public exposure and payouts. They also feel bringing companies up on charges is a good way to spark change. As the head of Catalyst, a group that works to advance women in business, Sheila Wellington explains, "Litigation is frequently the first wave of change.... We will be watching, and others will too."[44]

The New Face of Crises: CD Universe

From our look at Merrill Lynch, we can see how imperative it is for companies to evolve as culture changes. The nature of crises will change as a result of new trends. As we saw in Chapter 8, one of the most important developments over the past decade, the advent of the Internet, has generated new cultural concerns about security and privacy. The Internet has also created a new popular fixation with the mass accumulation and security of on-line information.

With serious Internet-related crises occurring early in the year 2000, the business world placed a new focus on IT security issues. Internet-related businesses needed protection from hackers, fraud, and other violations of privately held information. This was especially true in the case of companies that still needed to establish credibility with their customers, or, in the case of start-up companies, which had yet to build both reputation and trust. Security breaches can result in theft, viruses, and system downtime. Such incursions are extremely damaging because business-critical information can be lost or stolen by cyber-thieves. As we focus on the CD Universe case, consider how the cultural hot spots of personal privacy and security generated a corporate crisis.

The case of CD Universe, an on-line retailer of music CDs and a subsidiary of eUniverse, Inc., illustrates how a security breach can put a company in peril. The company was blackmailed in January 2000 after an extortionist claimed he had copied the credit card files of the Internet company's more than 300,000 customers.[45] A person identifying himself as Maxim claimed to possess the stolen customer information and demanded compensation of $100,000 in return for not posting the information on the Internet. The company did not respond to his demands, so he began placing the credit card files on the Internet.

How would you have responded to such a threat? CD Universe began by contacting the FBI to open an investigation. Brad Greenspan, chairman of eUniverse, asserted that eUniverse and CD Universe "[refuse] to bow down to this new breed of cyber-criminal... we have taken a stand against a new form of online blackmail on behalf of all legitimate e-commerce retailers."[46] And a growing breed it is. A July 2000 BBC report claimed that a computer hacker's tampering endangered astronauts' lives during a September 1997 voyage.[47] Such reports are backed by other high-profile incidents such as numerous attacks on Pentagon computers by Russian hackers in 1999.[48] Exaggerated or not, the reports were substantial enough to prompt then President Clinton to announce a $1.46 billion initiative to improve U.S. government computer security in 1999.

In the CD Universe investigations, an e-mail trail indicated that the extortionist was from Eastern Europe. This fact illustrates another danger of cyber-criminals: they operate beyond the jurisdiction of U.S. law, and so they are criminals without boundaries. The FDA role in the PepsiCo hoax proves how valuable national law can be when companies are addressing a crisis or stifling criminal activity perpetrated against them. When an attack is virtual and beyond the jurisdiction of any set of nationally enforced laws, the crisis can spin out of a company's control at even greater speeds. By transcending tangible borders, "The Internet creates a whole new class of criminals," commented Elias Levy, chief technology officer for SecurityFocus.com, a computer security firm. "On the Internet you can have criminals coming from countries where we have no extradition treaties....How do you prosecute these people, or even investigate their crimes?"[49]

With all of these questions looming, CD Universe decided to keep its customers and the public informed, above all else. Mr. Levy's company alerted journalists to the existence of a Web site that the extortionist had been using to distribute up to 25,000 stolen credit card numbers. At the site, called Maxus Credit Card Pipeline, a visitor could access a credit card number, a name, and an address with a single mouse click. To prove the authenticity of the stolen numbers, the extortionist e-mailed a reporter a list of 198 credit cards that were also available on his Web site. The reporter's calls to a random sample of people whose credit card numbers were on the list revealed that at least three credit card numbers were real.

In the midst of such a crisis, which constituency would you contact first? How would you contact them? The company's first reaction was to send e-mail notices to its customers alerting them to the theft of their information. The e-mail outlined the company's quick response to the security breach and its work with the credit card companies to help customers in case their stolen numbers were used. The Web site where the credit card information was being dispensed was shut down the same day the security breach was discovered. The blackmailer was using an Internet carrier based in Kirkland, Washington, without the carrier's knowledge.

Before the Maxus site was shut down, however, the hacker posted some additional customer information on the Internet, enabling several thousand visitors to download some 25,000 card numbers from the system. Although the FBI shut down the site on the same day the security breach was discovered, the potential damage that a hacker could do became all too evident. The man who ultimately identified himself as the blackmailer claimed he was 19 and from Russia. To break into CD Universe's database, he is said to have found and exploited a security flaw in the software that was used to protect financial information on the CD Universe Web site. Maxim also said he had hit other e-commerce Web sites in the same manner.

Organizations across the board—not merely Internet-based companies such as CD Universe—are vulnerable to cyber-violation. You need look no further than the 2000 "I Love You" virus—which cost businesses across a range of industries an estimated total of $10 billion in damages—for proof of this risk. And as long as hackers can rake in substantial dollars for their activities, they continue to pose a threat. For example, a Russian hacker successfully extracted $10 million from Citibank in the summer of 1994.[50] With thefts of that scale, the price tag for businesses is a hefty one. The FBI estimates that U.S. businesses lost $266 million in 1999 to hackers—a staggering figure that is more than double the average annual losses for the previous three years.[51] In the new economy that has emerged, the widespread public concern over personal security now has the power to substantially affect a company's bottom line. Whatever the crisis, we can see that some form of advance preparation is necessary.

PREPARING TO HANDLE A CRISIS

As we move on to describing how your company can best prepare for a crisis, we'll look at three main phases of planning:

Preparation: how to mobilize a crisis response structure before a crisis actually occurs

Documentation: how to make that structure concrete vis-à-vis a formal crisis document

Implementation: how to implement the plan and communicate effectively when a crisis rears its ugly head

Preparing for these three crucial phases ahead of time will allow your company to reduce vulnerability and panic.

How to Prepare in Advance for a Crisis

As shown by all the cases described earlier, any organization, no matter what industry or location, can find itself involved in the kinds of crises that we have been analyzing. Whether you're victimized by a tragic external event like Johnson & Johnson, hit with a media scandal like PepsiCo, or crippled by an undetected internal problem like Perrier— every organization is at risk. Today's rapidly changing culture means that all companies are up against new challenges and increased public scrutiny, as we saw with CD Universe and Merrill Lynch. If you are in an industry subject to crises routinely—the chemical industry, pharmaceuticals, airlines, mining, forest products, and energy-related industries such as gas and electric utilities—that risk is even greater. Regardless, you should always expect the unexpected.

Take, for example, the explosion that blew out three underground floors of the World Trade Center in New York in 1993, as well as the second terrorist attack on September 11, 2001. In 1993, over 50,000 people worked in the twin towers, and millions passed through the area each week. Only a handful of people were allowed back into the building two days after the 1993 blast (they were chosen by lottery) to gather up important papers and get individual businesses back on track. Large firms, such as the major accounting firm Deloitte & Touche, were able to move their operations to another location within a couple of days. Others, however, found themselves virtually out of business until the building was officially opened again over a week later. In the aftermath of the 1993 bombing, Morgan Stanley Dean Witter put in place a crisis plan, which the firm credits for saving the lives of many employees in September 2001.

After the 1993 bombing, many other organizations in the WTC developed crisis plans for an evacuation from the World Trade Center. Because evacuation plans were in place, many lives were saved in 2001 when the second, devastating terrorist attack occurred. You can motivate your colleagues in management to prepare for the worst by using anecdotal information about what has happened to unprepared organizations in earlier crises—such as the cases discussed in this chapter. With so many anecdotes to choose from, you should be able to find enough crises in each industry over the last 10 years to demonstrate the need for your company to be proactive in crisis prevention. Once the groundwork is laid for all levels of management to accept the notion that a crisis is a possibility, your organization should prepare as follows.

Brainstorm Ideas.   Schedule a brainstorming session that includes the most senior managers in the organization as well as the areas that are most likely to be affected by a crisis. In the case of the explosions at the World Trade Center in 1993 and 2001, after the loss of lives, the loss of crucial information was one of the worst outcomes of the explosion. Having your chief information officer involved in crisis preparation ensures that your company's data will be protected in the event of a crisis. The most important part of this brainstorming session is to get all areas of senior management directly involved in and comfortable with crisis preparation.

Assess Your Risk.   As mentioned earlier, some industries are more prone to crises than others. Now think about your own organization. Is it likely to be attacked, and by whom? Thinking back to the Merrill Lynch case, should the firm have foreseen an attack in the equality-conscious age in which we live? But how exactly can organizations determine whether they are more or less likely to experience a crisis? First, publicly traded companies are at risk because of the nature of their relationship with a key constituency, their shareholders. If a major catastrophe hits a company that trades on one of the stock exchanges, the chances of creating a run on the stock are enormous.

A privately held company does not have to worry about shareholders when a crisis hits, but it does have to worry about the loss of goodwill, which can affect sales. Often the owners of a privately held company become involved in communication during a crisis to lend their own credibility to the organization. So all organizations—public, private, and not-for-profit—are at some risk if a crisis occurs.

Set Communication Objectives for Potential Crises. The overriding objective of all crisis planning should be to maintain the flow of communication at all times—not just on paper, but in practice as well. Typically managers are more likely to focus on what kinds of things they will do during a crisis rather than on what they will say and to whom. Often the latter takes on more importance than the former when the crisis involves intangibles such as the loss of reputation rather than the loss of lives.

Consider Your Constituencies. Once companies have assessed the probability of potential crises, they need to determine which constituencies would be most affected by a crisis. Why is this issue so important? Since some constituencies are more important than others, organizations need to look at risk in terms of its effect on the most important constituencies. CD Universe recognized that its first priority was to keep its customers informed. And during the Tylenol crisis, the Johnson & Johnson Credo was invaluable in its rank ordering of constituencies. Ranking one constituency over another is much more difficult in the hectic, fast-paced environment of a crisis. Thinking about this issue in advance helps an organization further refine which potential crises it should spend the most time and money preparing for.

Analyze Your Channel Choice. Once this ranking of constituencies is complete, the participants in a planning session should start thinking about methods of communication, and what their communication objective will be for each crisis and constituency. Whether this objective will be achieved often depends on the communication channel you choose to convey the message. Would the mass distribution of a memo be too impersonal for a message you are sending to your employees? Would personal meetings or e-mails be a better choice? What would be the most efficient and most sensitive way to communicate with consumers or their families during a crisis? The choice of communication channel can often reflect how sensitive a company is to its consumers' needs and emotions. We saw earlier how Perrier's lack of proactive communication offended its customers, while Johnson & Johnson's caring, highly personalized reaction—involving a host of personal visits to hospitals and pharmacies nationwide—won over the hearts of many. In a time of crisis, constituencies crave information, and they are often very aware of how a company chooses to convey its message to them. Remember that the media is itself a constituency and should be treated as such.

Assign Different Teams to Each Crisis.   Another important part of communication planning in a crisis is determining in advance who will be on what team for each crisis. Different problems require different kinds of expertise. Communication experts need to be included, but your company should also consider who is best suited internally to deal with one crisis as opposed to another. For example, if the crisis is likely to have a financial focus, the chief financial officer may be the best person to lead a team dealing with such a problem. He or she may also be the best spokesperson when the problem develops.

On the other hand, if the crisis is tragic or of serious magnitude, for instance, involving the loss of human lives, such as the Alaska Airlines crash of 2000, the CEO is probably the best person to put in charge of the team and to serve initially, at least, as head spokesperson for the crisis. Indeed, Alaska Airlines chairman John Kelly addressed the press as soon as possible after the crash, telling a late-night press conference in Los Angeles: "We will do anything and everything to find out exactly what transpired."[52] Given the magnitude of the crisis, because of the loss of life, anyone other than the CEO would have lacked credibility with the general public and a media hungry for information.

Overall, assigning different teams to handle different crises helps the organization put the best people in charge of handling that crisis and the necessary communications. Appropriate team assignments also enable the company to get as many people involved as possible. The more involved managers are in planning and participating on a team in a crisis, the better equipped the organization will be to handle all the curve balls a crisis inevitably throws.

How to Combat Crises with a Plan

While organizations can deal with corporate communication using either a centralized or a decentralized approach for general purposes—when it comes to crisis, the approach must be completely centralized. A consolidated approach helps ensure that the flow of communication is as accurate and efficient as possible. Conflicting stories from the U.S. and European divisions became the main problem in the Perrier benzene scare and took the crisis to a new level. Such decentralized organizations often find efficient communications between divisions difficult, especially if they have not given interdivisional communication full consideration in a crisis-planning phase. Take the time to do so.

Every communications consultant will suggest that companies should develop a detailed plan for use in a crisis. These plans are formal in the sense that they are typically printed up and distributed to the appropriate managers who may have to sign a statement swearing that they have read and agree to the plan. Through this procedure the organization ensures that the responsible parties have acknowledged the plan, and that any disagreements about the plan are ironed out *before* rather than *during* a crisis. The last thing you want to have happen is for a plant manager to open the plan for the first time in the midst of a real crisis.

Be sure to incorporate the following elements into your formal plan to combat an imminent crisis:

• An approach to managing relations with the media
• A strategy for notifying employees
• A crisis headquarters location
• An official version of the plan

An Approach to Managing Relations with the Media.   Frank Corrado, president of a firm that deals with crisis communications, suggests that the cardinal rule for communicating with all constituencies in a crisis should be "Tell it All, Tell it Fast!"[53] To a certain extent this is true, but one should be extremely careful about applying such a rule too quickly with the media. Perhaps a friendly amendment to Corrado's rule might be "tell as much as you can as soon as possible" without jeopardizing the credibility of the organization. For example, Perrier's hasty communications with the media, in the absence of accurate information, were crippling mistakes.

If the organization has done a good job of building relations with the media when times are good, reporters will generally be understanding when something horrible happens. Having a reserve of goodwill with the media is what helped Johnson & Johnson during the Tylenol crisis. Generally, the person who has the best relationships with individual reporters is probably the person to get involved with them during a crisis. By agreeing ahead of time that all inquiries will be routed to a central location, organizations can avoid looking disorganized in a crisis.

A Strategy for Notifying Employees.   When a company faces a crisis, employees are analogous to families in a personal crisis. You wouldn't want a family member to hear about a personal problem from an outsider. Similarly, your company shouldn't want employees to find out from the media about something that affects the organization. Employee communication professionals should work out a plan for notifying employees and include this in the overall crisis plan.

A Crisis Headquarters Location.   Although crisis communications experts suggest that companies invest significant amounts of money for a special crisis center, all companies really need to do is to identify a space that can be easily converted for such an operation ahead of time. In addition, prior consideration should be given to gathering the appropriate technology (for example, computers, fax machines, cell phones, hookups for media transmissions) as quickly as possible when something bad happens. All pertinent internal and external constituencies should be notified about the location of the headquarters ahead of time. All information about the crisis should ideally be centralized through this office. Other lines of communication should then flow through the crisis headquarters for the duration of the crisis.

An Official Version of the Plan.   A detailed description of the company's approach to managing during the crisis should be included in the crisis plan document. It should contain more than just communication activities. It should discuss logistical details as well, for example, how and where the families of victims should be accommodated in the case of an airline crash. The plan should also have the go-ahead from everyone involved ahead of time. Obviously what your company includes in the plan depends on how complicated the possible crisis is and how much additional information (such as proprietary information) needs to be given to team members during that crisis.

Following the development of the overall plan, all managers should receive training about what to do if and when a crisis strikes. Several public relations firms and academic consultants now offer simulated crises so that managers can test their crisis management skills in experiential exercises. Managers searching for the right training should be sure that the simulation or training session includes a heavy emphasis on communication rather than just the management of the crisis itself.

How to Communicate During a Crisis

All of the planning that an organization can muster will only partially prepare it for an actual crisis because every crisis is different. But, if an organization's crisis management plan—the overall approach that is formalized in writing—is comprehensive enough, managers will at least start from a strong position.

Crises also have enough common elements that we can offer the following steps as a starting point for managing a crisis:

* Define the problem

- Gather the relevant information
- Centralize communications
- Communicate early and often
- Get inside the media's head
- Communicate directly with affected constituencies
- Keep the business running
- Make plans immediately after the crisis to avoid another crisis

Let's look at these steps using some of the examples mentioned earlier in this chapter.

Step 1: Define the Problem.   The first step is for the appropriate manager to define the real problem using reliable information, and then to set measurable communication objectives. After initially handing over control to the courts, Merrill Lynch, in the discrimination lawsuit case, decided to look into the claims on its own accord. This step allowed the firm to gain its own understanding of the problem. In Perrier's case, the company lacked sufficient information to define the problem in the first place, although its spokespeople tried to convince the public otherwise.

Not only do the right people need to be hired as outside crisis management specialists in the first place, but the right internal people need to be consulted at the right times. Everyone in the organization should, theoretically, know whom to contact when something happens. But in large organizations, this is unrealistic. Therefore the corporate communication department can serve initially as a clearinghouse. The vice president for corporate communications at the head office should know the composition of the company's crisis teams and be able to turn the situation over to the appropriate manager immediately.

Step 2: Gather the Relevant Information.   Directly related to defining the problem, the gathering of relevant information is crucial to addressing a crisis. This involves managing the information coming in from many sources. As Weatherup and Kessler continued to receive news of apparent Pepsi can tampering from all around the country, the FDA and FBI gathered the information, and Weatherup continued to refute claims that PepsiCo had contaminated its soft drinks. As information becomes available, someone should be assigned to mine this incoming information. If it is an industrial accident, how serious is it? Were lives lost? Have families already been notified? If the accident involves an unfriendly takeover, what are the details of the offer? Was it absurdly low? Have any plans been made to repel such an attack? Finding the answers to these questions may help an organization identify the key issues that need to be addressed.

Many corporations have been criticized for reacting too slowly during a crisis, even when the delay was caused by the company's desperate but fruitless attempt to gather information about the incident so that it could report the facts accurately to concerned constituencies. If the right information will take more than a few hours to secure, a company spokesperson should communicate this to the media and other key constituencies right away, to make it clear that the company is not stonewalling. No one will criticize your company for trying to find out what is going on, but you can face harsh treatment if constituencies think your company is deliberately obstructing the flow of information. In Merrill Lynch's case, the information gathering was initially left to the lawyers. The firm only began to gain some understanding of the crisis when it started obtaining information independently.

Step 3: Centralize Communications.   At the same time that managers are getting in touch with the right people and gathering information, corporate communication professionals should be making arrangements for getting a crisis center up and running. This location will serve as the platform for all communications during the crisis. Care should also be given to providing a comfortable location for media to use during the crisis. This would include adequate computers, phone services, fax machines, and so on. All communications about the crisis should come from this one, centralized location. In PepsiCo's case, about a dozen people gathered from production and manufacturing, scientific and regulatory affairs, and legal and public relations staff. The group began working around the clock; some slept in the office, while others got home only long enough for a shower, a change of clothes, and a nap. Meetings, like sleep, were catch-as-catch-can. As one veteran of the crisis remarked: "We would see each other wherever the Chinese food or pizza was located."[54]

Step 4: Communicate Early and Often.   Say whatever you can as soon as possible; as PepsiCo's spokesman Andrew Giangola states, "Our philosophy is simple...communicate fast and communicate frequently."[55] On the same note, however, never convey misinformation in haste merely to get a statement released.

Particularly if the crisis involves a threat to lives and property, the company should try to allay the fears that people will inevitably have about the situation—inside and outside the company. Employees, the media, and other important constituencies should know that the crisis center will issue updates at regular intervals until further notice. Companies need to put good inside people on the front lines rather than hired guns and should encourage managers to adopt a team approach with others involved in crisis communication. Perrier's CEO wasn't even involved in the crisis communication. Certainly, a strategy should have been in place that incorporated the company's chief player.

Step 5: Get Inside the Media's Head.   When considering all of these constituencies, don't underestimate the importance of the media. Imagining yourself in the shoes of a journalist shouldn't be too difficult. Much like members of corporations, members of the media work in an extremely competitive environment, which explains why each of them wants to get the story first. They are also more accustomed to a crisis environment than are managers. What they are looking for is a good story with victims, villains, and visuals. The Pepsi syringe hoax had all of these sensational elements. As we have seen, Weatherup recognized the visual effect syringes in cans would have on the public and decided to beat the media at its own visual game. Video footage of PepsiCo canning procedures, a grocery-store surveillance tape, and full-page newspaper ads are all examples of PepsiCo using the media as a vehicle to its own triumphant end. Perrier's decision to let the media keep the public informed—while failing to take any control of the messages the media was sending—robbed the company of the voice its consumers were hoping to hear in a time of crisis. As a result, in the Perrier case, the consumers were the victims and Perrier the villain. PepsiCo, however, managed to make itself out to be the victim, thereby capturing the sympathies of the cola-consuming public, and turning the visual emphasis of the media entirely in its favor.

Step 6: Communicate Directly with Affected Constituencies.   Using the media to get information can be useful, but it's more important to communicate with your employees, such as sales staff, site security, operators, and receptionists. These are likely to be the media's best sources in the crisis, as each employee acts as a goodwill ambassador for the firm. External constituencies need to be contacted as well, and with knowledge ahead of time of which constituencies need to be contacted first, your company will know who to be in touch with *right away*. These external constituencies include the other three key groups besides employees—customers, shareholders, and communities—as well as suppliers, emergency services, experts, and officials. Use all available technologies to communicate with them including e-mail, voice mail, faxes, direct satellite broadcasts, and on-line services. Perrier failed to even initiate a public-relations campaign; PepsiCo's final full-page newspaper ad just added a final touch to its already successful crisis communication strategy.

Step 7: Keep the Business Running.   For the managers who are directly involved, the crisis will most certainly be at the forefront of their minds, but for others, business must go on despite the crisis. Besides finding suitable replacements ahead of time for those who are on the crisis team, managers must try to anticipate the effects of the crisis on other parts of the business. For example, if an advertising campaign is under way, should it be suspended during the crisis? Have financial officers stopped trading on the company's stock? Is it necessary for the organization to move to a temporary location during the crisis? These and other questions related to the ongoing business need to be thought through by managers on and off the crisis team as soon as possible. Again, the pertinence of these measures is reflected in the contrasting outcomes of both Perrier's and PepsiCo's actions during their respective crises. Whereas PepsiCo has managed to maintain its soft-drink market share, Perrier's stake in the imported bottled water market has suffered considerably, from a 44.8 percent share in 1989 to a 20.7 percent share in 1990 to a 5.1 percent share in 1998.[56] MerrillLynch is still, despite its gender discrimination suit, considered one of the premier investment banks on Wall Street, having weathered the storm by keeping the business running. As a result, the firm is still a leading investment bank today.

Step 8: Make Plans Immediately to Avoid Another Crisis.   Post-crisis, make sure your company is better prepared for future events. Organizations that have experienced crises are more likely to believe that such occurrences will happen again. Generally, they also recognize that preparation is the key to handling the event successfully. They should try, therefore, to anticipate all the complications a future crisis could hold, and plan accordingly. Johnson & Johnson did just that and seamlessly handled its second Tylenol crisis in 1986—all thanks to the creation and implementation of a crisis plan honed following the 1982 tragedy. There is no better time than the period immediately following a crisis to prepare for the next one, because motivation is high to learn from mistakes made the first time around.

CONCLUSION

We all know that crises are a normal part of our private lives. Managers must realize that the same is true for organizations. Unfortunately, the short-term orientation of most managers prevents them from acknowledging the risks their organization faces. This is an open invitation for crises to come strolling through the front door.

After any crisis, from the attacks on the World Trade Center to the Diet Pepsi hoax, the question remains, would things have turned out differently if crisis preparation had gone into effect? After the devastating blast that leveled the twin towers in September of 2001, we learned that the crisis preparation put into effect in 1993 saved hundreds of lives, making possible the swift evacuation of hundreds of people from the buildings. Ignoring the advice of experts back in 1993 ended up costing a lot of people's lives, millions of dollars, and the disruption of hundreds of businesses. The management of any crisis is simplified by mastering the three phases of crisis management outlined in this chapter—mobilizing a crisis response plan before the crisis hits, documenting the plan formally, and, finally, implementing it effectively.

Prepare by initiating a crisis plan *in advance*, as Johnson & Johnson did to combat its 1986 crisis and PepsiCo did with its four-person core crisis team in 1993. You should also prepare by formalizing the plan in an official document much like Johnson & Johnson prioritized its constituencies through the Credo. And finally, communicate effectively with all constituencies—consumers, government officials, and, of course, the media—*during* the crisis, as PepsiCo did in 1993. But, above all else, getting senior managers to pay attention—and to always expect the unexpected—may be the most important part of crisis communication *before* rather than *after* a crisis develops.

ENDNOTES

CHAPTER 1

1. "How Big Mac Kept from Becoming a Serb Archenemy," *The Wall Street Journal*, September 3, 1999, p. B1.
2. "Merrill, Lawyers for Women in Bias Suit Keep Sparring," *The Wall Street Journal*, September 10, 1999, p. C1.
3. Leon E. Wynter, "Networks Need to Find a Better Balance with Minority Roles," *The Wall Street Journal*, September 8, 1999, p. B1.
4. "'Linux' Run-Up Wasn't Peanuts," *The Wall Street Journal*, September 1, 1999.
5. "Can the Big Guys Rule the Web? Ask Ford or Dunkin' Donuts," *The Wall Street Journal*, August 30, 1999, pp. A1, A6.
6. Robert L. Dilenschneider, "'Spin Doctors' Practice Public Relations Quackery," *The Wall Street Journal*, June 1, 1998, p. A18.
7. Adam Bryant, "Flying High on The Option Express," *The New York Times*, Money & Business, April 5, 1998, Section 3: pp. 1, 8.
8. "Executive Pay Up 571% from 1990 to 2000," *The Los Angeles Times*, September 2, 2001, p. W3.
9. "Decompensation: Executives Ordered to Return Millions," *The Wall Street Journal*, November 10, 1999, pp. A1, A12.
10. The address for this Web site is www.paywatch.org/front.htm.
11. Yankelovich Partners, Norwalk, CT.
12. *PR Reporter*, March 31, 1998, p. 2.
13. Robert Krumer, "Populism Meets Escapism and Escapism Wins," *The Boston Globe*, June 7, 1998, p. E7.
14. W. R. Bion, *Experience in Groups and Other Papers*. New York: Basic Books, 1961, p. 49.
15. National Household Survey on Drug Abuse, 1996.
16. Paul Argenti, Hooker Chemical Company [B] in the *Instructors Manual to accompany Corporate Communication* (2d Ed.). Boston: Irwin/McGraw-Hill, 1998, p. 42.

17. Kevin Johnson, "Firm to pay $129 million for Love Canal cleanup," *USA Today* December 22, 1995.

18. "Field Study Project" by Tuck Students for Field Studies in Business course at th Amos Tuck School, 1997.

19. *Reputation Management*, May/June, 1997, p. 8.

20. James Gleick, *Faster: The Acceleration of Just about Everything*. New Yorl Pantheon Book, 1999, p. 72.

21. Bruce McCall, "At Last, a New Magazine Idea—Oh Shut Up!" *Los Angeles Time* September 5, 1999, p. M3.

CHAPTER 2

1. John Chamberlain, "The Muck-rake Pack" in Herbert Shapiro, ed. *Tl Muckrakers and American Society*. Boston: D.C. Heath and Company, p. 50.

2. C. C. Regier, "The Balance Sheet," in Shapiro, p. 38.

3. Lincoln Steffens, "Shame of the Cities," in Shapiro, p. 62.

4. Richard Hofstader, "The Progressive Impulse," in Shapiro, p. 94.

5. Regier, p. 41.

6. Richard S. Tedlow, *Keeping the Corporate Image: Public Relations and Busines 1900–1950*. Greenwich, Connecticut: JAI Press, 1979, pp. 4–5.

7. Walter Lippman, "The Themes of Muckraking," in Shapiro, p. 20.

8. See Ray Eldon Hiebert, *Courtier to the Crowd: The Story of Ivy Lee and tl Development of Public Relation* (Ames, Iowa: Iowa State UP, 1966), pp. 47–48, and Tedlow, p. 36, for complete details of Lee's involvement in the operator. efforts to ward off a second strike and improve their reputation.

9. See Hiebert, pp. 53–69, for a detailed discussion of Lee's involvement with th railroads, an account to which we are indebted for our discussion.

10. Scott M. Cutlip, *The Unseen Power: Public Relations. A History*. Hillsdale, Nev Jersey: Lawrence Erlbaum, 1944, p. 52.

11. See Hiebert, pp. 64–65, for further discussion of Lee's work for the railroads.

12. Tedlow, p. 37.

13. Stuart Ewen, *PR! A Social History of Spin*. New York: Basic Books, 1996, pp. 78–8

14. Quoted in Cutlip, p. 154.

15. See Cutlip, pp. 143–153, for a detailed account on which this discussion is base

16. Ibid., p. 156.

17. See Hiebert, pp. 297–318, for a discussion of Lee's reputation.

18. "Transcript of Staff Conference, Ivy Lee & T. J. Ross," Oct. 4, 1934, pp. 2–3, 10–1. Ivy Lee Papers, Princeton, quoted in Hiebert, p. 315.

19. See Cutlip, pp. 162–163, for a detailed discussion.

20. Edward L. Bernays, *Biography of an Idea: Memoirs of Public Relations Couns Edward L. Bernays*. New York: Simon and Schuster, 1965, pp. 79–82.

21. See Ibid., pp. 102–129, for Bernays's discussion of the Russian Ballet and p 129–146 for his discussion of Caruso.

22. Ibid., pp. 143–144.

23. Cutlip, pp. 164–165.

24. Larry Tye, *The Father of Spin: Edward L. Bernays & the Birth of Public Relations*. New York: Crown Publishers, 1998, p. 157.

25. Bernays, *Biography of an Idea*, pp. 344–345.

26. See Cutlip, pp. 210–211, for a summary of Bernays's work.

27. Michael Schudson, *Advertising, The Uneasy Persuasion: Its Dubious Impact on American Society*. New York: Basic Books, 1984, p. 186.

28. Bernays, *Biography of an Idea*, p. 386.

29. Quoted in Bernays, *Biography of an Idea*, p. 387.

30. Tye, pp. 29–30.

31. See Bernays, *Biography of an Idea*, pp. 445–460, for Bernays's version of his involvement, upon which this discussion is partially based.

32. Ibid., p. 449.

33. Ewen, pp. 216–217.

34. Edward L. Bernays, *Crystallizing Public Opinion*. New York: Boni and Liveright, 1923, p. 57.

35. Ibid., p. 173.

36. Ibid., p. 171.

37. Ibid., pp. 216–217.

38. Edward L. Bernays, *Propaganda*. New York: Horace Liveright, 1928, p. 18.

39. Ibid., p. 22.

40. Ibid., p. 25.

41. Ibid., p. 42.

42. Ibid., p. 76.

43. Tedlow, pp. 29, 38.

44. See, for example, John C. Stauber and Sheldon Rampton, *Toxic Sludge is Good for You: Lies, Damn Lies, and the Public Relations Industry* (Monroe, Maine: Common Courage Press, 1995), on this crisis.

CHAPTER 3

1. Janis Forman, Interview with Phyllis J. Piano, May 10, 2001.

2. Janis Forman, Interview with Steven J. Harris, May 4, 2001.

3. Janis Forman, Interview with Elizabeth Heller Allen, May 14, 2001.

4. Hal Lancaster, "Managing Your Career: An Ex-CEO Reflects: H-P's Platt Regrets He Wasn't a Rebel," *The Wall Street Journal*, November 16, 1999, p. B1.

5. Matt Murray, "Why Jack Welch's Brand of Leadership Matters," *The Wall Street Journal*, September 5, 2001, p. B10.

6. Ibid., p. B1.

7. GE Annual Report for 2000, p. 9.

8. John A. Byrne, "A Close-up Look at How America's # 1 Manager Runs GE," *Business Week*, June 8, 1998, p. 90+.

9. Ibid., p. 90+.

10. Robert Slater, *Jack Welch and the GE Way: Management Insights and Leadership Secrets of the Legendary CEO*. New York: McGraw-Hill, 1999, p. 6.

11. Ibid., p. 52.

12. Byrne, p. 90+.

13. Slater, p. 53. This and the quotations that follow in this paragraph are quoted from the employee card.

14. Christopher A. Bartlett and Meg Wozny, "GE's Two-Decade Transformation: Jack Welch's Leadership," Harvard Business School, 2000, p. 4.

15. Ibid., p. 4.

16. James L. Heskett, "GE (A) ...We Bring good things to life." Harvard Business School, 2000, p. 11.

17. Kenton W. Elderkin and Christopher A. Bartlett, "General Electric: Jack Welch's Second Wave (A)." Harvard Business School, 1993, p. 11.

18. Ibid., p. 4.

19. Murray, p. B10.

20. Ibid., p. 114.

21. Slater, p. 267.

22. Ibid., p. 15.

23. Janis Forman, Interview with E. Ronald Culp, April 13, 2001.

24. Janis Forman, Interview with Elizabeth Heller Allen, May 14, 2001.

25. Janis Forman, Interview with Steven J. Harris, May 4, 2001.

26. Heyman Consulting, *State of U.S. Corporate Communications*, 2001, p. 18.

27. Janis Forman, Interview with David R. Drobis, March 26, 2001.

28. Janis Forman, Interview with Peter Fleischer, March 15, 2001.

29. Heyman, p. 22.

30. Janis Forman, Interview with Jack Bergen, August 28, 2001.

31. Ibid.

32. Janis Forman, Interview with Bill Margaritis, May 30, 2001.

33. Ibid.

34. Janis Forman, Interview with Bill Nielsen, April 16, 2001.

35. Ibid.

36. Francis J. Aguilar and Arvind Bhambri, "Johnson & Johnson: A Philosophy and Culture," Harvard Business School, 1986, p. 3.

37. Bill Nielsen, Presentation on the Corporate Communications Division, March 2001.

38. Ibid.

39. Janis Forman, Interview with Bill Nielsen, April 16, 2001.

40. Reported in Johnson & Johnson, *Worldwide News Digest.* Vol. 30, no. 1, February 21, 2001, p. 2. Also, "Perils of Corporate Philanthropy," *The Wall Street Journal*, January, 16, 2002, p. B1.

41. Janis Forman, Interview with Dennis Signorovitch, May 17, 2001.

42. Ibid.

43. Janis Forman, Interview with David R. Drobis, March 26, 2001.

44. Janis Forman, Interview with Dennis Signorovitch, May 17, 2001.

45. Ibid.

46. Ibid.

47. "Managing Corporate Communications in a Competitive Climate," a Conference Board Study by Kathryn Troy, 1996.

48. Heyman, p. 38.

49. Ibid., p. 38.

50. Janis Forman, Interview with E. Ron Culp, April 13, 2001.

51. Ibid.

52. John Iwata, "How 'One Voice' has changed IBM: The Downfall of IBM in the 90s was Dramatic but so was the Turnaround," *Arthur Page Society Journal, 16th Annual Spring Seminar*, pp. 26–28.

53. Ibid., p. 26.

54. Janis Forman, Interview with David R. Drobis, March 26, 2001.

55. Janis Forman, Interview with Steven Harris, May 4, 2001.

56. "Anti-org'l Activism on the Web is Grapevine in Real Time: Monitor, Manage, Blanket & Bulletproof Still Holds True." *PR Reporter*, October 20, 2000, p. 4.

57. Heyman, p. 6.

58. Heyman, pp. 21–22.

59. See Paul A. Argenti, "Introduction: Strategic Employee Communications," *Human Resources Management*, Fall/Winter 1988, vol. 237, no. 3 & 4, pp. 199–206, for further discussion of these issues.

60. Heyman, p. 24.

61. James C. Collins and Jerry I. Porras. *Built to Last*. New York: HarperCollins, 1997, p. 80.

62. Mary B. Schaefer "Chief Executive, Chief Communicator," *MIT Management*, Spring 1993.

63. Letter from Union Carbide's CEO, Robert B. Kennedy, to Executive List, dated March 5, 1992.

64. Janis Forman, Interview with John Onoda, April 10, 2001.

CHAPTER 4

1. Business and Economics: Henry Ford, *The Dictionary of Cultural Literacy*, January 1, 1988.

2. "Business Giants: The Businessman of the Century," *Fortune*, November 22, 1999, p 108+.

3. Collins and Porras, pp.52–53.

4. Ibid.

5. "A Corporate Collision; Ford-Firestone Feud Accelerated After Effort to Head It Off Failed," *The Washington Post*, June 20, 2001, p. E01.

6. Collins and Porras, p. xiv.

7. Majken Schultz, Mary Jo Hatch, and Mogens Holten Larsen, *The Expressive Organization*. Oxford: Oxford University Press, 2000, p. 118.

8. Cees B. M. van Riel, "Corporate Communication Orchestrated by a Sustainable Corporate Story," in Schultz, Hatch and Larson, p. 163.

9. Ibid.

10. Melanie Wells, "Cult Brands," *Forbes*, April 16, 2001, p. 201.

11. W. Chan Kim and Renee Mauborgne, "Creating New Market Space," *Harvard Business Review*, January 1, 1999, p. 83.

12. David A. Aaker, *Building Strong Brands*. New York: The Free Press, 1996, p. 109.

13. *Harvard Business School Case*, "The Body Shop International," April 5, 1994, p. 3.

14. The Body Shop 1996. Annual Report.

15. "The Body Shop International," p. 13.

16. Charles P. Wallace, "Can the Body Shop Shape Up?," *Fortune*, April 15, 1996, p. 118+.

17. Jerry Useem, "Conquering Vertical Limits," *Fortune*, February 19, 2001, p. 94.

18. "Who's Up Who's Down," *Fortune*, February 19, 2001, p. F5.

19. Melanie Wells, "Giving an Old Brand New Mystique." *Forbes*, April 16, 2001, p. 205.

20. van Riel, p. 158.

21. Kevin Lane Keller, *Strategic Brand Management*. New Jersey: Prentice Hall, 1998.

22. *PR News*, "This Just In...," March 12, 2001.

23. Rich Karlgaard, "Brand Hypocrisy," *Forbes*, April 16, 2001, p. 51.

24. Kevin L. Keller, "Building and Managing Corporate Brand Equity," in Schultz, Hatch and Larsen, p. 118

25. Bernd Schmitt and Alex Simonson, *Marketing Aesthetics: The Strategic Management of Brands, Identity, and Image*. New York: The Free Press, 1997, p. 17.

26. Wally Olins, "How Brands are Taking over the Corporation," in Schultz, Hatch, and Larsen, p. 55.

27. Ibid, p. 61.

28. Naomi Klein, *No Logo: Taking Aim at the Brand Bullies*. New York: Picador USA, 1999, p. 52.

29. Tom Peters, "Brands still rule supreme," *Advertising Age*, January 26,1998, p. 26.

30. Bernd Schmitt and Alex Simonson, *Marketing Aesthetics: The Strategic Management of Brands, Identity, and Image*. New York: The Free Press, 1997, p. 18.

31. Ibid, p. 22.

32. Ibid.

33. Keller, "Building and Managing Corporate Brand Equity," p. 118.

34. Keller, *Strategic Brand Management*, p. 165.

35. Klein, p. 3.

36. Ibid.

37. Ibid.

38. Ibid

39. Adam Tanner, "Activists embrace web in anti-globalization drive," *Reuters*, July 13, 2001.

40. Joe Chidley, "Tech will rise again," *Canadian Business*, June 11, 2001, p. 4.

41. John Musgreave and Graham Porter, "E-Business Futures Based On Reality," *The London Free Press*, May 21, 2001, p. 5.

42. Ibid.

43. "Tech Is Still The Growth Industry Have we hit bottom?" *Fortune*, November 27, 2000, p. 92+.

44. Ibid.

45. "Working for a tech firm after dot-com crash," *The Toronto Star*, May 12, 2001, p. ADV.
46. Howard Schultz. *Pour Your Heart into It*. New York: Hyperion, 1997.
47. James Lardner, "OK, here are your options." Vol. 126, *U.S. News & World Report*, March 1, 1999, p. 44.
48. Schmitt and Simonson, pp. 83–84.
49. Charles Fombrun. *Reputation: Realizing Value from the Corporate Image*. Boston: Harvard Business School Press, 1996, p. 5.
50. Ibid.
51. Ibid.
52. Useem, p. 94.
53. Belinda Luscombe, "Dusting Off Fashion's Old Bags," *Time*, June 25, 2001, p. Y2.
54. Ibid.
55. Nigel Cope, "Stars and Stripes," *Independent*, June 6, 2001.
56. Lauren Goldstein, "Dressing Up An Old Brand," *Fortune*, January 9, 1998, p.154+.
57. Ibid.
58. Cope.
59. Ibid.
60. Ibid.
61. Ibid.
62. Klein, p. 52
63. James S. O'Rourke, Bridgestone/Firestone Crisis Management, Mendoza College of Business, 2000, p. 1.
64. Caroline E. Mayer and Frank Swoboda, "A Corporate Collision; Ford-Firestone Feud Accelerated After Effort to Head It Off Failed," *The Washington Post*, June 20, 2001, p. E01.
65. *Fortune*, "Who's Up Who's Down," Fortune, February 19, 2001, p. 104.
66. *PR Reporter*, October 23, 2000, p. 1.
67. John Frank, *PR Week*, Feb. 19, 2001.
68. Ibid.
69. David Welch, "Crisis Management: Meet the new face of Firestone," *Business Week*, April 30, 2001, p. 64
70. "Can this brand be saved?," *Harvard Business Review*, p. 156.
71. Ibid.
72. Welch, p. 64
73. Mayer and Swoboda, p. E01.
74. Ibid.
75. Schmitt and Simonson, p. 24.
76. Klein, p. 21.
77. Wells, p. 200.
78. Ibid.
79. Klein. p. 21.
80. Ibid., p. 336.

CHAPTER 5

1. See Roland Marchand, *Creating the Corporate Soul: The Rise of Public Relations and Corporate Imagery in American Big Business* (Berkeley: The University of California Press, 1998), pp. 48–87 for a complete discussion of this topic.
2. Ibid., p. 59.
3. Ibid., pp. 63–69.
4. Ibid., p. 74.
5. Ibid., p. 86.
6. "Bitter dispute ends between Andersen Worldwide units," *Star-Tribune Newspaper of the Twin Cities–Minneapolis/St.Paul*, METRO, August 8, 2000, p. 1D.
7. Janis Forman, Interview with Jim Murphy, March 18, 2001.
8. Michael Siconolfi, "An Identify Crisis? First Boston Tinkers with Name Again—The Third Change in Six Years is Attempt to Emphasize Connection to Swiss Bank," *The Wall Street Journal*, July 3, 1996, p. B5.
9. See Norman Klein and Stephen A. Greyser, "Siemens Corporation (A): Corporate Advertising for 1992," Harvard Business School, 1996, and "Siemens Corporation (B): Corporate Advertising for 1996," Harvard Business School, 1996, for a full discussion of the Siemens advertising campaign throughout the 1990s.
10. Klein and Greyser, "Siemens Corporation (B): Corporate Advertising for 1996."
11. Ted Friedman, "Apple's *1984*: The Introduction of the Macintosh in the Cultural History of Personal Computers." Revised version of a paper presented at the Society of the History of Technology Convention, Pasadena, California, October 1997, www.duke.edu/-tlove/mac.htm, p. 4.
12. Ibid.
13. See Richard W. Lewis, *Absolut Book: The Absolut Vodka Advertising Story* (Boston: Journey Editions, 1996), pp. 105–136 for a discussion of Absolut and fashion.
14. Dale Buss, "Absolut ADvantage," *Business and Industry*, July 2000.
15. Ibid.
16. Annette Shelby, "Issue Advertising." Speech given to Tuck Corporate Communications Class, January 22, 1989.
17. Jess Bravin, "Hollywood Launches Messages of Peace," *The Wall Street Journal*, September 4, 2000, p. B17.
18. Mitchell Landsberg and Tim Reiterman, "Utilities Scramble to persuade Public of Need for Rate Hikes," *The Los Angeles Times*, January 27, 2001, p. A18.
19. Ibid.
20. Ibid.
21. Ibid.
22. Ibid.
23. David Kelley, "Critical Issues for Issue Ads," *Harvard Business Review*, July–August 1982, p. 81.
24. "Reaching the Compassionate Consumer," *American Demographics*, November, 1993, p. 26.
25. Les Blumenthal, "Weyerhaeuser updates image with new ads/campaign aims to give company a higher profile with Congress," *The News Tribune Tacoma Washington*, August 17, 1998, p. A1.

26. Craig Smith, "The Compassionate Consumer," *The Harvard Business Review*, May–June 1994, pp. 105–116.

27. Thomas F. Garbett, "When to Advertise Your Company," *The Harvard Business Review*, March–April 1982, p. 104.

28. Saul Hansell, "Web site ads, Holding Say, Start to Blare," *The New York Times*, March 17, 2001, p. A1.

29. Ibid., p.B2.

30. Carol Hymowitz, "In the Lead: Managers tell how to spot 'gold talent' in old and new hires," *The Wall Street Journal*, March 27, 2001, p. B1.

31. Joe Flint, "Super Bowl 30-Second Ad Reach," *The Wall Street Journal*, January 26, 2001, p. B8.

32. Janis Forman, Interview with Steven Parrish, April 9, 2001.

CHAPTER 6

1. Mary Schaefer, "Communication Is My Job," *IABC Communication World*, June/July 1993, p. 21.

2. CBS News Report, September 1996.

3. Sue Shellenbarger, "Workplace: Work-Force Study Finds Loyalty Is Weak, Divisions of Race and Gender Are Deep." *The Wall Street Journal*, September 3, 1993.

4. Schultz, Hatch, and Larsen, pp. 233–245.

5. Janis Forman, Interview with Maril McDonald, November 6, 1998.

6. G. Brooke, "Mr Assembler Goes to Chicago," *Inside Navistar*, July/August 1997, pp. 6-7.

7. Janis Forman, Interview with Maril McDonald, November 6, 1998.

8. Interview with Rob Frazier, October 15, 1999. A ll direct quotes from Rob Frazier come from this interview.

9. Roger D'Aprix, *Communicating for Change: Connecting the Workplace with the Marketplace*. San Francisco: Jossey-Bass Publishers, 1996, p. 3.

10. Paul A. Argenti, Interview with David McCourt,October 1999. All quoted material comes from this interview.

CHAPTER 7

1. "Keeping an Ear on Wall St.: Corporate Webcasts Earn a Growing Audience of Investors," *The Washington Post*, June 14, 2001, p. E1

2. "Is Yahoo Right to Bar Reporters from its Annual Meeting?" *Investor Relations Business*, May 14, 2001, p.1

3. Collins and Porras, p. 8.

4. "IR at 40: Future Is Bright," *PR News*, February 12, 2001, p. 1.

5. John Byrne, "Investor Relations: When Capital Gets Antsy," *Business Week*, September 13, 1999, p. 72.

6. "Most Investors Value Corporate Responsibility, Few Are Satisfied," *Investor Relations Business*, August 6, 2001, p. 1.

7. "Opening Doors for Investors," *Africa News Service*, July 24, 2001.

8. Patrice Hill, "On-line Investing Makes Market Accessible," *The Washington Times*, April 5, 1999, p. D12.
9. William Powers, "We're in the Money," *National Journal*, April 1, 2000.
10. "Opening Doors for Investors," *Africa News Service*, July 24, 2001.
11. "IR at 40: Future Is Bright," *PR News*, February 12, 2001, p. 1.
12. Ibid.
13. Byrne, p. 72
14. Ibid.
15. "Most Investors Value Corporate Responsibility, Few Are Satisfied," p. 13.
16. Lawrence B. MacGregor Serven, "Managing Shareholder Value Through Planning," *Financial Executive*, June 2001, p. 50.
17. "Panel OKs $3.2B Cendant Settlement,"*AP Online*, August 28, 2001.
18. Andy Serwer, "Street Life: Are Investors Ready to Check Back into Cendant? Henry Silverman's Fall and Rise," *Fortune*, January 24, 2000, pp. 183+.
19. "Opening Doors for Investors," *Africa News Service*, July 24, 2001.
20. "Few Companies Have Web Crisis Policies."*Investor Relations Business*, July 9, 2001, p. 1.
21. Ibid.
22. "Is Yahoo Right to Bar Reporters from its Annual Meeting?" *Investor Relations Business*, May 14, 2001, p. 1.
23. Ibid.
24. Ibid.
25. Ibid.
26. Byrne, p. 72.
27. Howard Armitage and Yijay Jog, "Creating and Measuring Shareholder Value: A Canadian Perspective," *Ivey Business Journal*, July 1999, p. 75.
28. Nina Munk, "In the Final Analysis," *Vanity Fair*, August 2001, p. 100.
29. Peter Elkind, "Can We Ever Trust Wall St. Again?" *Fortune*, May 14, 2001, p. 69.
30. Munk, p. 106.
31. Carol Loomis,"Lies, Damned Lies, and Managed Earnings," *Fortune*, August 2,1999, p. 74.
32. "Most Investors Value Corporate Responsibility, Few Are Satisfied." *Investor Relations Business*, August 6, 2001, p. 1.
33. "Investors Want Green Policies, but Not at the Price of Greenbacks," *Investor Relations Business*, July 23, 2001, p. 16.
34. Yankelovich Partners Survey, 2001.
35. "Most Investors Value Corporate Responsibility, Few Are Satisfied." *Investor Relations Business*, August 6, 2001, p. 1.
36. Ibid.
37. Ibid.
38. Armitage and Jog, p. 75.
39. "Most Investors Value Corporate Responsibility, Few Are Satisfied," p. 1.
40. Ibid.
41. "Everything IR Professionals Need to Know About Pitching the Press," *PR News*, February 12, 2001, p. 1.

42. Brett Nelson, "So What's Your Story?" *Forbes*, October 30, 2000, p. 274.
43. Ibid.
44. Armitage and Jog, p. 75.
45. L. Biff Motley, "Why Satisfying the Customer Is Good Business," *Bank Marketing*, April 2000, p. 44.
46. Collins and Porras.

CHAPTER 8

1. Tom Diemer and Stephen Koff, "White House Means Business: Company Owners Adore Bush Policies," *The Plain Dealer*, April 8, 2001, p. 1A.
2. John J. Fialka and David S. Cloud, "White House Review Freezes EPA Inquiry," *The Wall Street Journal*, June 28, 2001, p. A3.
3. David J. Vogel, "The Study of Business and Politics," *California Management Review*, Spring 1996, p. 154.
4. Murray L. Weidenbaum. *Business, Government, and the Public*. Englewood Cliffs, NJ: Prentice Hall, 1977.
5. Jonathan R. T Hughes, *The Governmental Habit: Economic Controls from Colonial Times to the Present*. New York: Basic Books, 1977, pp. 4–5.
6. Ibid.
7. Ibid.
8. David J. Vogel, "The Study of Business and Politics," *California Management Review*, Spring 1996, pp. 149, 153.
9. Jeffrey I. Cole et al., "Surveying the Digital Future," UCLA Center for Communication Policy, November 2000.
10. "How Sound Are Your Client's/Company's Privacy Policies? Get Them in Order to Earn Public Trust," *PR Reporter*, September 17, 2001, p. 4.
11. See Ken Auletta's *World War 3.0: Microsoft and Its Enemies* (New York: Random House, 2001) for a thoughtful analysis of the battle between Microsoft and the government.
12. A. Lee Fritschler, *Smoking and Politics: Policymaking and the Federal Bureacracy* (3rd edition). Englewood Cliffs, NJ: Prentice Hall, 1983, p. 38.
13. David Vogel, *Fluctuating Fortunes: The Political Power of Business in America*. New York: Basic Books, 1989, p. 31.
14. Ibid.
15. John M. Broder, "Cigarette makers in a $368 billion accord to curb lawsuits and curtail marketing: Major Concessions, Industry Would Pay for the Cost of Treating Smoking Diseases." *The New York Times*, June 21, 1997, pp. 1, 8.
16. Deirdre Shesgreen, "Usual Opponents Join Sides in Debate over Tobacco Legislation," *St.Louis Post-Dispatch*, August 22, 2001, p. A6.
17. Andrew Edglecliffe-Johnson, "Philip Morris backs tobacco legislation," *The Financial Times*, The Americas, June 15, 2001, p. 9.
18. Shesgreen, p. A.
19. Ibid.
20. Michael Stetz, "Smoking Battle is Blown Outdoors," *The San Diego Union-Tribune*, February 12, 2001, p. A1+.

21. "The Tobacco War Goes Global," *The Economist*, October 14, 2000.

22. Richard W. Stevenson, "A Nation Challenged: The Economy," *The New York Times*, September 22, 2001, p. C1.

23. James Dao, "Dogfight for Dollars on Capitol Hill, *The Los Angeles Times*, September 3, 2001, Money & Business, pp. 1, 7.

24. Grahan Wilson, *Interest Groups in the United States*. New York: Oxford University Press, 1981.

25. Mike Ryan, Carl L. Swanson, and Rogene A. Buchholz, *Corporate Strategy, Public Policy, and the Fortune 500: How America's Major Corporations Influence Government*. Oxford: Basil Blackwell, 1987, p. 93.

26. Janis Forman, Interview with Penny Cate, June 13, 2001.

27. "Shell Chemical's Employee Ambassadors Add Personal Element to Community Relations—and Help Assure Plant Survival," *PR Reporter*, August 30, 1999, p. 1.

28. "Mobilizing Employees as Community Members: Using Them as Constituents to Gain Public Approval for a Merger," *PR Reporter*, May 1, 2000, pp. 2–3.

29. Ibid.

30. "Study—Public Expects Social Responsibility from Org'ns, Will Punish Them Financially if They Don't Measure Up," *PR Reporter*, September 11, 2001, p. 2.

31. Janis Forman, Interview with Daryl Fraser, June 21, 2001.

32. Peter Davies, "Measures of Success Beyond the Bottom Line," *The Financial Times*, June 24, 1998, p. 11.

33. "Nominations are open for Awards for Excellence in Corporate Community Service," *PR Reporter*, June 28, 1999, p. 4.

34. "Study—Public Expects Social Responsibility from Org'ns, Will Punish Them Financially if They Don't Measure Up," *PR Reporter*, September 11, 2001, p. 2.

35. Curt Weeden, *Corporate Social Investing: The Breakthrough Strategy for Giving and Getting Corporate Contributions*. San Francisco: Berrett-Koehler, 1998, p. 39.

36. Description of the walkathon and Avon's charitable mission and its connection to the company's identity is based on data provided on Avon's Web site.

37. David A. Aaker and Erich Joachimsthaler, *Brand Leadership*. New York: The Free Press, 2000, p. 205.

38. Jean Strouse, "How To Give Away $21.8 billion." *The New York Times Magazine*, April 16, 2001, p. 58.

39. Steven Ballmer's letter, *Microsoft Corporation 2000 Annual Report of Giving*, p. 2.

40. Microsoft Press Release, September 12, 2001, p. 1.

41. Strouse, p. 63.

42. Quoted in Strouse, p. 59.

CHAPTER 9

1. Marshall McLuhan and Bruce R. Powers, *The Global Village: Transformations in World Life and Media in the 21st Century*. New York: Oxford University Press, 1989.

2. Sandi Sonnenfeld, "Media Policy—What Media Policy?" *Harvard Business Review*, July 1, 1994, p. 18.

3. "What the Internet Cannot Do," *The Economist*, August 19, 2000, p. 11.

4. Quoted in W. Terrence Gordon, Marshall McLuhan. *Escape into Understanding* (New York: Basic Books, 1997), p. 7.

5. "Days and Nights on the Internet: The Impact of a Diffusing Technology," *American Behavioral Scientist*, Vol 45, November 2002, p. 383.

6. "The Failure of the New Media," *The Economist*, August 19, 2000, p. 53.

7. "Truth vs. Fraudulent Info Another Big Web Problem," *PR Reporter*, October 27, 1997, p. 1.

8. "The Failure of the New Media," p. 53.

9. Steve Gibbs, "Testing the Water," *Wireless Review*, June 15, 2000, p. S7.

10. Gartner Dataquest Survey, 2001.

11. Rachel Beck, "Cos. Hear Disgruntled Voices on Web," *AP Online*, May 4, 1999.

12. Patrice Hill, "On-line Investing Makes Market Accessible; Web Users Trade in Brokerages for Internet," *The Washington Times*, April 5, 1999, p. D12.

13. "Wired China: The Flies Swarm in," *The Economist*, July 22, 2000, p. 24.

14. Steve Gibbs, p. S7.

15. Ibid.

16. Beck, "Cos. Hear Disgruntled Voices on Web."

17. "Bad News: Another Study Finds Media Really Has Problems," *PR Reporter*, April 7, 1997, p. 1.

18. Ibid.

19. Robin Cohn, "Learning from Crisis: As the Curtain Rises," *The Public Relations Strategist*, Summer 1996.

20. "CBS Reality Duo Grabs Ratings," *AP Online*, July 6, 2000.

21. Frank Farley, "Shows Test Limits of 'Low.'" *USA Today*, July 12, 2000, p. 14A.

22. Quoted in Drew Jubera, "CNBC's Buzz Is All Biz with 'SportsCenter' Twist: Network Injects Wall Street with Dash of 'Dilbert' Fun, Locker-Room: Camaraderie," *The Atlanta Journal and Constitution*, November 29, 1998, p. 1K.

23. Matthew Kauffman, "CNBC Rides Bull Market to Hight Ratings," *The Seattle Times*, June 10, 2000, p. B1.

24. David Bauder, "What's Bad for Business Is Very Good for CNBC, Others Covering Finances," *AP Online*, September 2, 1998.

25. Keith Girard, "Monday Morning: For All You Savvy Investors, Warren Says Watch TV," *Investment News*, June 17, 2000.

26. Rachel Beck, "Cos. Hear Disgruntled Voices on the Web."

27. Quoted in "How Do Your PR Efforts Measure Up in the Wired World?" *Interactive PR and Marketing News*, November 26, 1999.

28. "Measurement Helps Telecom Giant Think Quicker," *PR News*, September 27, 1999, p. 1.

29. Ibid.

30. "In Survey, Journalists Tell Companies How to Improve Media Relations in Cyberspace," *Interactive PR*, June 3, 1996.

31. Ron Alridge, "A Few Tips for Having Good Media Relations," *Electronic Media*, December 7, 1992, p. 48.

32. Sandi Sonnenfeld, "Media Policy—What Media Policy?" *Harvard Business Review*, July 1, 1994, p. 18.

33. Ibid.

34. Dan Bilefsky, "Join the Sultans of Spin Media Relations," *Financial Times*, July 13, 2000, p. 19.

35. Ibid.

36. Ibid.

37. John Holusha, "Packaging and Public Image: McDonald's Fills a Big Order," *New York Times*, November 2, 1990, p. A1.

38. Ibid.

39. Holusha, p. A1.

40. Ibid.

41. Jackie Prince and Richard A. Denison, EDF Scientists, "Launching a New Business Ethic: The Environment As a Standard Operating Procedure at McDonald's and at Other Companies," Environmental Defense Fund, www.edf.org.

42. Quoted in Holusha, p. A1.

43. Michael McCarthy, "McDonald's New Ads Aiming for Smiles All Around," *USA Today*, October 9, 2000, p. 7B.

44. Ibid.

45. Jonathan Gaw, "Web Sites Venting Customers' Fury over Buy.com's Pricing Fiasco," *Los Angeles Times*, February 22, 1999, p. 1.

46. P.J. Huffstutter, "Heard on the Beat: Costly Web Site Error," *Los Angeles Times*, February 15, 1999, p. 3.

47. Beck, "Cos. Hear Disgruntled Voices on the Web."

48. Huffstutter, p. 3.

49. Beck, "Cos. Hear Disgruntled Voices on Web."

50. Huffstutter, p. 3.

51. Gaw, p. 1.

52. Beck, "Cos. Hear Disgruntled Voices on the Web."

53. Huffstutter, p. 3.

54. Quoted in Paul Korzeniowski, "Consumers Vent on the Internet; Companies Deal with Fallout," *Investor's Business Daily*, January 27, 1999, p. A6.

55. Ibid.

56. Beck, "Cos. Hear Disgruntled Voices on the Web."

57. Amelia Kassel, "Guide to Internet Monitoring and Clipping," CyberAlert White Paper, www.cyberalert.com/whitepaper.html.

58. www.yousuck.com, *Reputation Management*, September/October 1999, p. 27.

59. Beck, "Cos. Hear Disgruntled Voices on Web."

60. Ibid.

61. Korzeniowski, p. A6.

62. Bilefsky, p. 19.

CHAPTER 10

1. Greg Gordon and Jim Parsons, "The Fall of a Wonder Drug," *Minneapolis Star Tribune*, September 21, 1997, p. 1A.

2. Quoted in Bruce Crumley, "Fizzz Went the Crisis: Perrier's Response to a Contaminated Product," *International Management*, April 1990, p. 52.

3. Robin Cohn, "Learning from Crisis: As the Curtain Rises," *The Public Relations Strategist*, Summer 1996.

4. Perrier Press Release, *The Perrier Group*, February 10, 1990.

5. "When the Bubble Burst," *The Economist*, August 3, 1991, p. 67.

6. Ibid.

7. "Poor Perrier, It's Gone to Water," *Sydney Morning Herald*, February 15, 1990, p. 34.

8. Crumley, p. 52.

9. Quoted in "Poor Perrier, It's Gone to Water," p. 34.

10. "Probers Suspect Fakery as Claims of Pepsi Tampering Mushroom," *The Star-Ledger*, June 17, 1993.

11. Quoted in Nancy Gibbs, "Let Them Drink Seltzer: The Champagne of Bottled Water Loses Its Sparkle," *Time*, February 26, 1990, p. 43.

12. "When the Bubble Burst," p. 67.

13. William Dawkins, "Cheese Puts the Smile Back into Perrier," *Financial Times*, July 10, 1991, p. 12.

14. Harold J. Leavitt, "Hot Groups," *Harvard Business Review*, July 1, 1995, p.1 09.

15. Brian O'Reilly, "Managing: J&J Is on a Roll," *Fortune*, December 26, 1994, p. 178.

16. David Birkland, "Couple Say They Found Used Needle in Pepsi," *The Seattle Times*, June 11, 1993, p. B2.

17. Sandi Sonnenfeld, "Media Policy—What Media Policy?" *Harvard Business Review*, July 1, 1994, p. 18.

18. Ibid.

19. Quoted in Laura Zinn and Mary Beth Regan, "Top of the News, The Right Moves, Baby," *Business Week*, July 5, 1993, p. 30.

20. Glenn Kessler and Theodore Spencer, "How the Media Put the Fizz into the Pepsi Scare Story," *Newsday*, June, 20, 1993, p. 69.

21. "Pepsi chief '99.9 percent' Sure Bottling Lines Are Tamper-proof," *The San Diego Union-Tribune*, June 16, 1993, p. A11.

22. John Schwartz, "Pepsi Punches Back with PR Blitz; Crisis Team Worked Around the Clock," *The Washington Post*, June 19, 1993, p. C1.

23. *Beverage Industry*, March 1999, p.14.

24. "Beverage Digest/Maxwell Ranks Soft Drink Industry for 2000," *PRNewswire*, February 15, 2001.

25. Geanne Rosenberg, "No more! Women Brokers Fight Back Against Economic Discrimination and Social Isolation," *On Wall Street*, April 1, 1999.

26. Ibid.

27. Quoted in "900 Accuse Merrill of Bias: More Women than Expected in Suit," *The Cincinnati Post*, March 3, 1999.

28. Mary Francis, "Taking Stock of Her Rights: Former Local Merrill Lynch Broker Is at Forefront of Class-action Gender-bias Suit," *The Indianapolis Star*, April 4, 1999, p. B1.

29. Ibid.

30. Rosenberg, "No More! Women Brokers Fight Back against Economic Discrimination and Social Isolation."

31. Quoted in "Claims Merrill Lynch Settlement: Cites Economic Discrimination," *Dow Jones News Service*, March 1, 1999.

32. Kimberly Seals McDonald, "Merrill Gets 900 Claims in Discrimination Case," *The New York Post*, March 3, 1999, p. 34.

33. Lorrie Cohen, "Lawsuit: Women Brokers Here Join Suit vs. Merrill Lynch," *The Tucson Citizen*, March 12, 1999, p. 9C.

34. Maggie Jackson, "Merrill Women File Bias Claims: Action Is Part of Sit Settlement," *Denver Post*, March 2, 1999, p. C2.

35. Rosenberg, "No More! Women Brokers Fight Back against Economic Discrimination and Social Isolation."

36. Kimberly Seals McDonald, "Merrill Gets 900 Claims in Discrimination Case," *The New York Post*, March 3, 1999, p. 34.

37. "More Suits Expected from Women in Securities Field," *The Houston Chronicle*, October 8, 1999, p. 3.

38. Betsy Stark and Peter Jennings, "Women on Wall Street against Bias: Merrill Lynch Discrimination Settlement," *World News Tonight*, March 2, 1999.

39. Rosenberg, "No More! Women Brokers Fight Back against Economic Discrimination and Social Isolation."

40. Ibid.

41. Beth Piskora, "Judge Told Merrill Discrimination Settlement Is Bull," *The New York Post*, September 15, 1999, p. 38.

42. "Merrill Lynch Accused of Failing to Fulfill Terms of Settlement," *The Wall Street Journal*, September 9, 1999, p. B10.

43. Beth Piskora, "NOW on Hot Seat over Merrill Award," *The New York Post*, September 18, 1999, p. 20.

44. "Claims Merrill Lynch Settlement: Cites Economic Discrimination," *Dow Jones News Service*, March 1, 1999.

45. John Markoff, "Thief Reveals Credit Card Data When Web Extortion Plot Fails," *The New York Times*, January 10, 2000, p. A1.

46. "eUniverse Confirms the Theft of Consumer Data from Its CD Universe Subsidiary," *PR Newswire*, January 10, 2000.

47. "NASA Disputes Report that Hacker Endangered Astronauts," *Associated Press*, July 3, 2000.

48. John Varoli, "In Bleak Russia, a Young Man's Thoughts Turn to Hacking," *New York Times*, June 29, 2000, p. G10.

49. Quoted in John Markoff, p. A1.

50. Varoli, p. G10.

51. Ann Harrison, "Cybercrime Cost Firms $266M in '99," *Computerworld*, March 27, 2000, p. 28.

52. "Airliner with 88 Aboard Crashes...," *Associated Press Newswires*, January 31, 2000.

53. Frank Corrado, *Media for Managers*. New York: Prentice-Hall, 1984.

54. John Schwartz, "Pepsi Punches Back with PR Blitz," *The Washington Post*, June 19, 1993, p. C1.

55. Patricia Winters and James Lyons, "Pepsi's Damage-Control Plan Was Right On, Baby," *New York Daily News*, June 18, 1993, p. 38.

56. *Beverage World*, July 1998, p. 12; "Year After Scare...," *USA Today*, February 18, 1991, p. 28.

INDEX

Note: Boldface numbers indicate illustrations.

ABOUT THE AUTHORS

Paul A. Argenti has taught management and corporate communication starting in 1977 at the Harvard Business School, from 1979-81 at the Columbia Business School, and since 1981 he has been a faculty member at Dartmouth's Tuck School of Business. Both *The Wall Street Journal* (2001) and *US News & World Report* (1994) have rated Professor Argenti's department number one in the nation. He has provided management and corporate communication consulting and training for over 75 corporations and nonprofit organizations in both the United States and abroad over the past 20 years. His clients cover a broad range—such as Goldman Sachs, Sony, and Martha Stewart. He has written over 75 case studies, and is the author of various articles for both academic and managerial journals. Professor Argenti also currently serves on the editorial board of *Journal of Business Communication* and is Associate Editor of *Corporate Reputation Review*.

Janis Forman (Ph.D) is the founder and director of the Management Communication Program at UCLA's Anderson Graduate School of Management. Professor Forman has been the communications faculty advisor for more than 100 Executive Program "Living Cases," extended international strategic studies for multinational organizations such as Microsoft, Disney, Nestle, Intel, SGS-Thompson, Sun Microsystems, and Hewlett-Packard, and for start-up firms in Chile, France, Finland, Australia and the United States. The entrepreneurial program in which she teaches was ranked first internationally by the *Financial Times* in 2002. She was named the outstanding researcher by the Association for Business Communication, an award based on her entire publication record and its pivotal role in extending research in her discipline and in educating managers. A consultant to a wide variety of organizations, Dr. Forman has been a visiting professor at the Hong Kong University of Science and Technology and at Dartmouth's Tuck School of Business. She is president of Forman & Associates, a firm specializing in corporate and management communications.

Argenti and Forman are coauthors of "The Communication Advantage" (in *The Expressive Organization*, Oxford University Press, 2000), and featured as an outstanding article in management in *The Financial Times Book of Management*. They are currently studying best practices in corporate communication at Accenture, Dell, FedEx, Goldman Sachs, Johnson & Johnson, and Sears under a grant from the Council of Public Relations Firms. Please contact the authors with comments or queries: paul.argenti@dartmouth.edu or janis.forman@ix.netcom.com.